MONS, ANZAC
AND KUT

MONS, ANZAC AND KUT

by

an MP
(Lieutenant Colonel
The Hon Aubrey Herbert)

Edited by Edward Melotte

Pen & Sword
MILITARY

First published in Great Britain in 2009 by
Pen & Sword Military
an imprint of
Pen & Sword Books Ltd
47 Church Street
Barnsley
South Yorkshire
S70 2AS

ISBN 978 1 84884 175 8

A CIP catalogue record for this book is
available from the British Library.

Typeset in Sabon by
Phoenix Typesetting, Auldgirth, Dumfriesshire

Printed and bound in England by
the MPG Books Group

Pen & Sword Books Ltd incorporates the imprints of Pen & Sword Aviation,
Pen & Sword Maritime, Pen & Sword Military, Wharncliffe Local History,
Pen & Sword Select, Pen & Sword Military Classics and Leo Cooper.

For a complete list of Pen & Sword titles please contact
PEN & SWORD BOOKS LIMITED
47 Church Street, Barnsley, South Yorkshire, S70 2AS, England
E-mail: enquiries@pen-and-sword.co.uk
Website: www.pen-and-sword.co.uk

Contents

Introduction

Mons, Anzac and Kut are the wartime diaries of an extraordinary man. Originally published anonymously as being 'By an MP', their author was the diplomat, politician, traveller, polyglot and poet – Aubrey Herbert. He was thrown, by both opportunity and design, into the heart of some of the key battles and campaigns that define the Great War. A unique personal account of the events in which he found himself thrown, his diaries are very much an expression of himself: impetuous, romantic, generous of spirit and humour and ardent in search of adventure. A man of broad acquaintance, well informed, perceptive and very much a part of the Establishment, his observations give the reader a strong sense of the emotions of those in the face of battle: the excitement at Mons, the sense of those early days of the war as a game, the horror of Gallipoli and the disappointment of Kut. The diaries never had great success – they were published in 1919, at a time when everyone wanted to forget the war and nothing could be more out of vogue than the spirit 'half-joy in life, half-readiness to die' in which so many had first rushed to arms. The Nation was bitter, as was Herbert, feeling betrayed by politicians and simply wanting to forget.

I first read the diaries as a teenager, a young aspirant in my great-grandfather's footsteps as an officer in the Irish Guards, and from reading them grew a spark, a desire to travel and to find adventure as he did. It seems appropriate therefore that when I read them again, twenty-five years later during the sweltering summer of 2003, that I was sitting in the Governor's house overlooking the River Tigris in Al Amarah in the Marsh Arab province of Maysan. A constant reminder of his own journey up the Tigris, the British War Cemetery, (sadly destroyed by the Mahdi Army 'rebels' the following year), lay a few hundred metres to the south. Re-reading *Mons, Anzac and Kut* I thought that there was much within it that had not changed and that Aubrey Herbert's observations gave a perspective of those long ago events that many today would find as enthralling as I did. The first diary was dictated in hospital from memory and rough notes made on the Retreat from Mons. For the writing of the second diary, idle hours were provided in the Dardanelles between times of furious action. The third diary, which deals with the fall of Kut, was written on the Fly boats of the River Tigris.

In the preface to the original version, Herbert stated that, *'this diary claims to be no more than a record of great and small events, a chronicle of events within certain limited horizons – a retreat, a siege and an attack. Writing was often hurried and difficult, and the diary was sometimes neglected for a period. If inaccuracies occur, the writer offers sincere apologies'*. He also withheld certain of his private thoughts, opinions and criticisms as well as *'concealing what, for the moment, at any rate, is better not revealed'*. I have edited *Mons, Anzac and Kut* to include many of these thoughts and criticisms, taking them from his diaries and certain of his private letters. Interesting, relevant and in many cases amusing, I believe that they add to the book without altering the spirit in which it was first produced, and therefore merit inclusion.

Also in the original, in the Retreat from Mons, only Christian or nicknames were generally used. In the case of the other two Expeditions names were used freely, though where it was considered advisable, at the time, they were occasionally disguised or initials substituted for them. I have, where possible, identified and footnoted those who he had previously mentioned only by initials or surname. If able to identify their role at that period I have included that, otherwise I have shown their title, rank and decorations at the time of their death.

And so to the author himself: Aubrey Herbert was born at Highclere near Newbury on 3 April 1880. He was the eldest son of the 4th Earl of Carnarvon's second marriage. His mother was Elizabeth, daughter of Henry Howard of Greystoke. He was born short-sighted, and could only read by holding a book to one eye so that its pages almost brushed his nose. Aided by a secretary who would read his work to him and to whom he in turn would dictate his notes, he was educated at Eton. Life was not happy for him at first – unable to join in the sporting activities of his peers he stood out and was bullied. Eventually, as his wit and determination were identified by others, his latter years became more enjoyable. His real passions as a boy were Somerset and the pack of twenty-one dogs, mongrels mostly, that he gathered around him in his holidays.

On leaving Eton he was taken to Wiesbaden to the great oculist, Dr. Pagenstecker, who operated on the lens of the blinder eye, restoring it to long sight, the better one continuing to be serviceable for reading. This operation gave him a new lease on life and he threw himself into his time at Balliol emerging with a First Class degree and a reputation for wild antics. Having completed his exams he was sent down from Oxford, the final straw being his dropping from a tree into the middle of a picnic declaring, 'I am a plum, I am ripe and therefore I must drop.'

Frustrated not to be able to serve in the South African war, he joined the Foreign Office and between 1903 and 1905 he was honorary attaché, first at the Embassy in Tokyo, then at Constantinople, after which he travelled extensively in the Ottoman provinces, from Bahrain in the East to the shores of Albania in the West. Despite enjoying his time in Japan he developed a much greater affinity for the Middle East and most especially the Turks.

His true love though was Albania and the Albanians. He visited the country regularly between 1907 and 1913 and became closely involved in Albanian politics, acting as an advisor to the Albanian delegation at the 1912 London Balkan Peace Conference. No one understood better the internal and external problems of the Albanians and it is probably fair to say that his greatest public achievement was that he contributed more than anyone to bringing into existence the modern independent state of Albania. In 2004 his efforts on behalf of the Albanians were finally recognised by the posthumous award of the President's Silver Medal. He was twice offered the throne of Albania. On the first occasion, just before the War, he was flattered but not seriously interested and this decision was reinforced by the then Prime Minister, Herbert Asquith (a family friend), who advised him to decline the offer. Seven years later, following the defeat of the Italian Army by the Albanians in September 1920, he received a second, unofficial, approach from the Albanian Government again offering him the throne. Tempted to accept this time, he discussed the offer with Philip Kerr, David Lloyd George's Private Secretary, and with Maurice Hankey, the Cabinet Secretary, pursuing the idea of acting under the banner of the League of Nations which had formed the previous year and of which he was a keen advocate. The first Secretary General, Eric Drummond, was a close friend. Herbert finally decided that he was not rich enough to become King but maintained his enthusiasm and love of the Albanian cause and his continual lobbying eventually led to the acceptance of Albania as a member of the League of Nations in December 1920.

He married in 1910 Mary Vesey, only child of Viscount de Vesci, and in 1911 entered Parliament as Conservative member for the Southern Division of Somerset, a seat he held until 1918. He subsequently represented the Yeovil Division of Somerset from then until his death. When war came he was determined to serve. His poor eyesight had prevented him serving in South Africa during the Boer War and he had resigned his Territorial commission in the North Devon Hussars in 1913 and, again due to his poor eyesight, was denied when he attempted to rejoin. Not to be discouraged, he simply had a uniform made and, aided by his wife's cousin, Tom Vesey (who was serving with the Regiment as were a number of other friends), stepped into the ranks of the Irish Guards as they marched out of Wellington Barracks and away to war. Reporting to the Commanding Officer on the boat to France, Herbert persuaded him to let him remain and was, albeit somewhat reluctantly, accepted into the Battalion, given the rank of Lieutenant and appointed as an interpreter. He landed with the 1st Battalion in France on 13 August 1914. Fighting with the Battalion in the Retreat from Mons he was wounded on 1 September during the rearguard action at the woods near Villers-Cotterets during the Battle of Le Cateau in which both the

Commanding Officer and Second-in-Command were killed. Captured by the Germans, he escaped when the Dressing Station was overrun by the French.

Having recovered from his wounds Herbert joined the Intelligence Bureau in Cairo in December 1914 and was subsequently attached to the New Zealand and Australian Division during the Gallipoli Campaign as an intelligence officer and interpreter working for General Godley (formerly an Irish Guardsman). Touched by the smell of the dead and the noise of the wounded crying for water between the trenches, he approached General Birdwood, the Corps Commander, about the possibility of an armistice for burying the dead and the bringing in of the wounded. Despite initial doubts about whether GHQ (*'living on its perfumed island* (and who) *did not consider how great was the abomination of life upon the cramped and stinking battlefield that was our encampment'*) would endorse it he was granted leave by Birdwood to speak to Sir Ian Hamilton, the Commander of the Mediterranean Expeditionary Force and went aboard HMS *Arcadian* where Hamilton was headquartered to present his case. Hamilton eventually agreed to Herbert's proposal in principle but stressed to Birdwood that he did so only on the basis that the Turks requested it. Somehow Herbert, in the subsequent negotiations managed to make both sides believe that the other sought the armistice. Compton Mackenzie, in his book *Gallipoli Memories,* wrote, 'It has never been perfectly clear who really did ask for this truce. Liman Von Sanders says we did; Sir Ian Hamilton says they did. My own opinion is that Aubrey Herbert alone was responsible for it'. However it was achieved, a temporary Armistice was eventually put in place on 24 May 1915 with Herbert wandering between the trenches as 'referee'. This led to one of those rare, if not unique occasions during war when soldiers (in this case the Turks) approach an enemy officer for orders. Gallipoli was a tragedy for Herbert, who loved the Turks (when in Parliament he always used to write his speaking notes in Turkish). His compassion for them, as well as two fine examples of his shambolic and eccentric nature are given by Compton Mackenzie. The first, in *Gallipoli Memories,* describes a conver-

sation with Aubrey Herbert on the deck of HMS *Arcadian* where
Herbert had gone to persuade Sir Ian Hamilton of the necessity
for the Armistice,

> *I had the chance of a long gossip with him as we walked
> round and round the deck in a series of rapid diagonals, for
> Aubrey was so short-sighted that he really could not see well
> enough to walk straight. I think he was holding forth
> passionately about the woes of the Turks and the beauty of
> their characters, gripping my arm from time to time and
> exclaiming 'My dear, we must do this,' or 'My dear, we must
> do that.'*
>
> *As we zigzagged along I suddenly became aware that a
> shape was following our course, though what that shape
> was, I did not dare for a moment to look round and
> ascertain, so acutely was I aware of a menace, an almost
> diabolical menace in its shadowing. At last I plucked up
> courage to turn my head. Imagine my dismay when I saw
> the Commander of the* Arcadian, *his cheeks an angry
> crimson, stalking along the deck after us with the air of one
> who is tracking a pair of assassins. The faintness of despair
> came over me. His eyes protruding like a Bateman admiral's
> were fixed upon a meandering line of ink-stains that
> stretched from one end of the deck to the other. I looked at
> Aubrey. Yes, there in the pocket of his service-jacket, or
> rather fixed to the outside of it, was a fountain-pen that
> was dripping with every step he took. I played a coward's
> part.*
>
> *'Aubrey,' I said, 'I must run now. And, by the way, I think
> your pen's leaking or something.'*
>
> *I cannot remember what steps were taken to restore the
> Commander of the* Arcadian *to consciousness; but I do
> remember that those ink-spots were still traceable when we
> went ashore ten days later.*

The second is in a letter from Mackenzie to Herbert remembering
a meeting they had on Mytilene,

How well I remember you, in the electric light of the gardens, which made more canary yellow than ever your canary yellow uniform. For luggage you had a typewriter, and you were wearing red Turkish slippers and the only thing that bothered you particularly was that you hadn't got a tie. I remember wondering why you should bother about a tie when you only had one button on your tunic. However, next morning we went to look for a tie together and you pounced on one at a local hosier's which you thought was just the thing and you still thought it just the thing even when I pointed out that it was covered with purple lozenges, lustrous as amethysts . . .

Herbert was a popular figure amongst his peers at Gallipoli. He in turn developed a great admiration for those with whom he served and he wrote a series of poems about them, including one to the poet Rupert Brooke, a close friend who was to die during the Gallipoli Campaign. Herbert developed a particular admiration for the New Zealanders who, he felt, had all the dash and *élan* of the Australians and the discipline of the Englishmen. One of his poems, *The New Zealander*, was subsequently to be published in *The Spectator* in 1916,

Samothrace and Imbros lie
Like blue shadows in the sky;
Scented come the wind from Greece
Slow winged as the Soul of Peace

All was still as evening came
With a whisper, sheathed in flame,
And the battlefield grew still
From the Valley to the Hill
Just beyond the ripple's reach
He was lying on the beach,
Dreaming half of things at home,
Mixing dreams with light and foam.

Three days he had smelt the dead,
Looked on black blood and on red,
Gripped and lain, and cursed and hated,
Feared, exulted, prayed, and waited.

From the dawn till dusk was dim
All the world had spied on him;
And the wind that sighed so low
Seemed the footstep of his foe.

And at night the fireflies dancing
Were the light of men advancing.
Swift his hands. His brain was cool.
"Hell," he said, "poor Tom's at school."
Then he rested on the beach
Just beyond the ripples' reach
Home and sunset in his dream
Till the shrapnel's quicker gleam

Found his heart, and found his head –
Found him dreaming, left him dead.
And they buried him at night
With men fallen in the fight
So he fought and went away
With the glory of the day,
And no hatred in his heart
When the great ways met to part.

On a beach without a name
He died sleeping, robbed of fame,
Just before the day grew dim.
Tom, his brother, envied him.

Eventually evacuated from Gallipoli after having fallen seriously
ill, Herbert returned home to recover before being sent back to the
Middle East to once again work with the Arab Bureau. With

T.E. Lawrence and the Head of British Intelligence in Mesopotamia, Colonel W.H. Beach, he journeyed up the Tigris where they made an unsuccessful attempt to buy the release of the British Garrison surrounded by the Turks at Kut-al-Amara. Afterwards he served as an intelligence officer at Salonika and later in Italy, and in the last months of the war he was the head of the English Mission attached to the Italian Army in Albania, where he held the temporary rank of Lieutenant-Colonel.

After the war Herbert returned to politics and the continued cause of the Albanians. For such an intelligent man he was to have a ridiculous end. His eyes began to deteriorate and convinced by someone that his sight would be repaired if he had his teeth pulled, he did so. He developed septicaemia and died at the age of 43 on 26 September 1923.

To describe the man himself, I must turn to the words of his friend Desmond MacCarthy[1]. MacCarthy wrote the original introduction to *Mons, Anzac and Kut* and described him thus,

He was well over medium height and slimly built. His normal carriage was stooping, his gait buoyant and careless, and he was apt to fling himself into chairs in any attitude of comfortable collapse and then to leap up again in the excitement of talk. All his movements were expressive. His dress was never intentionally unconventional, but unless he had taken special pains with his get-up, which he could seldom be induced to do, its general effect was decidedly unusual. He was untidy, his shirts bulged and his tie was apt to rise and obscure his collar. He would clap on his head any hat to hand regardless of the rest of his costume. He did not notice when his clothes were shabby, and strangers must often have been surprised to discover, as they must have done after a moment's conversation, that such an unpretentious-looking person was so politically adroit and so completely at home in the world.

1.   Sir Desmond MacCarthy (1877–1952).

His entry into a room was impetuous but never dramatic, and his greetings were exceptionally warm; his voice when he was pleased to see one became high and clear. He gave the impression of being completely unselfconscious, but at the same time exceptionally aware of other people. He was a flattering listener, and one of his distinctive gestures was that of bending towards the person to whom he was talking, or of drawing closer his chair in a manner which seemed to convey, Now, now we are going to understand each other. Then, he would listen with head slightly on one side, checking, now and then, an impulse to interrupt in precisely the way which stimulates most the volubility of others. Among friends he loved to promote laughter at his own expense. Many of his gestures were decidedly idiosyncratic. At meals while listening he would meditatively beat upon the palm of his hand with an unused knife. He would often seize a bottle from the table and apply it to his eye like a telescope to see now much more liquor there was still in it. And when an impulse to be confidentially emphatic possessed him, he would raise an arm and, stooping forward, bring it down slowly with the deliberate motion of one tolling a bell. This gesture of eagerly stooping forward was balanced by a movement equally characteristic, that of suddenly drawing himself backwards and erect. And at such moments an almost deprecating attitude of attention was instantly replaced by an impetuously alert dignity. He looked extremely well at such moments, valorous and self-assured.

A romantic figure, even amongst his peers, it is reputed that Herbert was the inspiration for the character Sandy Arbuthnot, a hero in several of John Buchan's novels including *Greenmantle*. The cameo character of the 'Honourable Herbert' in Louis de Bernières' novel *Birds Without Wings* is also clearly based on him: The 'Honourable Herbert' appears as a British liaison officer with the ANZAC troops serving at Gallipoli. A talented linguist, he is able to communicate with both Turks and Allies and arranges the burial of the dead, achieving great popularity with both sides – a description that clearly mirrors Herbert's own role.

Aubrey Herbert's character comes forth very clearly throughout the diaries: his love of daring, of adventure and of people; his generosity of spirit, of letting people off and of giving. But the value to him, in terms of his own happiness, of daring, adventure and generosity, depended greatly on finding others responsive to them. He lived in an age when his values were more common than they are today and when the approach to war (certainly at the beginning) was more chivalrous. Our journey to the Mesopotamia of 2003, whilst still inciting excitement did not, I believe, lead us there in the spirit 'half-joy in life, half-readiness to die' with which Herbert and his generation marched to war in 1914. While *Mons, Anzac and Kut* is a diary of its age, many of the observations and truths set out within it resonate as timelessly today as they did then, and on putting it down I for one was filled with admiration for its author, his experiences and his generation.

Edward Melotte
Jerusalem 2009

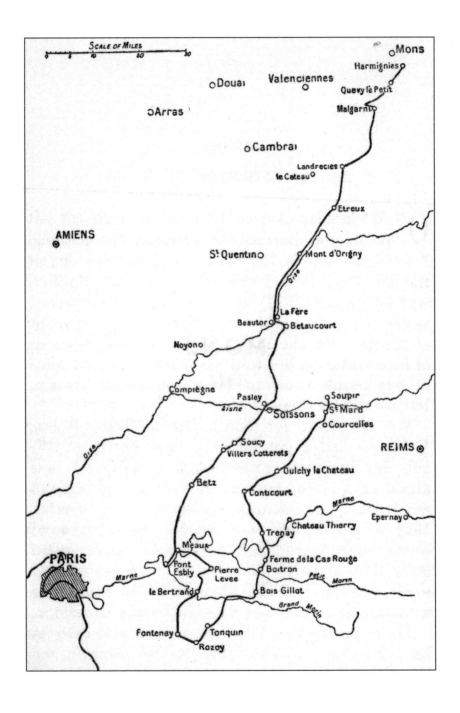

Chapter One

Mons
1914

On Wednesday, August 12th, 1914, my regiment[2] left Wellington
Barracks at seven in the morning. I fell into step in the ranks as
they went out of the gateway, where I said good-bye to my
brother, who left that day for Spain. It was very quiet in the
streets, as the papers had said nothing about the movement of
troops. On the march the wives and relations of men said good-
bye to them at intervals, and some of our people came to see us
off at the station, but we missed them.

We entrained for Southampton – Tom[3], Robin[4], Valentine[5]
and I got into the same carriage. We left Southampton without
much delay. I was afraid of a hitch, but got on to the ship
without any trouble. On board everybody was very cheerful.
Most people thought that the first big engagement would have
begun and very likely have ended before we arrived. Some were
disappointed and some cheered by this thought. The men sang
without ceasing and nobody thought of a sea attack.

The next day (the 13th) we arrived very early at Le Havre in a
blazing sun. As we came in, the French soldiers tumbled out of
their barracks and came to cheer us. Our men had never seen
foreign uniforms before, and roared with laughter at their colours.

2. 1st Battalion Irish Guards.
3. Tom Vesey (later Viscount de Vesci), a first cousin of Aubrey Herbert's
    wife.
4. Lord Robert Edward Innes-Kerr (1885–1958).
5. Lord Valentine Castlerosse (subsequently 6th Earl of Kenmare)
    (1891–1943).

Stephen Burton[6] of the Coldstream Guards rebuked his men. He said, 'These French troops are our Allies; they are going to fight with us against the Germans.' Whereupon one man said, 'Poor chaps, they deserve to be encouraged,' and took off his cap and waved it, and shouted, 'Vive l'Empereur!' He was a bit behind the times. I believe if the Germans beat us and invaded England they would still be laughed at in the villages as ridiculous foreigners.

We were met by a Colonel of the French Reserves, a weak and ineffective man, two Boy Scouts, and a semi-idiotic interpreter. We shed this man as soon as we were given our own two excellent interpreters. We had no wood to cook the men's dinners, and I was sent off with Jumbo and a hundred men to see what I could find. A French corporal came reluctantly with us. We marched a mile, when we found an English quartermaster at a depot, who let us requisition a heap of great faggots, which we carried back.

After breakfast I was sent with Hickie[7], the Quartermaster, to arrange for billeting the men. Hickie rode a bicycle and lent me his horse, which was the most awful brute I have ever mounted in any country. It walked ordinarily like a crab; when it was frightened it walked backwards, and it was generally frightened. It would go with the troops, but not alone, and neither whip nor reins played any part in guiding the beast. Hickie couldn't ride it. Some French soldiers threw stones at it and hit me. Finally we got a crawling cab, then a motor, and went off about eleven kilometres to the Café des Fleurs, where the camp was to be. It was a piping hot day. We got a house for the Colonel and Desmond[8] belonging to Monsieur Saville, who said he was a friend of Mr James Yoxall MP. He had a very jolly arbour, where we dined. In the afternoon the troops came marching up the steep hill in great heat. Hickie and I found a man rather drunk, with a very hospitable

6.   Killed on 20th July 1917 when serving as Battalion Second-in-Command, 1st Battalion Coldstream Guards.
7.   Lieutenant H. Hickie, 1st Battalion Irish Guards.
8.   Major Lord Desmond Fitzgerald (1888–1916). Adjutant of the 1st Battalion Irish Guards during the retreat from Mons. He was killed in March 1916, examining a new form of grenade in his tent when it exploded.

Frenchman. The Frenchman said: 'We have clean sheets and a well-aired bed, coffee, wine or beer for him, if he desires them.' There was no question about the man's desiring them. Hickie almost wept, and said: 'How can you keep an army together if they are going to be treated like this?' The sun had been delightful in the morning at Le Havre, but was cruel on the troops, especially on the Reservists, coming up the long hill.

The French had been very hospitable. They had given the men, where they had been able to do so free of observation, wine, coffee, and beer. The result was distressing. About twenty of the men collapsed at the top of the hill in a ditch, some of them unconscious, seeming almost dying, like fish out of water. The French behaved very well, especially the women, and stopped giving them spirits. I got hold of cars and carried the men off to their various camps. Jack Hamilton, Tom, and I slept all right in a tent on the ground. The next day I was sent down by the Colonel with the drum-major, to buy beer for the regiment at 1s. 1d a gallon, which seemed cheap. I met Stephen Burton while I was buying things. He told me we were off that night, that we were to start at 10, but that we should not be entrained till 04.30. I lunched with Churchill[9], the Consul, a man called Long, who talked very good French and English, and also saw Walsh, the Vice-Consul, whom I liked. I did not think much of Churchill, but he tried to help me get a horse from the Colonel of the Commissariat who was there. Long sent me back in his motor. At the camp, the Colonel complained that the beer had not come, and that the Drum-Major and the men had been lost. I commandeered a private motor and went back at a tremendous rate into the town, all but killing the drum-major at a corner. We had a capital dinner. Monsieur Saville gave us excellent wine, and the Colonel told me to make him a speech. We then lay down before the march.

9.   Major John ('Jack') Churchill DSO (1880–1947). Winston Churchill's brother. Churchill was serving on Field Marshal Lord French's staff (1914–1915). He subsequently joined Sir Ian Hamilton's staff at Gallipoli as the Naval Liaison Officer for the Mediterranean Expeditionary Force.

3

The next camp captured a spy, but nobody paid any attention. About 10.30 we moved off. It was a warm night with faint moonlight. Coming into the town the effect was operatic. As we marched or were halted all the windows opened and the people put their heads out to try and talk to us. At about half-past eleven it began to rain, but the men whistled the Marseillaise and 'It's a long way to Tipperary.' The people came out of the houses, trying to catch the hands of the men and walking along beside them. We were halted in front of the station, and waited endlessly in the rain. We then had an almost unspeakable march over cobbles, past interminable canals, over innumerable bridges, through what seemed to be the conglomeration of all the slums of all the world, to light that always promised us rest but never came. It poured without ceasing. At last we arrived at the station, and when we saw the train pandemonium followed. Everybody jumped into carriages and tried to keep other people out, so as to have more room. We were all soaked to the skin, and nobody bothered about anyone else. After that we got out and packed the men in. Tom, Charles Guthrie, Jack, Hickie, and I got into one carriage. Lieutenants who tried to follow were hurled out. It was very cold. Tom had a little brandy, which did us some good. At about 5 a.m. we moved off. The next day we arrived at Amiens.

Saturday, the 15th, we arrived at Amiens to see a great stir and bustle. We had not had much to eat. We found several officers of the Coldstream Guards in their shirt-sleeves, who had got left trying to get food. I got masses later on at a wayside station, and a stream of people to carry it, and returned with rousing cheers from the men. At every station we were met by enormous crowds that cheered and would have kissed our hands if we had let them. They made speeches and piled wreaths of flowers upon the Colonel, who was at first very shy, but driven to make a speech, liked it, and became almost garrulous. At Arras we had the greatest ovation of all. An old man in the crowd gave me a post-card, which I directed to a relation at home and asked him to post. This he did, adding a long letter of his own, to say that I was well and in good spirits. This letter and my post-card got past the censor.

4

Late that night we came to a place called Wassigny, where, after a lot of standing about, we went up to a farmhouse. Hickie and I lay down on the floor in a sort of an office at about half-past two, with orders to be off at five. The Colonel slept outside, half on and half off a bench. He never seemed to need sleep.

We left the next morning, Sunday, the 16th, at five, for Vadencourt. I was wearing Cretan boots, and my feet already began to trouble me.

At Vadencourt we met the Maire and his colleague, Monsieur Lesur. He took us first of all to the most beautiful place for a camp, a splendid field by a river for bathing, wooded with poplars, but no sooner had we got there than we were told the Coldstreamers had the right to it.

In Vadencourt everybody helped us. The people threw open their houses, their barns and their orchards. They could not do enough; but it was a long business and we had not finished until 1 o'clock, by which time we were pretty tired. Then the troops turned up, and we had to get them into billets. After that we lunched with the Colonel. The French cottages were extra-ordinarily clean, never an insect, but plenty of mice rioting about at night. There were many signs of religion in all these cottages. Most of the rooms were filled with crucifixes and pictures of the Saints. The priests seemed to have a great deal of influence. Vadencourt was very religious, and the morning we went off they had a special service for the men, which was impressive. All the people seemed saintly, except the Maire, who was very much of this world. Shields[10], our doctor, who was stroke of the Cambridge Eight and a heavy weight boxer of renown and who came from Sherborne, gave us a lecture and persuaded the reluctant to be inoculated for typhoid. It was the only unpleasant day we spent at Vadencourt.

The men had fraternized with the people and, to the irritation of the Colonel, wore flowers in their hair and caps. There was no

10.   Lieutenant Hugh Shields RAMC. Mentioned in Despatches in October 1914, he was Killed in Action at Ypres whilst tending a wounded man on October 26th 1914.

drunkenness – in fact the men complained that there was nothing strong enough to make a man drunk. Generally there was not much to do, though one day the men helped with the harvest. The people couldn't have been kinder. It was, as one of the men said, a great 'overtation.' Every day there was a paper published in amazing English. In one paper we found a picture of Alex Thynne[11], with contemptuous and angry references to a speech he had made against English tourists going to France; he wanted them to go instead to Bath, in his constituency, and so to please both him and his constituents.

It was a quiet life. There was little soldiering, and that, as someone said, was more like manoeuvres in the millennium than anything else. Everywhere corn was offered for our horses and wine for ourselves, but there was a great fear underlying the quiet. We were constantly asked whether the Germans would ever get to Vadencourt, and always said we were quite sure they would not. We used to mess at the inn close to my house. Of French troops we saw practically nothing, except our two interpreters, Charlot, who talked very good English, and Bernard, a butcher from Havre, a most excellent fellow, who was more English than the English, though he could only talk a few words of the language. There was also another interpreter, head master of a girls' school in Paris. He said to me: 'Vous trouverez toutes espèces d'infames parmi les interprets, même des MPs.'

One day Hugo Gough said that it would be interesting, before going into battle, to have our fortunes told. I told him he could not get a fortune-teller at Vadencourt. 'Not at all, there is one in the village; I saw it written over her shop, "Sage Femme".' I was very comfortable in my house, which was just out of bounds, but not enough to matter.

Monsieur Louis Prevot came in one day, with a beautiful mare, brown to bay, Moonshine II, by Troubadour out of Middlemas. He said that she could jump two metres. Her disadvantages were that she jumped these two metres at the wrong time and in the wrong

---

11.   Lieutenant Colonel Lord Alexander Thynne DSO (1873–1918). MP for Bath.

place, that she hated being saddled and kicked when she was groomed: while Monsieur Prevot was showing me how to prevent her kicking she kicked right through the barn door. I bought her for £40. I think Prevot thought that the French Authorities were going to take his stables and that I was his only chance. When she settled down to troops she became a beautiful mount.

That day I went with Hickie through Etreux to Boué, foraging. I drove with a boy called Vanston behind a regular man-killer. It was far worse than anything that happened at Mons. Vanston talked all the time of the virtue of Irish women, of the great advantage of having medals and the delight old men found in looking at them, of the higher courage of the unmarried men and his keen anxiety to get into battle, and of the goodness of God. Hickie was upset because he thought that the man-killing horse was going to destroy the Maltese cart, which was, apparently, harder to replace than Vanston or me.

The night before we left the Colonel gave us a lecture. As an additional preparation for the march we were also inoculated against typhoid which made some people light-headed.

We left Vadencourt on August 19th, Hickie and Hubert both ill, travelling on a transport cart. I rode ahead, through pretty and uneventful country. At Oisy, Hickie was very ill, and I got him some brandy. We were to camp beyond Oisy. When we got to the appointed place the Maire was ill and half dotty. Stepney[12] and I laboured like mad to find houses, but at last, when our work was finished we found that they had already been given to the Coldstreamers. Some of the people were excellent. One old fellow of seventy wept and wished that his house was a big as a barn that he might put up the soldiers in it. A rough peasant boy took me round and stayed with us all the afternoon and refused to take a penny. But some of them were not so kind. In the end, billets were not found for a number of officers and men, who slept quite comfortably in the new-mown hay. We passed a big monastery where two Germans, disguised as priests, had been taken and shot the week before. I slept in a house belonging to three widows, all

12.   Major H.A. Herbert-Stepney. Killed 1918.

7

like stage creatures. They had one of the finest cupboards I have ever seen.

The next morning (20 August) we marched off to Maroilles – a big dull town, and again some of the people were not overpleased to see us. Here we had an excellent dinner. I slept at a chemist's. Hickie was sent back from Maroilles to Amiens with rheumatic fever. We got up at 4 o'clock the next morning (21 August), and had a pretty long march to Longueville by Malplaquet.

As we crossed the frontier the men wanted to cheer, but they were ordered to be quiet, 'so as not to let the Germans hear them.' This order gave an unpleasant impression of the proximity of the Germans.

The men began to fall out a great deal on the road. The heat was very great. Many of the Reservists were soft, and the feet found them out. Their rough clothes rubbed them. Tom carried rifles all day, and I carried rifles and kit on my horse, while the men held on to the stirrups.

By this time the Maires of France seemed to be growing faint under the strain of billeting. We never saw the Maire of Longueville. The country made a wonderful picture that I shall never forget. We marched past fields of rich, tall grass, most splendid pasture, and by acres and acres of ripe corn which was either uncut or, if cut, uncarried.

There was any amount of food for our horses, but one felt reluctant at first at feeding them in the standing corn. I went ahead when I could to forage for the mess, and because Moonshine danced continuously and produced confusion.

We lived chiefly on hard-boiled eggs, chocolate and beer, but we did better than most other companies, because generally, as Valentine said, the officers' vocabulary was limited to 'omelette' and 'bière.'

Longueville is a very long town, with fine houses, and we did capitally there, but the men were tired. No. 3 dined luxuriously at a farm. Hugo Gough and I billeted at two houses close to each other. At 6 o'clock I went to get some rest, when my servant told me that the order had come to stand to arms at once, as the Germans were close upon us.

I went outside and heard one cannon boom very faintly in the distance. Women were wringing their hands and crying in the streets, and the battalion was order to stand to arms. Then, after a time, we were ordered to march at ten, and went back to quarters. At this time we began to curse the Germans for disturbing the peace of Europe.

The women of the village brought us milk, bread, everything they could for the march. While we were dining the order came to make ready for a German attack. We went out at once. Bernard took me up and down various roads, and we put iron and wire and everything we could lay hold of, across them, making a flimsy defence. When we returned we heard that we were to march at 2 a.m., and at 11 those who could lay down to sleep. The woman in my house was very kind in getting bread and milk. At 2 o'clock we began marching. The horses were all over the place. Moonshine nearly kicked a man behind her heels, and Tom just missed being killed by the ammunition horse in front. It was very dark.

We marched to a place called Senlis. Dawn came, and then an enemy aeroplane appeared over us, which everybody at once shot at. Moonshine broke up two companies in the most casual way. The aeroplane went on. In Belgium the people were very good to us, during the week-end that we spent there. They were honest and pathetic. There were no signs of panic, but there was a ghastly silence in the towns.

Beyond Senlis we were halted on a plain near a big town which we did not then know was Mons. We were drawn up and told that the Germans were close to us and that we had to drive them back. Valentine and I lay down under the shelter of a haystack, as it was raining. It was a mournful day in its early hours. At about 10 a.m. I was sent for by the Colonel, who had been looking for me, he said, for some time. He told me to ride after Stepney to Quevy-le-Grand. I rode fast, and caught up Stepney. We stabled our horses and went round the town. Soames, a Staff officer, told us we could have both sides of the road – as we understood, the pompous main road. Unfortunately he meant both sides of an insignificant road we had not even noticed. We took one of the biggest and

9

most beautiful farms I have ever seen for Headquarters, and proposed to put seven or eight officers in it. We, then, as usual, found that this house and all the rest had been given to the Coldstreamers, and we went to hunt for other billets. I thought I heard cannon, faint and dim. As we went on with our work the noise grew louder and louder. There was a big battle going on within four or five miles. Then in came the battalion from Senlis (which was burnt twenty-four hours later) at about twelve, and got into billets, while, at last, we had luncheon. Valentine and I were eating an omelette and talking Shakespeare, when suddenly we saw the battalion go past. We both got cursed because we had not been able to prophesy that the battalion would start within twenty minutes. We marched on till about half-past three, through rising and falling land, under a very hot sun. We were getting nearer to the battle. The sky was filled with smoke-wreaths from shells. 'We are going slap-bang at them,' said Hubert[13]. At 3.30 we found ourselves on a hill, by a big building which looked like a monastery. The road was crowded with troops and frightened peasants. Below the road lay the green valley with the river winding through it, and on the crest of the wooded hills beyond were the Germans.

We left our horses and marched down to the valley. As we passed the village of Harveng I inconsiderately tried to get a drink of water from a house. The men naturally followed, but we were all ordered on, and I had nothing to drink until 7 o'clock the next morning. The men, or some of them, got a little water that night.

From behind us by the monastery the shells rose in jerks, three at a time. The Germans answered from the belt of trees above the cliffs. Our feelings were more violently moved against German as the disturber of Europe. I went into the first fight prepared only for peace, as I had left my revolver and sword on my horse. Tom said: 'For goodness sake don't get away from our company; those woods will be full of Germans with bayonets to-night.' We never doubted that we should drive them back. The Colonel called the

13.   Major Hubert Crichton (1874–1914), Second-in-Command, 1ˢᵗ Battalion Irish Guards.

10

officers together and told us that the trees above the chalk cliffs were our objective. We then lay down in some lucerne and waited and talked. The order to move came about 5.30, I suppose. We went down through the fields rather footsore and came to a number of wire fences which kept in cattle. These fences we were ordered to cut. My agricultural instinct revolted at this destruction. We marched on through a dark wood to the foot of the cliffs and skirting them, came to the open fields, on the flank of the wood, sloping steeply upwards. Here we found our first wounded man, though I believe as we moved through the wood an officer had been reported missing.

The first stretch was easy. Some rifle bullets hummed and buzzed round and over us, but nothing to matter. We almost began to vote war a dull thing. We took up our position under a natural earthwork. We had been there a couple of minutes when a really terrific fire opened. We were told afterwards that we were not the target – that it was an accident that they happened to have stumbled on the exact range. But even if we had known this at the time, it would not have made much difference. It was as if a scythe of bullets passed directly over our heads about a foot above the earthworks. It came in gusts, whistling and sighing. The men behaved very well. A good many of them were praying and crossing themselves. A man next to me said: 'It's hell fire we're going into.' It seemed inevitable that any man who went over the bank must be cut neatly in two. Valentine was sent to find out if Bernard was ready on the far left. Then, in a lull, Tom gave the word and we scrambled over and dashed on to the next bank. Bullets were singing round us like a swarm of bees, but we had only a short way to go, and got, all of us, I think, safely to the next shelter, where we lay and gasped and thought hard.

Our next rush was worse, for we had a long way to go through turnips. The prospect was extremely unattractive; we thought that the fire came from the line of trees which we were ordered to take, and that we should have to stand the almost impossible fire from which the first bank had sheltered us. This was not the case, as the German trenches, we heard afterwards, were about 300 yards behind the trees, but their rifle fire and their shells cut across. We had not gone more than about 100 yards, at a rush and uphill, when a shell burst over my head. I jumped to the conclusion that I was killed and fell flat. I was ashamed of myself before I reached the ground, but looking round, found that everybody else had done the same.

The turnips seemed to offer a sort of cover, and I thought of the feelings of the partridges, a covey of which rose as we sank. Tom gave us a minute in which to get our wind – we lay gasping in the heat, while the shrapnel splashed about – and then told us to charge, but ordered the men not to fire until they got the word. As we rose, with a number of partridges, the shooting began again, violently, but without much effect. I think we had six or seven men hit. We raced to the trees. Valentine was so passionately anxious to get there that he discarded his haversack, scabbard and mackintosh, and for days afterwards walked about with his naked sword as a walking-stick.

When we reached the trees in a condition of tremendous sweat we found an avenue and a road with a ditch on either side. We were told that our trenches were a few yards over the farther hedge, faced by the German trenches, about 250 yards off. There was fierce rifle and machine-gun fire. Night fell; the wounded were carried back on stretchers; we sat very uncomfortably in a ditch. I was angry with Tom for the only time on the march, as he was meticulous about making us take cover in this beastly ditch when outside there was a bank of grass like a sofa, which to all intents and purposes was safe from fire. We were extremely thirsty, but there was nothing to drink and no prospect of getting water. After some time we moved down the road upon which we lay, getting what sleep we could. In the earlier part of the night there were fierce duels of rifle fire and machine guns between the two trenches. It sounded as if the Germans were charging. Our men in the road never got a chance of letting off their guns. Most of us dozed coldly and uncomfortably on the hard road. I woke up about 2 a.m., dreaming that a mule was kicking the splash-board of a Maltese wagon to pieces, and then realized that it was the German rifle fire beyond the hedge, hitting the road. I walked up the road for a few yards and heard two men talking, one of whom was, I suppose, Hubert, and the other must have been Curry who commands the Grenadiers. Hubert said: 'Have I your leave, sir, to retire?' 'Yes, you have; everybody else has gone; it is clear that we are outflanked on the left, and it is suicide to stay.' the battalion was then ordered to retire; No. 3 Company, doing rearguard, was ordered back to the fields which we had already crossed. I said to Tom: 'I hear upon the best authority that this is suicide.' Tom said: 'Of course it is; we shall get an awful slating.' We moved back. There was a faint light and a spasmodic rifle fire from the Germans as we went back to the fields we had crossed. We could not make out why they did not open on us with shrapnel, as they had the range. We lay down on the new-cut hay, which smelt delicious. It seemed almost certain that we should be wiped out when dawn came, but most of us went fast asleep. I did. At 4 o'clock we were hurried off. We went down into the blinding darkness of the wood by the road we had gone the evening before. We went through the wood, past the monastery, up into the village. There we waited. The road was blocked, the villagers were huddled, moaning, in the streets.

The men were very pleased to have been under fire, and compared notes as to how they felt. Everyone was pleased. But they felt that more of this sort of thing would be uncivilized, and it ought to be stopped by somebody now. In the dawn we crossed a high down, where we expected to be shelled, but nothing happened. We were very tired and footsore.

At 7 o'clock we got to Quevy-le-Petit and had a long drink, the first for seventeen hours. The smell of powder and the heat had made us very thirsty. Two companies were set to dig trenches. We were held in reserve, and all the hot morning we shelled the Germans from Quevy-le-Petit, while their guns answered our fire without much effect. One shell was a trouble. The remainder of the Regiment (men without officers) who had had a bad time at Mons had a shell burst over them and rushed through our ranks, taking some of our men with them. This was put right at once.

We were told that a tremendous German attack was to take place in the evening; we disliked the idea, as, even to an amateur like myself, it was obvious that there was hardly any means of defence. To stay was to be destroyed, as the Colonel said casually, causing 'une impression bien pénible.'

We wrote farewell letters which were never sent. I kept mine in my pocket, as I thought it would do for a future occasion. They began to shell us heavily while we helped ourselves from neighbouring gardens. We did this with as much consideration as possible, and Valentine and I went off to cook some potatoes in an outhouse by a lane.

The peasants were flying, and offered us all their superfluous goods. They were very kind. Then an order to retire came, and in hot haste we left our potatoes. We retired at about 1 o'clock in the afternoon and marched to Longueville, or rather to a camp near it called Bavai. We reached this camp at about 10.30 at night.

Moonshine behaved like the war-horse in the Bible. She had hysterics which were intolerable; smelling the battle a long way off. She must have done this the night before, when it was much nearer and I had left her with Ryan, for when I found her again she had only one stirrup. A sergeant-major captured her and picketed her for the night.

The orchard in which we camped blazed with torch-light and camp-fires and was extremely cheerful. Every now and then a rifle went off by accident, and this was always greeted with tremendous cheers. I was very tired, and threw myself down to sleep under a tree, when up came the Colonel, and said: 'Come along, have some rum before you go to bed.' I went and drank it, and with all the others lay down thoroughly warm and contented in the long, wet grass, and slept soundly for three hours. Next morning we were woken about 3 o'clock, but did not march off till 6 o'clock.

From Bavai we marched to Landrecies. Hubert rode ahead with me to do the billeting. We pastured our horses in the luxuriant grass and got milk at the farms. We did not see much sign of panic amongst the people, but coming to a big railway station we saw that all the engines of the heavy ammunition wagons had been turned round. Hubert saw and swore. In the morning we occupied a farm where I tried to buy a strap to replace my lost stirrup. We lay about under haystacks and talked to the farmer and his son.

After about an hour it was reported that two hundred Germans were coming down the road, and Eric went off after them, with machine guns.

The retreat had begun in real earnest. This whole retreat was curiously normal. Everybody got very sick of it, and all day long one was hearing officers and men saying how they wanted to turn and fight. I used to feel that myself, though when one was told to do so and realized that we were unchaperoned by the French and faced by about two million Germans, it did something to cool one's pugnacity, and one received the subsequent order to retire in a temperate spirit. Men occasionally fell out from bad feet, but the regiment marched quite splendidly. There was never any sign of flurry or panic anywhere. I think that most people, when they realized what had happened, accepted things rather impersonally. They thought that as far as our Army in France was concerned, disaster, in the face of the enormous numbers that we had to fight, was inevitable, but that this disaster was not vital as long as the Navy was safe.

My dates are not quite accurate here, as I cannot account for one day. It was Sunday, August 23rd, that we had the fight at Mons; I remember several men said: 'Our people are now going to Evening Service at home,' as we marched out; and it was Tuesday, September 1st, that we had the fight in which I and the others were taken prisoners.

Hubert and I arrived at Landrecies about 1 o'clock. Going in, we met Soames, a Staff officer, who told us where we could quarter the men. We went to a big house belonging to a man called Berlaimont, which Hubert wanted to have as Headquarters. Berlaimont was offensive and did not wish to give his house. We went on to the Maire, who gave us permission to take it. After lunch we went on billeting, finding some very fine houses. We had a mixed reception. Berlaimont gave in ungraciously, and wrote up rather offensive orders as to what was not to be done: 'Ne pas cracher dans les corridors.' In other houses, too, they made difficulties. I said: 'After all, we are better than the Germans.' They soon had the chance of judging. The troops came in to be billeted. At 6 o'clock fire suddenly broke out in the town, and the cry was raised that the Germans were upon us. I ran back and got my sword and revolver at Headquarters, and going out, found a body of unattached troops training a Maxim on the estaminet that was my lodgings. I prevented them firing. Troops took up positions all over the town. The inhabitants poured out pell-mell. It was like a flight in the Balkans. They carried their all away in wheelbarrows, carts, perambulators, and even umbrellas. I met and ran into Monsieur Berlaimont, very pale and fat, trotting away from the town; he said to me with quivering cheeks: 'What is it?' I said: 'It is the Prussians, Monsieur Berlaimont and they will probably spit in your corridors.'

We had some dinner in a very hospitable house. At 8 o'clock there was some very fierce fighting; the Coldstreamers had been ordered outside the town. The Germans came up, talking French, and called out to Monk, a Coldstream officer: 'Ne tirez pas; nous sommes des amis,' and 'Vive les Anglais.' A German knocked Monk under a transport wagon. Then our men grasped what was happening; they charged the Germans and the Germans charged them, three times, I believe. They brought up machine guns. Afterwards one of our medical officers said that we lost 150 men, killing 800 to 1,000 Germans. It was there that Archer Clive[14] was killed.

Just before dinner I met an officer of the regiment. I asked him if he had a billet. He told me he could not get one, and I said he could have mine and that I would find another. However, I found that my kit had already been put into the estaminet, and took him up to the market-place to find a lodging. We first went to an empty café, where all the liquor was left out, with no master or servants. We left money for what beer we drank. I then found a room in a tradesman's house. After dinner I went down to the main barricade with Jack. Wagons, including one of our own that carried our kit, had been dragged across the road and defences were put up like lightning. We loopholed the houses and some houses were pulled down. It was an extraordinarily picturesque scene. The town was pitch-black except where the torches glowed on the faces and on the bayonets of the men, or where shells

14. The Hon Archer Windsor-Clive (1890–1914).

flashed and burst. I thought of the taking of Italian towns in the seventeenth century. The Germans shelled us very heavily. It did not seem as if there was much chance of getting away, but no one was despondent. At about 1 a.m. there was a lull in the firing, and I went back to lie down in my room. There I fell asleep, and the shelling of the town did not wake me, though the house next to me was hit. About 2.30, in my sleep I heard my name, and found Desmond calling me loudly in the street outside. He said: 'We have lost two young officers, come out and find them at once. The Germans are coming into the town and we shall have to clear out instantly.' I said to him: 'I don't know either of the officers by sight and if I did it is far too dark to see them.' 'Well,' he said, 'you must do your best.' I went out and walked about the town which was still being shelled but I was far more afraid of being run over in the darkness than of being hit. Troops were pouring out in great confusion; foot, artillery, transport mixed, and there were great holes in the road made by the German shells. I met Eric Gough who said: 'Come along with me to Guise'; also the driver of a great transport wagon who said he had no orders, and begged me to come with him; he felt lonely without an officer.

It was quite clear to me that it was impossible to find these two officers. I met Desmond by Headquarters and told him so; he said: 'Very well, fall in and come along.' The regiment passed at that moment. Hubert and Tom told me to fall in, but I would not leave Moonshine, though there did not seem to be much more chance of finding her than the officers. My groom and servant had both disappeared. The houses were all locked and deserted. I battered on a door with my revolver. Two old ladies timidly came out with a light. They pointed to a house where I could find a man, but at that moment a Frenchman came up, whom I commandeered. I went off to Headquarters to see if a sergeant was left.

There was nobody there. The dinner left looked like Belshazzar's feast. I had a good swig of beer from a jug. My saddle and sword had gone. I went out with the Frenchman and saw that the troops were nearly out of the town. I determined to stay, if necessary, and hide until I could find my horse, but the Frenchman turned up trumps and we found her. We were terrified

17

of her heels in the dark. I thanked the old ladies and apologized for having threatened them with my revolver. There was no question of riding Moonshine bareback. I went back to get a saddle, below Headquarters, but the Germans were there, so the Frenchman swore. It was too dark to see, but they weren't our men. I took her back to where the medical officer was billeted. He had been waiting with a dying man and was about to leave the town. I asked him to let one of his men lead her, and went forward to see if I could get a saddle. In this I failed. As I got out of the town dawn was breaking. For some obscure reason one of our gunners fired a shell. Everybody said: 'I suppose that is to tell them where we are.' We all thought that the German artillery fire must catch us going out of the town. For the second time they let us off. By that time we had grasped the fact that they could outmarch us, but we did not know that they had come on motorcars, and ascribed their greater pace to what we believed to be the fact – that we were entirely unsupported by the French. My regiment were a good long way ahead. I joined an officer who was leading a detachment, and he was anxious that I should stay with him. As I walked along, pretty footsore, an unshaven man came up and asked me if I liked this sort of thing better than politics. I didn't say much, as I heard the soldiers discussing politicians in the dark at Landrecies, cursing all politicians every time a shell fell, and saying: 'Ah, that's another one we owe to them. Why aren't they here?' He offered me a horse. He was the Colonel of the Irish Horse, Burns-Lindow[15]. I took the horse gratefully, which had a slight wound on its shoulder and was as slow as an ox, poor beast. This drove me almost mad after Moonshine, and, meeting another officer, I fell into conversation with him. I asked if he saw anything wrong in my taking the saddle off this horse and putting it on to Moonshine when I found her. He said it was certainly against the rules. He told me he was the Commander of the Division and I then recognized Douglas Haig[16]. I got away

15.   Lt Col I.W. Burns-Lindow DSO.
16.   Field Marshal Douglas Haig, 1st Earl Haig KT GCB OM GCVO KCIE ADC (1861–1928). Commanding 1 Corps BEF.

from him as soon as possible and finding another officer of the Irish Horse persuaded him to help me to take off the saddle and put it on to Moonshine, whom I had regained, fairly chastened. I found the Colonel, and we rode on to Etreux. Here we brought down an aeroplane after it had dropped a bomb on us. The officers tried to prevent the men shooting, but the noise made their commands useless. The CO was very angry. He said: 'I will teach you to behave. Off you go and dig trenches.' One of the men said as we marched off: 'If that was a friendly aeroplane, what did it want to drop that bomb on us for?' He was quite right. It had done this, and the shell had fallen about thirty yards away. Our fire prevented us hearing it. Stephen came down in a Balaclava helmet and said that officers were the best shots at aeroplanes because pheasants had taught them to swing in firing.

At Etreux we were ordered to dig trenches, which we did. After this I slept under a hedge, where Bernard, the Frenchman, gave me some rum, which was very welcome, as it was raining. At about 9 o'clock I felt Hubert, very angry, thumping me, as he thought I was a private who had taken his haversack to lie on.

The next morning everybody was in tremendous spirits. They had slept very well in the trenches and those outside had been housed in nests of straw. The officers were called up and spoken to by the Colonel. He read out a message from Joffre to say that the British Army had saved France. He told us that the retreat had been inevitable and had given the French time to take up adequate defensive positions. The impression I think most of us had was that we had been used as bait. Then we were once more ordered to retire.

As I rode along in the morning going to La Fère an aeroplane passed fairly close over us; everybody fired at it at once; thousands of rounds must have been fired, and I found it useful in teaching Moonshine to stand fire. She took her first lesson well, though she broke up the formation of half a company. We often saw aeroplanes, and they were nearly always shot at, whether they belonged to friend or foe.

That day we marched to Origny, where we camped below a hill with a steep cliff to it. I went into the town and bought eggs, brandy, etc. There was every kind of rumour about: that we were completely surrounded by the Germans; that there were millions of them in front and behind; also that there had been a great French defeat at Charleroi.

We were all very jolly. At night the artillery poured past with the sound of a great cataract. We lay down on the hillside, and every man going to get straw to cover him walked over Tom's face, who swore himself almost faint with rage. All our kit had been lost at Landrecies, and many of us had not great-coats.

We started at dawn; but had to wait to let other troops pass us. I was sent back to look for communicating files of the regiment that had been lost. I found them with difficulty and brought them on. The Germans were too near to us. That day we marched through great avenues of tall poplars and through a pleasant smiling country to La Fère. Moonshine began to grow lame. I stayed behind to get food for my company and lost the regiment, only finding them again after long wanderings and with the greatest difficulty. We camped near La Fère.

The regiment forgot its tiredness in a hunt after a strange horse which strayed into our camp and which Eric finally captured for transport. Both Desmond and he tried hard to take my saddle from me; for the saddle which I had first put upon Moonshine was Hickie's harness. Then Hickie was invalided, and I lost his saddle at Landrecies and then got the saddle from Burns-Lindow, Colonel of the Irish Horse. I beat them in argument, but thought they were quite capable of taking the saddle in spite of that.

We stopped some time to smoke and rest. The men were drawn up on a torrid cornfield. Valentine was overdone. He volunteered, like the man in the Bible, to get water. Finding that he would have to wait in a long queue, he returned without the water. Tom's anger beat all records. A deputation from another regiment came and asked him to repeat what he had said. They were surprised to find that it was his brother-in-law who had provoked these comments.

I saw John Manners and George Cecil, and gave them cigarettes. Near a great factory of some kind we marched past Sir Douglas Haig. I hurried past him.

La Fère was an old fortified city. We were told we were to have a rest and the next day's march was to be a very short one. We camped near Berteaucourt. It was very hot. I hobbled up to the village to get provisions, and found a French girl, the daughter of a farmer, who talked fair English. Near the village I spoke to a number of people. I told one peasant I thought it was a mistake that everybody should fly from their houses if they did not mean to clear out altogether, and that it was an invitation to the Germans to loot and burn. He said: 'Monsieur, I quite agree with you. Moi, je vais agir en patriote quand ils viendront. Je vais tout bonnement descendre dans ma cave.' The next day (the 29th) we camped above the village of Pasly. On the road I got boracic cream for my horse's cracked heel. We passed through a big town, Coucy, crowded with curious, frightened, silent people. It had a very fine castle. I bought some cigarette-holders, with cinema pictures inside, for the Colonel. People pressed chocolate and all they could into my hands, taking payment unwillingly. Moonshine lost a shoe, but I managed to get her shod there. Reluctantly at Pasly I lent her to Robin, who went off to post his men in the village. The moment he had gone the OC sent for me and told me we had got outside the area of our maps, and asked if I could get him a map. I started off at once to walk to Soissons. When he discovered where I was going he said it was out of the question; so I walked down to Pasly either to get a map there or to take the Maire's carriage and drive to Soissons. In Pasly there was a tenth-rate Maire and a schoolmaster. They provided me with an ancient map, the date of which was 1870. It did not even mark the monument of the schoolmasters whom the Germans had lightheartedly shot on their last visit to the village.

I found a half-wit, and paid him to carry up some wine, bread and eggs.

We camped above a quarry and talked of what was going to happen. There seemed only two alternatives. One was that we should get into Paris and take first-class tickets home to England, and the other that we should stay and get wiped out. For we still saw no French troops; we still believed ourselves to be 100,000 against a force of anything from one to two millions.

21

Eric had met a Lancer who had been full of German atrocities. I met him and talked to him afterwards. His stories sounded improbable. Eric had also seen an extraordinary thing happen that morning. He had seen an aeroplane which we were bombarding. It was flying in the blue sky when it was struck. It was there, and then it was not. It just disappeared.

August 31st. We got up fairly early, and I rode with Eric past caves in which there were houses and quarries down the steep hill-side to the plain of Soissons. It was a beautiful morning, very peaceful, and the air was scented. There was bright sunlight over the marching soldiers and the fields of green, tall grass. The CO told me that our camping ground was at Coeuvre. I asked leave to ride into Soissons and see if I could not get clean shirts and hand-kerchiefs to replace what we had lost at Landrecies.

Soissons was like a sunlit town of the dead. Four out of five houses were shut. Most of the well-to-do people had gone. It was silent streets and blind houses. The clattering which Moonshine made on the cobbles was almost creepy. I stopped first of all at a saddler's shop and tried to get a proper bridle. The saddler was a rough democratic Frenchman, not a bad fellow, the sort of man who made the Republic. He took me to a boot shop which was my first need, where the people were very kind, and I bought a capital pair of boots for twelve francs. I went into the 'Lion d'Or.' they refused me a stall for Moonshine on the ground that the land-lord and all his family were going. I insisted and bought her some fodder, also some food for myself. They drove hard bargains.

Out of doors I met some English officers having breakfast. They had only just arrived. I left a man called Gustave to look after Moonshine and went out to spend a most laborious morning of shopping. After going to many different shops I found a bazaar like a mortuary, with two old women and a boy. They said to me: 'Take whatever you want and pay as much or as little as pleases you. If the Germans come we shall set fire to this place.' They pressed every kind of souvenir on me, but it was extraordinary, with plenty lying round, how difficult it was to get what one needed. I was buying mostly for other people. It was like being turned loose in Selfridge's – boots, scissors, pocket-knives, electric torches, watches, bags, vests, etc. I also bought an alpenstock, as I had lost my sword and thought it might be useful as a light bayonet.

I then went and had a bath, the first proper one since England. The heat was very great. I felt dirty and wanted to shave my beard, as the men said every day that I became more like King Edward. I then intended to go to the Cathedral, but found the few English soldiers in the town moving out hurriedly. They said the Germans were coming in an hour. So I gave up the Cathedral and went and had lunch in a jolly little inn. There were some very excitable Frenchmen, one of whom asked me if I would sell him a lucky sixpence for a franc which he could wear round his neck. I suppose he was really pathetic; at the moment he only irritated me. He said: 'J'ai confiance – même s'ils vont à Paris j'aurais confiance.' 'But,' he said, 'where is the French Army?' They were all saying that by this time.

I went back to my boot shop. All the women there were crying. They insisted upon giving me some wine. At the hotel I found the hotel-keeper and his family going off, squeaking with anger at the ostler, Gustave, who was helping me to carry all I had bought in two great bags. The weight was very oppressive in the heat, and I was afraid of making Moonshine's tender foot worse on the hard road. Before I had got outside the town I had to get off and read-just everything, with the help of some very kind French people. While I was doing this, Westminster[17], with Hugh Dawnay[18], drove up in his beautiful car. I suggested his taking my things on to Coeuvre. He said, unfortunately he had other orders, and wanted to know where to lunch. I told him where I had lunched, but said that he would probably have to share his lunch with the Germans if he went into the town, as they must now be close behind us.

Riding on, I met some French troops, evacuating the town and with them a man of my regiment, who had hurt his knee. He could

17.　　Hugh Grosvenor, 2nd Duke of Westminster GCVO DSO (1879 –1953).
18.　　Major the Hon Hugh Dawnay DSO (1875–1914).

not walk, so I put him under the charge of a French sergeant. While I was talking to him two other men of my regiment came up. They had fallen out on the previous day and had had nothing to eat since yesterday's breakfast. I took them into a French house, where the people were very hospitable; gave them food at once and insisted on giving them champagne, which they said was 'déchampagnisé.' The men ate like wolves. One of them was a splendidly built fellow, called Sheridan.

Then we marched slowly on in the heat, for about two hours, when Sheridan said: 'What is it is happening yonder, sir?' pointing to the horizon about a mile away. Soon rifle fire broke out, and Sheridan said: 'There are Uhlans coming down the road.' There was a wood on our left, and we made preparations to get into this; the other man had fallen behind. They were both very done, but Sheridan was like a different man at the prospect of a fight. Our people, however, or rather the French, drove the German cavalry back at this moment, and we went on quietly. I was glad to be able to turn to the left, as the fighting on our right was pretty hot and I was weighed down with all the extra things I carried.

I fell into conversation with a medical officer, and asked him if he knew where Coeuvre was. Then an RAMC Colonel came up and looked at my kit very suspiciously. He asked me who the General in command of the Division was. I said I had forgotten his name; I could not keep my head filled with these details. He said to me: 'You don't seem to know who you are.' I said to him: 'I know who I am; I don't know who you are, I don't want to. I hope to God I shall never see you again. Go to hell and stay there.' This made him angry, and he said: 'Your regiment is ahead on the left, but the Germans are in front of you, if you wish to rejoin them,' pointing in the direction from which I had come.

All this time I had been waiting for Sheridan and other numerous stragglers behind me, and at this point I turned round and rode off to see what had happened, thoroughly irritated with the RAMC Colonel. This apparently convinced him that I really was a German, as the engagement in the rear was going on fairly close, and he came after me with a Major of the KRR, who was unhappy. He said: 'Will you come with me to my Colonel?' I said:

'I will go with you anywhere to get away from this fussy little man, but if you think that a German spy would come on a race-horse, dressed like the White Knight, with an alpenstock, you are greatly mistaken.' He promised to have my stragglers looked after, and then I rode up to his regiment with him, when Blank came up and shook hands. We had not met since Eton. He cleared my character. After that I went on as fast as I could. I picked up some more of my regiment, including a sergeant who had sprained his ankle. I told him to ride, but found a motor and put him in that.

Soon we were stopped by a sentry in a wood, as it was growing dark. He said that his officer had told him to stop all on the road and send for him. Then came General Monro[19], who was also stopped. He was with a sad man. He forced his way through, and I asked permission to take on the men of my regiment. He told me that I should find my regiment at Soucy, and gave me the permission I wanted. In a few moments I met the officer who had had us stopped. He said the Germans were very close to us. We could hear firing nearby.

I reached my regiment as night was falling. They were delighted with my arrest. We spent our last night very comfortably, though there was heavy dew. Tom, who had been frightfully overdone, always carrying rifles, was recovering, and everyone was cheerful and very keen to have a fight. Until now only Hickie had been invalided. The rum at night after a long march made a wonderful difference. The men got in very tired, footsore, cold and hungry, and had to sleep on the wet ground. A tot of rum sent them to sleep, and sent them to sleep feeling warm. Teetotalism on the march is an excellent thing, better still to drink nothing, but that nip at night made the difference between health and sickness, comfort and misery.

September 1st. The next morning we got up at 2 o'clock. The Army was passing all round us already. It was like the sound of deep, slow rivers. For the first and last time we took a wrong turning, only for a couple of hundred yards. This was the only

19. General Sir Charles Monro Bt GCB GCSI GCMG ADC (1860–1929). Commanding the 2nd Division BEF.

mistake I saw at all in the long march. After two hours we halted, and S. and I sat under a dripping tree and talked about the West Country. At the beginning S. had said to me: 'I shall be very disappointed if I go home without seeing a fight, but the worst of it is you can't make an omelette without breaking eggs, and I don't want to see my friends killed.' I said to him: 'You are going to get your omelette all right now.' Some constituents passed me. They said: 'This be terrible dangerous. Do'ee come along with we.'

Moonshine would eat nothing, and this worried me. I had become very fond of her.

At about 6 o'clock we halted on what I knew to be a tragic plain. In my mind I associate this plain with turnips, though I am not sure that any grew there. There was stubble, high and wet lucerne, and a mournful field where corn had been cut but not carried. We sat about on the wet, muddy ground for breakfast, while a thin, dismal rain fell.

The CO called us round and gave us our orders. He said: 'We are required to hold this wood until 2 o'clock in the afternoon. We may have to fight a rearguard action until a later hour if there is a block in the road. We are to retire upon Rond de la Reine.' After this we breakfasted on hot cocoa; it tasted of vaseline or paraffin, but it was warm.

It was apparent that if the First Division took long over their luncheon we should be wiped out. By this time everyone had got their second wind, their feet were hard and they were cheerful. Jumbo said he could go on walking forever. I talked to Alex[20] and agreed that we had seen a great deal of fun together. He had said, while we were crossing the Channel, that it was long odds, not, of course, against some of us coming back, but against any particular one of us seeing it through. This was now visibly true; we believed that we were three divisions against twenty-one or even twenty-eight German divisions. I wrote two letters, one of them a eulogy of Moonshine. I went to Desmond, asking him to post them. He said crossly: 'You seem to think that Adjutants can work miracles.

20.   Field Marshal H.R. Alexander, 1st Earl Alexander of Tunis KG OM GCB GCMG CSI DSO MC PC PC CD (10 December 1891–16 June 1969).

Charles asks for letters under fire, you want to post them on the battlefield. It is quite useless to write letters now.'

He then borrowed some of my paper and wrote a letter. I have the picture in my mind of Desmond constantly sitting, in very tidy breeches, writing and calling for sergeants. We had little sleep. He never seemed to sleep at all. He was woken all the time and was always cheerful. We had nothing to do for a bit, and I read scraps about cemeteries from Shakespeare, to irritate the others. They remained cheerful. Then we moved off to the wood. Nobody had any illusions about the immediate future. One man said to me: 'I may live to see many battles; I think I shall, for I am very keen on my profession, but I shall never forget this plain or this morning.' It must have been about 7.30 when we went into the wood. No. 4 Company held the extreme right; they were protected by a wall, which they loopholed, and a wire fence outside. No. 3 Company was next on a road that ran through the heart of the wood to Rond de la Reine. I did not see Tom; I thought I was sure to see him some time in the morning. Stubbs was behind No. 3 Company, down in the village (I forget the name). The CO said to me: 'I want you to gallop for me to-day, so stick to me.' I lost him at once in the wood behind No. 4, but rode right down to a deserted farm and, swinging to my right, found him at the cross-roads.

I had seen a good deal of him the last days. He had a very attractive personality, and it was a delight to hear him talk about anything. I asked him what chance he thought we had of getting more than half of us away. He said he thought a fairly good chance. Then he said to me: 'How is your rest-cure getting on now? There is very little that looks like manoeuvres in the millennium about this, is there?' I had told him some time before that I looked upon this expedition as a rest-cure, as in some ways it was. We talked about Ireland and Home Rule, riding outside the wood. The grey, damp mist had gone and the day was beautiful.

He sent me first to Hubert, Second-in-Command, with the order that in the retreat every officer was to retire down the main road, with the exception of Stubbs, who was to retire as he liked. I imagine that he was afraid that men would be lost in the wood.

By this time the firing had begun, some way off, but our men could see the Germans coming over the rising land. The CO ordered me to find Colonel Pereira of the Coldstream Guards and tell him that, as soon as our own troops, now fighting the Germans in front of him, would fall back through his lines, after this he was to fall back himself.

I went off at a hand gallop, and had got halfway there, with the wood on my left and open land on my right, when the Germans began shooting at about three-quarters of a mile. Our men were firing at them from the wood, and I felt annoyed at being between two fires and the only thing visible to amuse our men and the Germans. I turned into the wood, and, galloping down a sandy way, found the road filled with refugees with haunted faces. We had seen crowds of refugees for days, but I felt sorrier for these. I suppose it was that the Germans were so very near them. I gave my message to Pereira, who advised me to go back through the wood, but I knew the other way and thought I should soon be past the German fire. I had not, however, counted on their advancing so quickly. When I came to the edge of the wood they were firing furiously – shrapnel, machine-gun and rifle fire. Our men had excellent cover, and were answering. I then tried to make my way through the wood, but it was abominably rough. There were ferns and brambles waist-high, and great ditches; the wood was very beautiful with its tall trees, but that, at the moment, was irrelevant. Moonshine stood like a goat on the stump of a tree that made an island among the ditches, and I turned back to take the way by the open fields. When I got outside the fire had grown very bad. I raced for an orchard that jutted out of the wood. Bullets hummed and buzzed. Coming to it, I found that there was wire round it. I then popped at full speed, like a rabbit, into the wood again, through a thicket, down an enormous ditch, up the other side, bang into some barbed wire, which cut my horse. It was like diving on horseback. I turned round and galloped delicately out again, riding full tilt round the orchard.

I found the Colonel, who was standing under shelter at the cross-roads to the left of the road, facing the enemy, that led through the heart of the wood. He mounted the bank and

watched the Germans advancing. I sat under the bank with Alex.
The German shells began to fall close to us, knocking the trees
about in the wood. There were some sergeants very excited and
pleased at the idea of a fight. They said: 'Now has come the time
for deeds, not words.' They felt that they were the men of the
moment.

We considered whether the Germans were likely to charge
down the road along which I had come, but thought we could
hold them effectively in check from our corner and that the fire
from the wood would reach them.

It was, I suppose, now about 10.30. Desmond, the Colonel and
I rode back into the big, green wood. It was very peaceful. The sun
was shining through the beech-trees, and for a bit the whole thing
seemed unreal. The CO talked to the men, telling them to reserve
their fire till the Germans were close on them. 'Then you will kill
them and they won't get up again.' That made them laugh. The
German advance began very rapidly. The Coldstreamers must
have begun falling back about this time. The Germans came up in
front and on our left flank. There was a tremendous fire. The
leaves, branches, etc., rained upon one. One's face was constantly
fanned by the wind from their bullets. This showed how bad their
fire was. My regiment took cover very well, and after the first
minute or two fired pretty carefully. Moonshine was startled to
begin with by the fire, but afterwards remained very still and
confidential. Desmond did not get off his horse; he told me to lead
my horse back into the wood and then come back to the firing
line. The Colonel then told me to gallop up to the Brigadier to say
that the retreat was being effectively carried out; that there were
two squadrons advancing and he did not know what force of
infantry. In this estimate he was very much out, as subsequent
events proved. Eric, now at home wounded, said to me: 'The
Germans seemed hardly to have an advance guard; it was an army
rolling over us.' When I found the Brigadier he wanted to know if
the CO seemed happy about things. I said I thought on the whole
he did. There were bullets everywhere and men falling, but the fire
was still too high. One bullet in about half a million must have hit
a man. I reported to the Colonel. Our men had then begun to

retire down the main road to Rond de la Reine. A galloper came
up and, as far as I heard, said that we were to hang on and not
retreat yet. This officer was, I think, killed immediately after
giving his message. The Colonel said that the Coldstreamers had
already begun to retreat, that we couldn't hold on there, but must
go back to the position we had left. We were ordered to resume
the position which Hubert had been told to leave. The Germans
were by this time about 250 yards away, firing on us with
machine guns and rifles. The noise was perfectly awful. In a lull
the CO said to the men: 'Do you hear that? Do you know what
they are doing that for? They are doing that to frighten you.' I said
to him: 'If that's all, they might as well stop. As far as I am
concerned, they have succeeded, two hours ago.'

The men were ordered to charge, but the order was not heard
in the noise, and after we had held this position for some minutes
a command was given to retreat. Another galloper brought it, who
also, I think, was shot. Guernsey[21], whom I met with his company,
asked me to gallop back and tell Valentine he must retire his
platoon; he had not received the order. I found Valentine and got
off my horse and walked him some yards down the road, the
Germans following. He, like everybody else, was very pleased at
the calm way the men were behaving.

I mounted and galloped after the Colonel, who said: 'If only we
could get at them with the bayonet, I believe one of our men is as
good as three of theirs.' He started in the direction of the
Brigadier. Men were now falling fast. I happened to see one man
drop with a bayonet in his hand a few yards off, and reined in my
horse to see if I could help him, but the CO called me and I
followed him. The man whom I had seen was Hubert, though
I did not know it at the time. The CO said: 'It is impossible now
to rescue wounded men; we have all we can do.' He had a
charmed life. He raced from one place to another through the
wood; cheering the men and chaffing them, and talking to me;
smoking cigarette after cigarette. Under ordinary conditions one

21.   Captain Heneage Finch, Lord Guernsey (1883–1914). Killed in Action
on the 14th September.

would have thought it mad to ride at the ridiculous pace we did over the very broken ground, but the bullets made everything else irrelevant. At about 1 o'clock we went up to the Brigadier at the corner of the road. The fighting there was pretty hot. One of the men told the Colonel that Hubert was killed. The Colonel said: 'Are you sure?' The man said: 'Well, I can't swear.' I was sent back to see. The man said he was about 400 yards away, and as I galloped as hard as I could, Guernsey, I think, called to me: 'To the right and then to the left.' As I raced through the wood there was a cessation of the firing, though a number of shots came from both sides. They snapped very close. I found Hubert in the road we had been holding. I jumped off my horse and put my hand on his shoulder and spoke to him. He must have been killed at once, and looked absolutely peaceful. He cannot have suffered at all. I leant over to see if he had letters in his pocket, when I heard a whistle 25 or 30 yards behind me in the wood. I stood up and called: 'If that is an Englishman, get outside the wood and up to the corner like hell; you will be shot if you try and join the rest through the wood. The Germans are between us.' I bent over to pick up Hubert's bayonet, when again a whistle came and the sound of low voices, talking German. I then thought the sooner I was away the better. As I swung into the saddle a shot came from just behind me, missing me. I rode back as fast as Moonshine could go. The lull in the firing had ceased, and the Germans were all round us. One could see them in the wood, and they were shooting quite close. The man who finally got me was about 15 or 20 yards away; his bullet must have passed through a tree or through Bron's greatcoat, because it came into my side broken up. It was like a tremendous punch. I galloped straight on to my regiment and told the Colonel that Hubert was dead. He said: 'I am sorry, and I am sorry that you are hit. I am going to charge.' He had told me earlier that he meant to if he got the chance.

I got off and asked them to take on my horse. Then I lay down on the ground and an RAMC man dressed me. The Red Cross men gave a loud whistle when they saw my wound, and said the bullet had gone through me. The fire was frightfully hot. The men who were helping me were crouching down, lying on the ground.

While he was dressing me a horse – his, I suppose – was shot just behind us. I asked them to go, as they could do me no good and would only get killed or taken themselves. The doctor gave me some morphia, and I gave them my revolver. They put me on a stretcher, leaving another empty stretcher beside me. This was hit several times. Shots came from all directions, and the fire seemed to be lower than earlier in the day. The bullets were just above me and my stretcher. I lost consciousness for a bit; then I heard my regiment charging. There were loud cries and little spurts of spasmodic shooting; then everything was quiet and a deep peace fell upon the wood. It was very dreamlike.

It is really very difficult to reconstruct this fight. I think every man's attention was fixed like iron on doing his own job, otherwise they would all have noticed more. I carry in my mind a number of very vivid pictures – Desmond on his horse, Valentine and I discussing fatalism, the CO smoking cigarettes in the cinema holders I had bought for him a few days before.

As I lay on the stretcher a jarring thought came to me. I had in my pocket the flat-nosed bullets which the War Office had served out to us as revolver ammunition. They were not dum-dum bullets, but they would naturally not make as pleasant a wound as the sharp-nosed ones, and it occurred to me that those having them would be shot. I searched my pockets and flung mine away. I did not discover one which remained and was buried later on – but neither did the Germans. It was first hearing German voices close by that jogged my memory about these bullets, and the Germans were then so close that I felt some difficulty in throwing the bullets away. The same idea must have occurred to others, for later I heard the Germans speaking very angrily about the flat bullets they had picked up in the wood, and saying how they would deal with anyone in whose possession they were found.

The glades became resonant with loud, raucous German commands and occasional cries from wounded men. After about an hour and a half, I suppose, a German with a red beard, with the sun shining on his helmet and bayonet, came up looking like an angel of death. He walked round from behind, and put his serrated bayonet on the empty stretcher by me, so close that it all but touched me. The stretcher broke and his bayonet poked me. I enquired in broken but polite German what he proposed to do next; after reading the English papers and seeing the way he was handling his bayonet, it seemed to me that there was going to be another atrocity. He was extraordinarily kind and polite. He put something under my head; offered me wine, water, and cigarettes. He said: 'Wir sind kamaraden.' Another soldier came up and said: 'Why didn't you stay in England – you who made war upon the Boers?' I said: 'We obeyed orders, just as you do; as for the Boers, they were our enemies and are now our friends, and it is not your business to insult wounded men.' My first friend then cursed him heartily, and he moved on.

The Germans passed in crowds. They seemed like steel locusts. Every now and then I would hear: 'Here is an officer who talks German,' and the crowd would swerve in like a steel eddy. Then: 'Schnell Kinder!' and they would be off. They gave a tremendous impression of lightness and iron. After some hours, when my wound was beginning to hurt, some carriers came up to take me to a collecting place for the wounded. These men were rather rough. They dropped me and my stretcher once, but were cursed by an officer. They then carried me some distance, and took me off the stretcher, leaving me on the ground. The Germans continued to pass in an uninterrupted stream. One motor cyclist, but with a bayonet in his hand, was very unpleasant. He said: 'I would like to put this in your throat and turn it round and round,' waving it down to my nose. That sort of thing happened more than once or twice, but there were always more friends than enemies, though as night fell the chance of being left without friends increased. As it grew dark, I got rather cold. One of the Germans saw this, covered me with his coat, and said: 'Wait a moment, I will bring you something else.' He went off, and, I suppose, stripped a dead Englishman and a dead German. The German jersey which he gave me had no holes in it; the Englishman's coat had two bayonet cuts.

The wounded began to cry dreadfully in the darkness. I found myself beside Robin, who was very badly wounded in the leg. The Germans gave me water when I asked for it, but every time

I drank it made me sick. At, I suppose, 9.30 or 10 p.m. they took us off into an ambulance and carried us to a house that had been turned into a hospital. I was left outside, talking to a Dane, who was very anti-German, though he was serving with them as a Red Cross man. He cursed them loudly in German. He said it was monstrous that I hadn't been attended to, that the Germans had had a defeat, and would be beaten. I said: 'Yes, it's all true, but please stop talking, because they'll hear you and punish me.'

Just before 12 o'clock they carried me into the hospital on to the operating table, and dressed my wound quickly.

Then I was helped out to an outhouse and lay beside Robin. It was full of English and German wounded. They gave us one drink of water and then shut and locked the door and left us for the night. One man cried and cried for water until he died. It was a horrible night. The straw was covered with blood, and there was never a moment when men were not groaning and calling for help. In the morning the man next to Robin went off his head and became animal with pain. I got the Germans to do what was possible for him. I asked the Germans to let me out, and they helped me outside into a chair, and I talked to an officer called Brandt. He sent a telegram to the German authorities to say that Robin and I were lightly wounded, and asking them to let our families know. He would not let me pay. I would have liked to have done it for everyone, but that wasn't possible. They took us away in an ambulance at about 11 o'clock. It was a beautiful September day, very hot indeed. The heat in the covered ambulance was suffocating, and Robin must have suffered horribly. He asked me the German for 'quick,' and when I told him, urged the Germans on. There were great jolts.

At Viviers I found Shields, who said to me: 'Hello, you wounded, and you a volunteer, too?' – as if a volunteer ought to be immune from wounds. We were carried upstairs and told that Valentine and Buddy, whom I had last met under the cedars, were in the same hospital. Valentine had the point of his elbow shot away just after I had left him. He raised his hand to brush a wasp off his neck, and only remembered pitching forward when a bullet struck his elbow. He woke up in a pool of blood. A German came up and took the flask of brandy that I had given him after my visit to Soissons. He gave Valentine a drink, and then, when Valentine had said he did not want any more, swigged the whole of the rest off. It was enough to make two men drunk, solidly, for hours. Later, five Germans came up to Valentine and ragged him. One of them kicked him, but an officer arrived, took all their names, promised Valentine they should be punished, and attached an orderly to him for the night. Buddy was badly wounded in the back and arm. He found his servant in the church at Viviers. Then we all met at the house in Viviers. The doctors gave Robin and me a strong dose of morphia. That afternoon a German doctor, whose name was Hillsparck, came in and woke me. He gave me a gold watch with a crest on it, and a silver watch and a purse of gold (£8 in it). He said that a Colonel to whom the watch belonged had been buried close by in the village of Haraman, and asked me if I could say who he was. We heard that the Colonel had been killed, and I imagined it must have been him, but we could not tell, as apparently every single man of the seventy odd who had charged with him had been killed. The doctor left this watch with me. In the hospital we believed that the General of the Division, Monro, and also our own Brigadier, General Scott Kerr[22], were wounded, and that the Colonel[23] and Tysdale were killed.

Our experiences on the field were all the same. We were all well treated, though occasionally we were insulted. In hospital an old *ober-stadt* was in command of the doctors. He was very good to us. The English doctors were Wetherell in command, Sinclair next, Rankin and Shields. They were all good doctors. Wetherell, Rankin and Shields were excellent fellows. Rankin, who has been killed since, himself wounded, was dressing the wounded on the field and was recommended for the VC. Shields has been killed in the same way, and I believe would have been recommended but that his CO was also killed. They were both the best sort of man you can find.

22. Brigadier Robert Scott-Kerr DSO (1859–1942). Commanding 4th Guards Brigade.
23. Lieutenant-Colonel The Hon George Morris (1872–1914), Commanding Officer 1st Battalion Irish Guards.

35

Sinclair was rather an ass, though Needham said that this was not possible as he was such a good surgeon. They used to dress the wounds every morning and one got callous very soon to the cries that one heard just outside the window. After a couple of days I moved into Buddy and Valentine's room. A little way down the street there was the château, full of wounded Germans. Our men were carried there to be operated upon.

Wetherell and the other doctors who went to help discovered that there were 311 wounded Germans as against 92 of our own, so we didn't do badly.

Every morning the German sentries used to come in and talk to us. My German and Buddy's was very weak, but we managed to get along all right. Downstairs those who were lightly wounded sat outside in the chairs they took from the house, in the sunny garden. It was a fairly luxurious house, with paper marked 'F.H.' I thought it was a girls' school, for the only books we could find were the *Berger de Valence* and Jules Verne. My side was painful the first few days. Then they cut me open and took out the bullet, which was all in bits. It was rather hard lines on the others to perform an operation in the room, but I felt much better for it. The food difficulty was rather acute. There was very little food, and what there was was badly cooked. We lived principally on things that Sinclair called 'chupatti' – thick, unleavened biscuits. The men began to give trouble. There was nobody in command of them. There was an ex-comedian who was particularly tiresome. We had to ask the Germans to punish one man for us. About the fourth day one of the orderlies escaped – Drummer McCoy. He passed for four days through the German lines, and on one occasion watched a whole Army Corps go by from the boughs of a tree. Then he found the French, who passed him on to the English, where he went to the Staff and told them of us. That is how we were picked up so quickly on the 11th.

Here is a copy of my diary for September 9th:

The people are beginning to return, but not the priest, who is with the Army. We want him for the regiment. Up till this time only six of the wounded have died. The Germans tell us every kind of story – the United States are declaring war on Japan, Italy on

36

France, Denmark on England, etc. etc. Also that Paris has been given twelve hours to accept or reject the German terms, and if the French Government is obdurate the town will be bombarded. We are told that we are to be taken as prisoners to Magdeburg. It is a week since I have had a cigarette.

Thursday, September 10*th.* We are all very anxious to get news home, but there is no chance. Last night S. Herbert died. I had a Testament, and Valentine and I found verses which W. read over his grave. Valentine has bad pain. Three bones broken in his arm and the point of his elbow gone. Buddy is better, but hit cruel hard. Robin has a bad wound, and is very restless. They don't like giving us morphia. Luckily I have got my own medicine chest, which is a good thing for all of us, as I can give the others sleeping draughts. Last night a French cavalry patrol came within two miles of us. Early this morning there was rifle fire close by. It sounded in the wood that we suppose is Haraman. We think the Germans may evacuate this place at any time. The bandages have given out. Stores are not coming in. There is a big aeroplane depot quite close by, and the whole air is full of aeroplanes. It looks and feels as if there might be a big battle round here soon. They have shot an old man wandering about the aerodrome. But he was asking for it.

9 *a.m.* The aeroplanes are being shifted from the depot. Last night we heard that arms were issued to all the wounded Germans in hospital who could carry them. This morning the Germans are digging trenches hard. There are Red Crosses everywhere. The doctors want us to go down to the cellars if we are shelled. The French women in the village say that the French are coming. The firing is increasing.

9.15 *a.m.* The German hospital across the way is ordered to be ready to move at once.

10.25 *a.m.* An order has come for all prisoners to parade at the church at 12 o'clock. The German lightly wounded are being sent on. We are very anxious as to whether they mean to take us, too. More of our wounded who have died are being buried.

11.10 *a.m.* A German doctor has come. He said: 'They are going and taking all (of our) prisoners, 18 (of our) lightly wounded, and leaving 25 (of their) badly wounded.' French

37

wounded are now coming in. We have no more bandages at all. A German sentry with whom I had talked has just come in. I asked him some days ago to buy some handkerchiefs. He said: 'I have not been able to buy you any handkerchiefs, or to get the cigarettes you wanted, but here is one of my own handkerchiefs, which I have washed. We have got to go.'

8 *p.m.* The last order is that the previous orders are countermanded and the Germans are to stay on ten days.

Friday, September 11*th.* Our English prisoners were marched off this morning. We are full of speculation as to what has really happened. Valentine, Buddy, and I are well.

10.10 *a.m.* There are many machine guns about four miles away.

10.30 *a.m.* There is a heavy rifle fire within a mile. It is very trying lying here in bed. We have nothing to read except *The Rajah's Heir* which V. sent to me and which has become known as the treasure-house of fun. It is a sort of mixture of Hymns Ancient and Modern and the *Fairchild Family.*

2 *p.m.* There is a Maxim within a few hundred yards of the house. Rifle volleys outside in the garden. A rising wind and rain threatening.

3 *p.m.* Heavy rain. The French are visible, advancing.

3.10 *p.m.* The French are here. They came in in fine style, like conquerors; one man first, riding, his hand on his hip. The German sentries who had been posted to protect us wounded walked down and surrendered their bayonets. The German doctors came to us for help. I offered to go, but Wetherell went. The French infantry and cavalry came streaming through. Our wounded went out into the pouring rain to cheer them. They got water from our men whose hands they kissed. The German guns are on the skyline. The Germans are in full retreat, and said to be cut off by the English.

5 *p.m.* A heavy bombardment of the German guns began from here. I have come upstairs to a long low garret with skylights, in order to leave Valentine and Buddy more room. Through the skylight one can see every flash of the French and German guns. The doctors all come up here to watch with their field glasses through my skylights.

Saturday, September 12*th*. Yesterday, when Wetherell went down, he found the German doctors receiving cavalier treatment from the French. He explained to the French that they had treated us with the greatest kindness; after that the French treated with courtesy the old *ober-stadt*. Shields carved a great wooden tombstone for the thirteen men who had died up to date. It is a month to-day since I left England.

This afternoon Colonel Thompson, English Staff Officer attached to General Manoury, who had been attached to the Serbian Army through the last war, came in. McCoy, who had escaped, had found him and told him about us at Viviers. He said he would take me into Villers Cotterets after he had done some other business. We talked a lot about the Balkans, but I finally went back and lay down in my garret and shall not get up again to-day.

Sunday, September 13*th*. I went off with Thompson this morning. We passed through the wood where we had had the fight, and a long grave of 120 men was shown to me by McCoy.

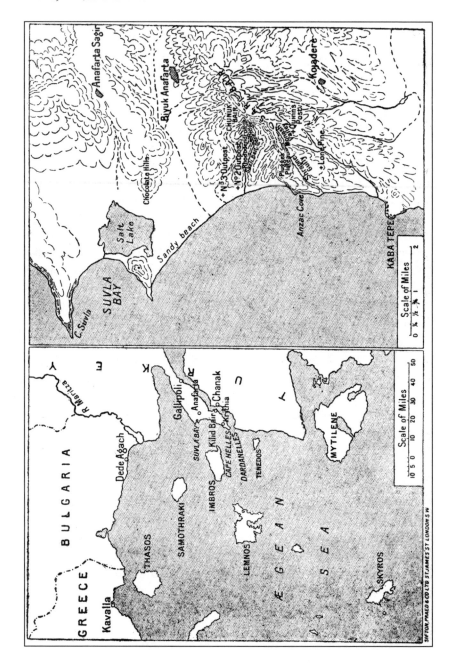

Chapter Two

Anzac
1915

When I was passed fit for Active Service, after some time in hospital, I left England for Egypt with five other officers. Four of these had strange histories. One is, perhaps, the most romantic figure of the War, another now governs a great Province, while two, after many adventures, were prisoners of war in Turkey, for different but dreary periods.

I was sent to the East because it had been my fortune to have travelled widely, and I had a fairly fluent smattering of several Eastern languages. On arriving at Gilbraltar about December 14th, 1914, we heard the first news of submarines. One of these was reported to have passed through into the Mediterranean a few days previously.

When I reached Egypt just before Christmas, superficially everything was calm. This calm did not last very long. I was given Intelligence work to do, under Colonel Clayton, who had played a very great part in achieving our success in the East. Reports constantly came in from Minia, Zagazig and Tanta of Turkish and German intrigues. General Sir J. Maxwell commanded the Forces in Egypt. Prince Hussein had just been proclaimed Sultan, and Egypt had been declared to be under British protection. Rushdy Pasha was Prime Minister and a triumvirate of Sir Milne Cheetham at the Residency, Sir R. Graham as Adviser to the Ministry of the Interior, and Lord Edward Cecil as Adviser to the Ministry of Finance, directed the Government.

It was difficult to believe that the Egyptian, who then had all the advantages, really meant mischief. Most people, I think, agreed with Lord Cromer, and believed that his policy of making taxes light and easy for the Egyptian had succeeded, but the East is never logical, as we all know, and the natural consequence constantly does not follow the parental cause. Mecca rose to join us after Kut had fallen; the rebellion in Egypt only took place when the English had achieved a complete victory over Turkey, and held Palestine and Syria. I quote the following incident as an illustration of the difficulty of sometimes following this mentality:

A Syrian reported to me that a great Egyptian family, whom I will call the Ashakas, had conspired to bring 15,000 rifles into the country and to engineer a rising. The rifles were to be imported from the Greek islands and from Greece, by means of Greek sponge-fishers. One of these, who had the pleasant and appropriate name of Son-of-the-Dagger, met me in a café in an obscure side street in Cairo. There he revealed the conspiracy, explaining that only the landing-place for the arms had still to be decided upon. He and his companions were to receive a commission on every rifle landed, and he wanted to know what the British Government would be ready to pay for his betrayal of his patrons.

On reporting this to the proper authorities, I was told that they were aware of the existence of this plot. The next day frantic messages from the Greek came, and I met him, disturbed in his mind. He said that the Ashakas had become suspicious of him and the other Greeks, and that he feared for his life. He asked to be arrested immediately after the seizure of the arms and thrown into prison with the Egyptians, and then to be flogged before them, in order to convince them that he was acting honourably by them. He was very anxious to be paid for both pieces of treachery, by the Egyptians and by us. On making my report to the authorities I learned that the Ashakas had betrayed the Greeks by denouncing them as traitors.

The whole affair had been a result of Levantine nerves. The Ashakas in the past had been strong Nationalists. When the war between the Turks and ourselves broke out, in spite of the fact that it seemed possible, and indeed likely, that Egypt might again become a Turkish province, their politics changed, and they hastily became Anglophile, but their past record haunted them.

They feared the British Government almost as much as the Turks, and yearned to prove themselves loyal.

After much thought it appeared to them that the simplest way of achieving this would be to supply valuable military information to the British. That, however, was an article which they did not possess, and they therefore hit upon the idea of getting up a bogus conspiracy in order to be able to denounce it. This seemed the simplest way to safeguard themselves, and they hurriedly adopted the plan. The instruments that they chose were subtle Greeks, who were more proficient in the art of intrigue than the Ashakas, and had an even more degraded morality. It took only a few days for the Ashakas to realize the infidelity of the Greeks, and to inform against them still more hurriedly, but meanwhile the Greeks had spoken first. In the end, when the hair of the Ashakas had turned grey, they made a clean breast of the whole affair to the British authorities, and were, I believe, forgiven.

'Happy is the country that has no history' is a proverb which is often untrue, but Egypt was certainly happy, compared with the rest of the world, early in 1915. Then history moved rapidly towards us. The thunder of the guns in France was no longer something remote and irrelevant. The Turks massed across the desert, and prepared to attack the Canal. Many of the English thought that we were living on a sleeping volcano, but there was general confidence, and no one doubted our power to cope with the situation. The Turks attacked skilfully and bravely, but the odds against them were too heavy. They were, however, able to shell HMS *Harding* in the Canal, and a few of their men swam across to Egypt. Complete serenity reigned in Cairo. I remember going to the Opera that night. General Sir John Maxwell was listening, quite unruffled, to the performance. I heard a civilian say in a scandalized voice to him: 'They have gone and broken the *Harding*. What next?' To which Sir John answered: 'Well, they'll have to mend it, I suppose.' Two ladies landed at Port Said and had their train shelled as it steamed slowly along the banks of the Canal to Cairo. They wondered placidly if this was the normal state of things in Egypt.

These attacks added to the labours and quickened the energies of the Intelligence in Egypt, but still there were only vague rumours to be heard. One of these foretold that there was to be a general rising of Islam on April 27th.

I remember long conversations with a specialist with regard to this possibility; he disbelieved in it, then or at any time, for, as he said very rightly, Islam had to contend with great difficulties from the point of view of communications – waterless deserts, impassable seas, mountain ranges, unbridged by our telegraph. My friend, who was remarkable, would not have an office like any other man in his position; he disconcerted friend and foe alike by changing his address every few days, and when one wished to see him, and after the unusual event of catching him, he would make an appointment such as: 'The third lamp-post in the Street of Mohammed Ali at dusk.' When he had gone beyond recall, one remembered that the Mohammed Ali Street was several miles long, and that he had not said at which end was the appointed lamp-post; so he was well qualified to speak of the disadvantages accruing from lack of communications.

Prisoners began coming in, but not much was to be obtained from them. They were mostly shattered and rather pathetic men. The first to arrive were some escaped Syrian schoolmasters, who had been conscripted by the Turks, and gave a very graphic account of a hot and harrassing journey ahead of their comrades to Egypt, where their friends and relations lived. Then came a blind old gentleman of eighty, who fell into our front-line trench. It had been his habit, every two years, to visit his son in Egypt, and he had not realized that there was a war going on.

Amongst the Turkish prisoners of the first attack there was one old quartermaster seriously ill, whose manners and courage made him the friend of all his captors, but, like the rest, he told us nothing. There was probably more information amongst the prisoners who had been interned, if they had been willing to speak, but they were not. I met one of these to whom fate had been unusually cruel. He was an Albanian whose home had been in Montenegro. When the amiable Montenegrins seized the land of the Albanians, he had been beaten and cast out; thence he had

44

gone to Turkey, but the Albanians had been the first to attack the Turks, and were, indeed, the main cause of the ruin of the Ottoman Empire, so in Turkey he was bastinadoed and thrown into prison. Somehow he managed to escape and arrived in Egypt. In Egypt he was arrested as a Turk, and again thrown into prison. In prison he was continually beaten by his fellow-prisoners, who were Turks, as an Albanian and an enemy of Islam.

There were no tangible proofs of a conspiracy; one used sometimes to get black looks in the bazaar, and scowls from the class of the Effendis. On the other hand, we were very strongly supported by men of the type of the late Sultan Hussein and Adly Yeghen Pasha.

It would be difficult to meet a more attractive or courteous gentleman than the late Sultan. He was of the advanced school of enlightened Islam; neither his literary tastes, his philosophy, nor his pleasure in European society allowed him to forget his own people for a moment. Adly Yeghen Pasha, then Minister of Education, is an exceptional and outstanding figure in Egypt, with a marked personality. The other Ministers mixed freely with European society, and there was no sign of anything but friendliness.

At the end of February I was sent on the battleship *Bacchante*, commanded by Captain Boyle[24], which lay for about a fortnight off Alexandretta, occasionally bombarding telegraphs, or wagons that were said to be loaded with artillery wheels. One morning we saw two carts crawling along, drawn by bullocks, carrying the alleged wheels of artillery northward from Alexandretta. In order to warn the two drivers shells were fired from the great battleship a hundred yards ahead of them. The men left their oxen, taking refuge in a neighbouring ditch, while the oxen went slowly forward alone, like automata. Our guns then fired upon the carts, which were about half a mile distant, and one of the oxen was immediately hit. On this one of the two Turks left the ditch, cut the wounded animal free, and continued to lead the two carts.

24.   Rear Admiral The Hon Sir Algernon Boyle KCB CMG, MVO (1871–1949).

45

Again our guns fired ahead of him to give him warning, but he went on steadfastly at about a mile an hour to what was certain death. In the end he was left lying by his dead oxen and his broken cart. We had given him every chance that we could, and if the admiration of a British ship for his courage could reward a dead Anatolian muleteer, that reward was his.

Life outside Alexandretta was uneventful. Occasionally a Turkish official came out to discuss various questions that arose. He used to sway and bow from the tiller of his boat while I swayed and bowed from the platform below the gangway of the cruiser. It is perhaps worth saying that when I expressed to him Captain Boyle's regret for the death of the Turkish muleteer it was an event that he would not condescend to notice.

We discovered one curious fact of natural history, that with a searchlight you can see the eyes of dogs or jackals at night more than half a mile away. A previous ship had reported that men came down to the shore with electric torches, and it was only after some days that we discovered that these will-o'-the-wisp appearances were in reality the eyes of dogs.

But though life was uneventful, it was very pleasant on the ship, and all were sorry when the cruise came to an end.

I remember the last night at dinner in the wardroom the name of a distinguished Admiral occurred in the conversation. He was a man who had a great reputation for capacity and also eccentricity that came mainly from his habit of concentrated thinking. When he was deep in thought and his eyes caught any bright object, he would go up to it like a magpie and play with it. He would sometimes go up and fiddle with the button of a junior officer on the quarter-deck, looking at it very attentively, to the great discomfort of the junior officer, or even with that of a stranger to whom he had been introduced. The legend grew from this idiosyncrasy, that those may believe who wish to. It was said that one night at a dance he sat out for a long time with a girl in a black dress. His eye caught a white thread on her shoulder, and unconsciously while he talked he began pulling at it. The story goes on to say that when the girl went home she said to her mother: 'I know I went out with a vest to-night, and now I wonder what has happened to it.'

I remember at the same dinner Dr. Levick, who had been with Captain Scott in the Antarctic voyage, told a curious story of prophecy. He had been to a fortune-teller after the idea of going with Captain Scott had occurred to him, but before he had taken any steps. The fortune-teller gave a description of the melancholy place where he was to live for two years, of the unknown men who were to be his companions, and particularly one who had strangely flecked hair.

I returned to Cairo and office work with some reluctance. Friends of mine and I took a house, which somehow managed to run itself, in Gezireh. It was covered with Bougainvillea and flowers of every colour, and was a delight to see. Sometimes it lacked servants completely, and at other times there was a black horde. Gardeners sprang up as if by enchantment, and made things grow almost before one's eyes.

I quote from my diary of March 18th, 1915:

News to-day that King Constantine won't have Greece come in and that Venizelos has resigned. At a guess, this means that either Greece of King Constantine is lost. If Constantine goes, Venizelos might shepherd his son through his minority.

March 14th. I left Luxor Tuesday night, after a wonderful time. My guide was a Senoussi – something-or-other Galleel. He had a tip of white turban hanging, which he said was a sign of his people. He was rather like one of the Arabs out of a Hichens book, and I expect about as genuine. A snake-charmer came with us. He gave me the freedom of the snakes as a man is given the freedom of a city, but as one scorpion and two snakes – one of them a so-to-speak soi-disant cobra – stung and bit him during the day, it's not likely to be of much help to me. He did some very mysterious things, and called snakes from every kind of place – one from a window in the wall, a five-foot long cobra, and a Coptic cook found its old skin in the next window.

In justice to the snake-charmer it ought to be said that he was only stung and bitten as a consequence of a quarrel with an archaeologist.

In Egypt every archaeologist looks upon the local magician or snake-charmer as his competitor, and hates him. When the archaeologist is telling the tourist the history of Rameses II the attention of the tourist is distracted by a half-naked man doing the mango trick. My archaeologist friend, irritated by the presence of the snake-charmer, declared that his snakes were all doped and his scorpions were tame town scorpions, green, and not yellow like the country scorpions. He found a bucolic scorpion under a stone, of the proper colour, which instantly stung the snake-charmer; he then insisted upon stirring up his snakes with a stick, with the unfortunate results that have already been mentioned.

The Egyptian has always seemed to me harder to understand than his neighbours. It may be because there is less in him to understand. The Greeks, Turks, and Arabs have all got very salient characteristic qualities, but though the characteristics of the Egyptians are probably as strongly marked, they are less conspicuous to the foreigner's eye; in other words, the Egyptian has less in common with the outer world than any of the Asiatic, or even African, peoples who surround him. Lane, in his *Modern Egyptians,* says that they refused to believe that the ordinary traveller was not an agent for the Government, because they could not understand the desire for travel, and their character had not changed since his day. Here is a story of Egyptian guile and credulity:

An Egyptian was anxious to get some job profitable to himself done, and he went to one of the kavasses (guards) at the Agency for advice. The kavass professed himself able to help. He said: 'The man for you to go to is Mr. Jones, that high English official. He will get what you want done, but I warn you that Mr. Jones is an expensive man. Give me three hundred pounds, and I will see what can be done.' The three hundred pounds was duly paid, and for a long time nothing happened. The petitioner grew impatient and importunate, and was eventually satisfied for the moment by an invitation to lunch with a Levantine who passed himself off as Mr. Jones. At luncheon the Levantine, who was of German extraction, wore his hat, banged his fist on the table, smoked a pipe, interrupted, and generally acted as an Englishman abroad is supposed by some to behave. Then occurred an interval of inaction; the petitioner again grew restive, and this time complained to the authorities. Finally the transaction was discovered, and the kavass was sent to gaol.

Events moved in Egypt. The Australian and New Zealand troops poured in, and splendid men they were. But there was little love lost between the Australians and the Egyptians, though the British troops and the natives fraternized occasionally. The native Egyptian was, it must be admitted, constantly very roughly treated, for the average Australian, while he was at first apt to resent superiority in others, felt little doubt about his own claim to it. The Australian and New Zealand Corps was commanded by General Birdwood[25], and the New Zealand and Australian Division by General Godley[26].

I joined the New Zealand Division as Interpreter and Intelligence officer, and we all made preparations to start early in April. I was anxious to buy a beautiful snow-white Arab, that had won most of the races at Cairo, from a friend of mine, but General Godley spoke simply but firmly. 'You aren't the Duke of Marlborough,' he said. 'You can't have that white pony unless he's dyed, and even then it would wash off in any rainstorm. You may get yourself shot, but not me.' I agreed with the less reluctance because I had found that the pony pulled furiously and would certainly lead any advance or retreat by many miles.

The day for our departure approached. The golden sunlight and tranquillity of Egypt was tragic in its contrast to what was coming.

Every Intelligence officer was a Cassandra with an attentive audience. In every discussion there was, as far as I saw, unanimity between military, naval, and political officers, who all wished the landing to take place at Alexandretta, and deplored (not to use a stronger word) the project of the Dardanelles, which the Turks had been given ample time to fortify.

---

25.   Field Marshal William Birdwood, 1st Baron Birdwood GCB GCSI GCMG GCVO GBE CIE DSO (1865–1951).
26.   General Sir Alexander John Godley GCB KCMG (1867–1957).

The heat increased and the English officers' wives, who had come to Egypt to be with their husbands, were given a taste of a ferocious khamsin that affected their complexions. In the spring of 1915 this wind came in waves and gusts of lurid heat. It was like a Nessus shirt, scorching the skin and making slow fire of one's blood. After the khamsin, which had the one advantage of killing insects with its heat, locusts came. They made a carpet on the ground and a shadow against the sun. Life was intolerable out of doors, and they followed one into the recesses of the house. A friend of mine said to me: 'What on earth had they got to grumble about in Egypt in the time of the Pharaohs? They had one plague at a time then; we are having all the lot at once.'

I quote from my diary:

Yesterday I saw Todd, who had been on the *Annie Rickmers* when she was torpedoed off Smyrna. The crew was Greek. There were five Englishmen on board, and a good many wounded. The Greeks were all off at once, taking all the boats. They had no interpreter with them. He said the English in Smyrna were angry at being bombarded, and came aboard with Rahmy Bey, the Vali, to complain. Rahmy was always Anglophile.

Early in April Sir Ian Hamilton came and went. He had a great review of the troops in the desert on a glorious day. It was a splendid sight, and one I should have enjoyed better if I had not been riding a mountainous roan horse that bolted through the glittering Staff.

Many old friends, Ock Asquith[27], Patrick Shaw-Stewart[28], Charles Lister[29] and Rupert Brooke[30], had come out to Egypt in the Naval Division, and we lunched, dined, and went to the Pyramids by moonlight.

The first week in April we made our preparations for leaving,

---

27.   Brigadier Arthur Asquith DSO (1883–1939). Son of the Prime Minister, Herbert Asquith.

28.   Lieutenant Commander Patrick Shaw-Stewart RN (1888–1917).

29.   2nd Lieutenant the Hon Charles Lister (1887–1915).

30.   Sub Lieutenant Rupert Brooke RND (1887–1915). Brooke died of septicaemia, resulting from an infected mosquito bite before even reaching Gallipoli.

and I went to say good-bye to native friends. One of them was an old Albanian Abbot of the Bektashi sect, whose monastery was in the living rock in a huge cave behind the Mokattan Hills. He had a fine face and a venerable beard, and I spent much time talking to him, drinking his coffee, by a fountain in the cool garden outside his home. I was sorry to say good-bye to the delightful Zoo in Cairo, with the hawks calling unceasingly in the sunlight, and a hundred different birds. Another pleasure there was Said, an attractive and intellectual hippopotamus, who performed a number of tricks.

On April 10th I went to Alexandria to report aboard the German prizeship *Lutzow*, and on the 12th we sailed. We discovered that night at dinner that the puritanical New Zealand Government had ordained that this boat should be a dry one, but it made no difference to our mess, which was very pleasant. On April 13th we made a new discovery, that the boat was even drier than we expected, as there was not enough water, and the men had to shave in salt water. On April 15th we came into Lemnos Harbour, with a keen wind and a rustling deep blue sea, and white-crested waves, with cheer on cheer from French and English warships, from German prizes with British crews, from submarines, and even from anchored balloons.

The next day I went ashore with a couple of other officers to buy donkeys, who were to carry our kits. Mudros was not too bad a town, and was a very curious spectacle in those days. There were great black Senegalese troops with filed teeth who chased the children in play, though if the children had known what their home habits were the games would probably have ceased abruptly. There were Greeks dressed in fantastic costume and British troops of all sorts. Many old friends from the East were there, among them Colonel Doughty Wylie, who in a few days was to win his VC and lose a life of great value to his country.

I met a friend, Bettelheim, nicknamed 'Beetle,' whose life had been one long adventure. When last I had seen him he had been an official in Turkey, and in a rising had been dragged from his carriage on Galata Bridge in Constantinople by the mob, with his companion, the Emir Arslan. Emir Arslan was torn to pieces, but 'Beetle,' with his marvellous luck, escaped.

Many of us lunched together under a vine, drinking excellent wine at a penny a glass. Everybody was extremely cheerful, and there was great elation in the island air. The talk was, of course, about the landing. A friend of mine said: 'This is a terrible business; entire Staffs will be wiped out.' He seemed to think that the Staffs were the most important thing.

After lunch I went to see the Mayor, to help me buy all that I wanted. He was rather shaky with regard to his own position, as Lemnos had not yet been recognized by us as Greek, and our recognition was contingent on the behaviour of the Greek Government. He was a very good linguist, talking French, a little English, Italian, Greek, Turkish, and Arabic. I think it was he who quoted to me the story of the Khoja Nasr-ed-Din. Nasr-ed-Din was lent a saucepan by a friend; he returned it with another small saucepan, saying it had produced a child. Next year the friend offered a huge saucepan at the same date, which the friend considered the breeding-time of saucepans. Later on, when his friend applied for the return of the saucepan, Nasr-ed-Din said: 'It is dead.' His friend expostulated: 'How can a saucepan die?' 'Well,' said Nasr-ed-Din, 'if it can have a child, why can't it die?'

Lemnos itself, though then it was a pageant, is on the whole a dreary island. The land was green, as all lands are in the spring, but there was not the carpet of anemones that one finds in Crete, Cyprus, and other islands, nor was there even asphodel.

On Friday, April 16th, we heard that the *Manitou* had been torpedoed, and that a number of men had been drowned. This was not the case, though she had had three torpedoes fired at her.

At this time we believed that we were to make three simultaneous attacks, the New Zealanders taking the centre of the Peninsula. A rather melancholy call to arms was issued by General Birdwood, the pith of which was that for the first few days there would be no transport of any kind. This made it all the more necessary to obtain the donkeys, and with the help of the Mayor of Mudros I bought six, and one little one for £1 as a mascot. It was a great deal of trouble getting them on board. The Greek whose boat I had commandeered was very unfriendly and I had to requisition the services of some Senegalese troops.

Diary. April 21*st*, 1915. *Mudros.* Inner Bay. Monday, the 19th, I tried to dine on HMS *Bacchante*, but failed to find her. Dined on the *Arcadian.* Came back with Commodore Keyes. Met Maxwell (a journalist turned censor). He said that the Turks had thirty 15-inch howitzers on Gallipoli, also wire entanglements everywhere. The general impression is that we shall get a very bad knock, and that it may set the war back a year, besides producing an indefinite amount of trouble in the East.

Tuesday, April 20*th*. I went ashore to get porters, but the Mayor was in a nervous state, and I failed. I tried to get back in a dinghy with a couple of Greeks, and we nearly got swamped. A gale got up. Finally made the *Imogen*, tied up by the *Hussar*, and at last reached my destination. Great gale in the night. I hope we don't suffer the fate of the Armada. It is said that our orders are to steam for the outer harbour at once.

It was curious to see the *Imogen*, once the Ambassador's yacht at Constantinople. In those days she was treated with reverent care. The Mediterranean had to be calmed by the finest weather before she travelled. Now she had to sink or swim with the rest. Her adventures did not end at Lemnos. Travellers may see her name written proudly on the harsh cliffs of Muscat in the Persian Gulf, and to-day she is probably at Kurna, the site of the Garden of Eden.

On Thursday, April 22nd, I was able to get two Greek porters, Kristo Keresteji (which being interpreted means Kristo the Timber-merchant) and Yanni, of the little island of Ayo Strati. Kristo was with me until I was invalided in the middle of October. He showed the greatest fidelity and courage after the first few days. The other man was a natural coward, and had to be sent away when an opportunity offered, after the landing.

Diary. Friday, April 23*rd.* I have just seen the most wonderful procession of ships I shall ever see. In the afternoon we left for the outer harbour. The wind was blowing; there was foam upon the sea and the air of the island was sparkling. With the band playing and flags flying, we steamed past the rest of the fleet.

Cheers went from one end of the harbour to the other. Spring and summer met. Everybody felt it more than anything that had gone before. After we had passed the fleet, the pageant of the fleet passed us. First the *Queen Elizabeth*, immense, beautiful lines, long, like a snake, straight as an arrow. This time there was silence. It was grim and very beautiful. We would rather have had the music and the cheers. This morning instructions were given to the officers and landing arrangements made. I have to do prisoners. We leave to-night. The Australians have to land first. This they should do to-night. Then we land and the attack is left to us. Arrangements were made as to action to be taken if one of our ships is sunk by shellfire. The naval guns will have to cover our advance, and the men are to be warned that the naval fire is very accurate. They will need a little reassuring, if it goes just over our heads. The 29th land at Helles, the French in Asia near Troy. This seems curious as they can't support us or we them. The Naval Division go north and make a demonstration. The General is to go on board the *Queen* with Tahu. Admiral Thursby[31] is on the *Queen*. Hughes, Braithwaite, Shaw, Cazalet, Thoms, Reed and I go off together to-morrow afternoon if all turns out as it should. It won't. The general opinion is that very many boats must be sunk from the shore. Having got ashore we go on to a rendezvous. We have no native guide. There were to have been some flags, yellow and red, for us to show if we are getting mopped up by our own naval guns, but they aren't forthcoming. This has depressed some people. Winston's name fills everyone with rage. Roman Emperors killed slaves to make themselves popular; he is killing a lot of free men to make himself famous. If he hadn't tried that coup, [*the naval bombardment of 19th February*] but had co-operated with the Army we might have got to Constantinople with very little loss.

The sea was very quiet between Lemnos and Anzac on April 24th. There were one or two alterations in plans, but nothing very material. We expected to have to land in the afternoon, but this was changed, and we were ordered to land after the Australians,

31.   Admiral Sir Cecil Thursby KCB KCMG (1861–1936).

who were to attack at 4.30 a.m. Some proposed to get up to see the first attack at dawn. I thought that we should see plenty of the attack before we had done with it, and preferred to sleep.

Diary. Sunday, April 25th. I got up at 6.30. Thoms, who shared my cabin, had been up earlier. There was a continuous roll of thunder from the south. Opposite to us the land rose steeply in cliffs and hills covered with the usual Mediterranean vegetation. The crackle of rifles sounded and ceased in turns. Orders were given to us to start at 8.30 a.m. The tows were punctual. We were ordered to take practically nothing but rations. I gave my sleeping-bag to Kyriakidis, the old Greek interpreter whom I had snatched from the *Arcadian*, and took my British warm and my Burberry. The tow was unpleasantly open to look at; there was naturally no shelter of any kind. We all packed in, and were towed across the shining sea towards the land fight. We could see some still figures lying on the beach to our left, one or two in front. Some bullets splashed round.

As we were all jumping into the sea to flounder ashore, I heard cries from the sergeant at the back of the tow. He said to me: 'These two men refuse to go ashore.' I turned and saw Kristo Keresteji and Yanni of Ayo Strati with mesmerized eyes looking at the plops that the bullets made in the water, and with their minds evidently fixed on the Greek equivalent of 'Home, Sweet Home.' They were, however, pushed in, and we all scrambled on to that unholy land. The word was then, I thought rather unnecessarily, passed that we were under fire.

It was difficult to understand why the Turkish fire developed so late. If they had started shelling us during our landing as they shelled us later, our losses would have been very heavy. We frequently owed our salvation in the Peninsula to a Turkish weakness and a Turkish mistake. They were constantly slow to appreciate a position and take full advantage of it, and their shrapnel was generally fused too high. Hardly any man who landed escaped being thumped and bumped on different occasions by shrapnel, which would, of course, have killed or seriously wounded him if the burst had not been so high. I remember on the afternoon of the first landing a sailor was knocked down beside me, and I and another man carried him to what shelter there was. We found that, while the bullet had pierced his clothes, it had not even broken his skin. Said the sailor: 'This is the third time that that's 'appened to me to-day. I'm beginning to think of my little grey 'ome in the West.' So were others.

We had landed on a spit of land which in those days we called Shrapnel Point, to the left of what afterwards became Corps Headquarters, though later the other spit on the right usurped that name. I took cover under a bush with a New Zealand officer, Major Browne. This officer had risen from the ranks. He fought through the whole of the Gallipoli campaign, and in the end, to the sorrow of all who knew him, was killed as a Brigadier in France.

The shrapnel fire became too warm to be pleasant, and I said: 'Major, a soldier's first duty is to save his life for his country.' He said: 'I quite agree, but I don't see how it's to be done.' We were driven from Shrapnel Point to the north, round the cliff, but were almost immediately driven back again by the furious fire that met us.

Diary. We were being shot at from three sides. All that morning we kept moving. There were lines of men clinging like cock-roaches under the cliffs or moving silently as the guns on the right or left enfiladed us. The only thing to be done was to dig in as soon as possible, but a good many men were shot while they were doing this. General Godley landed about twelve, and went up Monash Gully with General Birdwood. We remained on the beach. We had no artillery to keep the enemy's fire down. We spent a chilly night, sometimes lying down, sometimes walking, as the rain began to fall after dark, and we had not too much food. My servant, Jack, who was a very old friend, and I made ourselves as comfortable as we could.

There was a great deal of inevitable confusion. We were very hard pressed; as every draft landed it was hurried off to that spot in the line where reinforcements were most needed. This naturally produced chaos amongst the units, and order was not re-established for some time. It was a terrible night for those in authority. I believe that, had it been possible, we should have re-embarked that night, but the sacrifices involved would have been too great. Preparations for the expedition had been totally inadequate. The chief RAMC officer had told me the ridiculously small number of casualties he had been ordered to make preparations for, and asked my opinion, which I gave him with some freedom. As it was, we had to put 600 men on the ship from which we had disembarked in the morning, to go back to hospital in Egypt, a four days' journey, under the charge of one officer, who was a veterinary surgeon.

Diary. Monday, April 26th. At 5 o'clock yesterday our artillery began to land. It's a very rough country; the Mediterranean macchia everywhere, and steep, winding valleys. We slept on a ledge a few feet above the beach. Firing went on all night. In the morning it was very cold, and we were all soaked. The Navy, it appeared, had landed us in the wrong place. This made the Army extremely angry, though as things turned out it was the one bright spot. Had we landed anywhere else, we should have been wiped out. I believe the actual place decided on for our landing was a mile further south, which was an open plain, and an ideal place for a hostile landing from the Turkish point of view.

Next morning I walked with General Godley and Tahu Rhodes[32], his ADC, up the height to the plateau which was afterwards called Plugges Plateau. The gullies and ravines were very steep, and covered with undergrowth. We found General Walker, General Birdwood's Chief of Staff, on the ridge that bears his name. Bullets were whining about, through the undergrowth, but were not doing much harm, though the shelling on the beach was serious.

Diary. We believed that the Turks were using 16-inch shells from the Dardanelles, and we were now able to reply. The noise was deafening, and our firing knocked down our own dugouts. The Generals all behaved as if the whole thing was a tea-party. Their different Staffs looked worried for their chiefs and themselves. Generals Godley and Walker were the most reckless, but General Birdwood also went out of his way to take risks. The sun

---

32.   Capt (Arthur) Tahu Rhodes DSO MVO, Grenadier Guards.

was very hot, and our clothes dried while the shrapnel whistled over us into the sea.

At noon we heard the rumour that the 29th were fighting their way up from Helles, and everybody grew happy. We also heard that two Brigadiers had been wounded and one killed.

The Australians had brought with them two ideas, which were only eliminated by time, fighting and their own good sense. The 'eight hours' day' was almost a holy principle, and when they had violated it by holding on for two or three days heroically, they thought that they deserved a 'spell.' Their second principle was not to leave their pals. When a man was wounded his friends would insist upon bringing him down, instead of leaving him to the stretcher-bearers. When they had learned the practical side of war, both these dogmas were jettisoned. In Egypt the Australians had human weaknesses, and had shown them; in Gallipoli they were the best of companions. Naturally, with the New Zealand Division, I saw more of the New Zealanders, who had the virtues of the Australians and the British troops. They had all the dash and *élan* of the Australians and the discipline of the Englishmen.

Diary. Tuesday, April 27th. Last night, or rather this morning at about 1 o'clock, I was called up by Cunningham. He said: 'We are sending up 40,000 rounds of ammunition to Colonel Pope.' Greek donkey-boys, with an Indian escort, were to go up with this ammunition. I asked if any officer was going, and was answered 'No'; that there was no officer to go. I said that I would go if I could get a guide, but that I did not talk Hindustani, and that the whole thing was risky, as we were just as likely without a guide to wander into the Turks as to find our own people; also that if we were attacked we should be without means of communicating, and that the Greeks would certainly bolt. At the Corps Headquarters I found an absolutely gaga officer. He had an ADC who was on the spot, however, and produced a note from Colonel Pope which stated that he had all the ammunition he wanted. The officer, in spite of this, told me to carry on. I said it was nonsense without a guide, when Pope had his ammunition. He then told me to take the mules to one place and the ammunition to another. I said that I had better take them both back to my Headquarters, from which I had come. He then tried to come with me, after saying that he would put me under arrest, but fell over two tent-ropes and was nearly kicked by a mule, and gave up in mute despair.

I may add that this officer was sent away shortly afterwards. The next night he was found with a revolver stalking one of the Staff officers, who was sleeping with a nightcap that looked like a turban, to shelter his head from the dew. My persecutor said that he thought he was a Turk.

Diary. Tahu, Jacky Hughes[33] and I slept crowded in one dugout on Monday night. The cliff is becoming like a rookery, with ill-made nests. George Lloyd[34] and Ian Smith have a charming view, only no room to lie down in. Everybody's dugout is falling on his neighbour's head. I went round the corner of the cliff to find a clean place to wash in the sea, but was sniped, and had to come back quick. The Gallipoli Division of Turks, 18,000 strong, is supposed to be approaching, while we listened to a great artillery duel not far off. An Armenian who was captured yesterday reported the Gallipoli Division advancing on us. On Tuesday night things were better. I think most men were then of the opinion that we ought to be able to hold on, but we were clinging by our eyelids on to the ridge. The confusion of units and the great losses in officers increased the difficulty.

This was the third day of battle. My dugout was twice struck. A tug was sunk just in front of us. The interpreters have all got three days' beards which are turning white from worry. The shells to-day did not do so much damage; they whirled over us in coveys, sometimes hitting the beach and flying off singing, sometimes splashing in the sea, but a lot of dead and wounded were carried by.

33.   Lieutenant-Colonel John Hughes CMG DSO (1866–1954). Commanding officer The Canterbury Battalion, New Zealand Infantry.
34.   George Lloyd, 1st Baron Lloyd GCSI GCIE DSO PC (1879–1941). A Liberal Unionist politician and close friend of AH. Lloyd and AH had explored the state of the Bagdad Railway together in 1906. Lloyd was a staff officer on Hamilton's staff during the Gallipoli campaign. Later Governor of Bombay and Secretary of State for the Colonies.

About this time the spy mania started, which is one of the inevitable concomitants of war. Spies were supposed to be everywhere. In the popular belief, that is 'on the beach,' there were enough spies to have made an opera. The first convincing proof of treachery which we had was the story of a Turkish girl who had painted her face green in order to look like a tree, and had shot several people at Helles from the boughs of an oak. Next came the story of the daily pigeon post from Anzac to the Turkish line; but as a matter of fact, the pigeons were about their own business of nesting.

We had with us, too, a remarkable body of men who were more than suspect, and whose presence fed the wildest rumours. These were called Zionists, Zionites, and many other names. They were the Jewish exiles from Syria, who looked after the mules, and constituted the Mule Corps, under Colonel Patterson, of lion-hunting fame[35]. They performed very fine service, and gave proof of the greatest courage. On several occasions I saw the mules blown to bits, and the men of the Mule Corps perfectly calm, among their charges. One night it did seem to me that at last we had got the genuine article. A panting Australian came to say that they had captured a German disguised as a member of the Mule Corps, but that he had unfortunately killed one man before being taken. When I examined this individual he gave his name as Fritz Sehmann, and the language in which we conversed most easily was German. He was able to justify himself in his explanation, which turned out to be true. He had been walking along the cliff at night with his mule, when the mule had been shot and fallen over the cliff with Fritz Sehmann. Together they had fallen upon an unfortunate soldier, who had been killed by the same burst.

It was a work of some difficulty to explain to the Colonial troops that many of the prisoners that we took as, for instance, Greeks and Armenians, were conscripts who hated their masters. On one occasion, speaking of a prisoner, I said to a soldier: 'This man says he is a Greek, and that he hates the Turks.' 'That's a

35.   Colonel J.H. Patterson DSO: Hunter, author and Zionist, best known for his book *The Man-Eaters of Tsavo* (1907).

likely story, that is,' said the soldier; 'better put a bayonet in the brute.'

The trouble that we had with the native interpreters is even now a painful memory. If they were arrested once a day, they were arrested ten times. Those who had anything to do with them, if they were not suspected of being themselves infected by treachery, were believed to be in some way unpatriotic. It was almost as difficult to persuade the officers as the men that the fact that a man knew Turkish did not make him a Turk. There was one moment when the interpreters were flying over the hills like hares.

Diary. Wednesday, April 28th. I got up at 4 a.m. this morning, after a fine, quiet night, and examined a Greek deserter from the Turkish Army. He said many would desert if they did not fear for their lives. The New Zealanders spare their prisoners.

Last night, while he was talking to me, Colonel Chaytor was hit by a bit of shell on his hat. He stood quite still while a man might count three, wondering if he was hurt. He then stooped down and picked it up. At 8 p.m. last night there was furious shelling in the gully. Many men and mules hit. General Godley was in the Signalling Office, on the telephone, fairly under cover. I was outside with Pinwell, and got grazed, just avoiding the last burst. Their range is better. Before this they have been bursting the shrapnel too high. It was after 4 p.m. their range improved so much. My dugout was shot through five minutes before I went there. So was Shaw's. Colonel Chaytor was knocked down by shrapnel, but not hurt. The same happened to Colonel Manders. We heard that the Indian troops were to come to-night. Twenty-three out of twenty-seven Auckland officers killed and wounded.

11 *a.m.* All firing except from Helles has ceased. Things look better. The most the men can do is to hang on. General Godley has been very fine. The men know it.

4.30 *p.m.* The Turks suddenly reported to have mounted huge howitzer on our left flank, two or three miles away; that meant being pounded to death. We rushed all the ammunition off the beach, men working like ants, and the Australians as mild as milk asking for orders. No nonsense about being free and equal. That's past. They worked hard in silence. We were absolutely enfiladed and they could have (a) pounded us, mules and machinery to pulp or (b) driven us into the gully and up the hill, cutting us off from our water and at the same time attacking us with shrapnel. The ships came up and fired on the new gun and proved either that it was a dummy or had moved or been knocked out. It was a cold wet night.

The material which General Birdwood and General Godley had to work upon was very fine. The Australians and the New Zealanders were born fighters and natural soldiers, and learnt quickly on Active Service what it would have taken months of training to have taught them. But like many another side-show, Anzac was casual in many ways, as the following excerpt from this diary will show:

Diary. Thursday, April 29th. Kaba Tepé. I was woken at 2.30 a.m., when the New Zealanders stood to arms. It was wet and cold, and a wind blew which felt as if it came through snowy gorges. The alarm had been given, and the Turks were supposed to be about to rush the beach from the left flank in force. Colonel Chaytor was sent to hold the point. He told me to collect stragglers and form them up. It was very dark, and the stragglers were very straggly. I found an Australian, Quinn, and told him to fetch his men along to the gun emplacement, beyond the graves, on the point where Chaytor was. Everyone lost everyone.

I found Chaytor with an Australian officer. He said to him, 'Go out along the flank and find out where the Canterbury Battalion is and how strong. On the extreme left there is a field ambulance. They must be told to lie down so that the Turks will not shoot them.' I said: 'Let me go out. I will look after them and if necessary interpret.' He agreed and we started. I heard the Australian officer ordering the Canterbury in support to retire. I said: 'But are your orders to that effect? A support is there to support. The Canterburys will be routed or destroyed if you take this support away.' He said: 'Well, that's a bright idea.' He went back, and I heard him say: 'This officer thinks you had better stay where you are.' I don't know if he was a Colonel or what he was and he didn't know what I was.

I found the field ambulance, a long way off, and went on to the outposts. The field ambulance were touchingly grateful for nothing, and I had some tea and yarned with them till morning, walking back after dawn along the beach by the graves. No one fired at me.

When I got back I heard the news of Doughty's[36] death, which grieved me a great deal. He seems to have saved the situation. The description of Helles is ghastly, of the men looking down into the red sea, and the dying drowned in a foot of water. That is what might have, and really ought to have happened to us.

One hears the praise of politicians in all men's mouths . . . .

I was brought a Turkish officer's note-book and the photograph of his little girl. His name was Mulazim Evvel, 1st Lieutenant, 1st Company, 1st Battalion, 72nd Regiment. Hussein Effendi; also Mehmed Debe 15th Platoon, 8 Company of 27th Regiment. I showed the photograph to the General; he dropped it as if a wasp had stung him. Also a little pocket book with bottles of horrible sticky sickly scent. 3,000 casualties at Helles we hear.

In the last twenty-four hours I have expected (1) peace for a time (2) death from the big howitzer (3) to be once again a prisoner of war with the field ambulance. We have blue hot weather and cold grey weather; and the ordinary man has passed from anxiety to weariness; the Generals have been tortured with anxiety, some of it in some of them quite unselfish.

I have done my best to prevent the killing of prisoners. They realize now, the Australians I mean, that what is sauce for the goose is sauce for the gander, and they cannot expect to receive quarter if they give none. I spent the afternoon with Chaytor wishing that poor Doughty hadn't been killed, and wondering how many more of my friends have gone the same way.

A beautiful night, last night, and a fair amount of shrapnel. Every evening now they send over a limited number of howitzers from the great guns in the Dardanelles, aimed at our ships. That happens also in the early morning, as this morning. To-night an

36.   Lieutenant-Colonel Charles 'Dick' Doughty-Wylie VC CB CMG (1868–1915). Doughty-Wylie's grave lies close to where he was killed. His is the only solitary British or Commonwealth war grave on the Gallipoli.

aeroplane is to locate these guns, and when they let fly to-morrow we are to give them an immense broadside from all our ships.

At this time the weather had improved, but we were living in a good deal of discomfort. We were not yet properly supplied with stores, the water was brackish, occasionally one had to shave in salt water, and all one's ablutions had to be done on the beach, with the permission of the Turkish artillery.

The beach produced a profound impression on almost all of us, and has in some cases made the seaside distasteful for the rest of our lives. It was, when we first landed, I suppose, about 30 yards broad, and covered with shingle. Upon this narrow strip depended all our communications: landing and putting off, food and water, all came and went upon the beach – and the Turkish guns had got the exact range. Later, shelters were put up, but life was still precarious, and the openness of the beach gave men a greater feeling of insecurity than they had in the trenches.

Diary. Our hair and eyes and mouths are full of dust and sand, and our nostrils of the smell of dead mules. There were also colonies of ants that kept in close touch with us, and our cigarettes gave out. Besides these trials, we had no news of the war or of the outer world.

Diary. Tahu and I repacked the provisions this morning. While we did so one man was shot on the right and another on the left. We have been expecting howitzers all the time, and speculating as to whether there would be any panic if they really get on to us. The Turks have got their indirect, or rather enfilading, fire on us, and hit our mules. One just hit a few yards away. There is an extraordinary unreality about this whole situation; so much of the war that I have seen has been unreal as a picture or a romance. Mons, Landrecy and Compiègne were all like dreams in a sense, but they had nothing of the opéra bouffe about them. This is different. Here Imbros and Samothrace are clear and delicate between the blue sea and the hot sky. The riband of beach is crowded with transport and Jews, Greeks, Armenians, New Zealanders, Australians, scallywag officers and officers that still manage to keep a shadow of dandyism between their disreputable selves and immaculate past. And there is the perpetual ripple of the waves that is sometimes loud enough to make the nervous mistake it for shrapnel which is perpetual, splashing in the sea or rattling on the beach. There is very little noise on the beach in the way of talk and laughter. The men never expected to be up against this. When we left Lemnos we saw one boat with an arrow and in front of it 'TO CONSTANTINOPLE AND THE HAREM'. Precious few of those poor fellows will see Constantinople, let alone the Harem.

May 1st. A dawn too beautiful to tell, but defiled by a real hymn of hate from the Turks. Last night the *Torgut Reiss* sent us some shells. This morning it was supposed to be the *Goeben* that was firing. I woke to hear the howitzers that have been haunting men's minds here droning over us, and watched them lifting great columns of water where they hit the sea. Then there came the sigh and the snarl of shrapnel, but that to the other is like the rustle of a lady's fan to the rumble of a brewer's dray. This hymn of hate went on for an unusually long time this morning from the big stuff. A lot of men were hit all round and it has been difficult to wash one's face in the sea. All the loading, unloading etc., is done at night. The picket boats are fairly well protected. The middies are the most splendid boys, but this position is an awful one. We are all so cramped and the mules add to the congestion. We shall have a plague of flies before we are done if we don't have a worse plague than that. I don't know how the Australians will stand it. The New Zealanders are all right. The first charge has bucked the Australians tremendously, and it was a very fine performance, that storming of the hill, but they are uncivilised and are not gentlemen as so many uncivilized people are. Still all this has taught and sobered them.

Smith and I talked for hours last night of what we would do if we live through this. George has gone back. His dugout, where he can't sleep because there isn't room for Smith and him, has a very nice window on the sea. I don't know why it should be called George's dugout as he doesn't sleep there and Smith does. Colonel White, Rickes, who is a bad levantine cad, and Murphy all hit at breakfast this morning, but not hurt. One of the Greek donkey boys says he is a barber. This would be a great advantage, but he is obviously a nervous man and starts when shrapnel bursts.

We are making no headway but holding on. The fleet of hydroplanes don't seem much use at spotting, or so say the soldiers. An order has come from Kitchener that we are to take prisoners. I am glad of this. Skeen is less fanatical now, and I have worried away at this on intelligence lines. For how can you get information if you murder all your prisoners? There is a fleet of boats in front of us and even more at Helles; the Turks must feel uncomfortable, but another landing between us would be pretty risky. They are fighting splendidly. Opinions are divided as to what would happen if we fought our way to Maidos. Many think we could be shelled out again by the *Goeben*. This expedition needed at least three times the number of men. The Indians have not come and the Territorials cannot come for a long time.

General Godley wants to change Headquarters for us. Colonel Artillery Johnston's battery is on our right, facing the Turks, and only a few yards away. The Turks spend a lot of time shooting at it, missing it, and hitting us. Another man killed just now. Shrapnel, heaps of it, is coming both ways on us. Nobody speaks on the beach. We have two tables on the top of the dugout. One is safe, and the other can be hit. The punctual people get the safe table.

Bennett, a naval brigade man, has lunched. He says that Rupert Brooke died at Lemnos. I am very sorry; he was a good fellow, and a poet with a great future. Bennett was blown up by a shell yesterday. His nerve has obviously gone, he ducked whenever a shell came and when I filled his cigarette case I saw how bad he was. He has to go back to-night. I am sorry for him. While we lunched a man had his head blown off twenty yards away. The attack we were to have made is off for to-day. I am getting rather bored at the General refusing to allow me to go to these things; still I don't mind so much as it is the Turks we are fighting. I hear that Tenedos and Lemnos are to go to Russia. This seems to me absolutely wild extravagant diplomacy. Orders have come that we are to entrench impregnably. We are practically besieged, for we can't re-embark without sacrificing our rearguard, and if the howitzers come up we shall be cut off from the beach and our water. A lot more men have been killed on the beach.

Sunday, May 2nd. 6 a.m. Shrapnel all round as I washed. Beach opinion is if this siege lasts they must be able to get up their heavy guns. The Indians have gone to Helles, and the Naval Division is being taken away from us. New Turkish Divisions are coming against us. There are no chaplains here for burial or for anything else.

Waite took a dozen prisoners this morning, gendarmes, nice fellows. They hadn't much to tell us. One of them complained that he had been shot through a mistake after he had surrendered. There ought to be an interpreter on these occasions.

It is a fiery hot day, without a ripple on the clear sea, and all still but for the thunder coming from Helles. I bathed and got clean. The beach looks like a mule fair of mutes, for it is very silent. We are to attack to-night at seven. We have now been here a week, and advanced a hundred yards farther than the first rush carried us. There is a great bombardment going on, a roaring ring of fire, and the Turks are being shelled and shelled.

At night the battleships throw out two lines of searchlights, and behind them there gleam the fires of Samothrace and Imbros. Up and down the cliffs here, outside the dugouts, small fires burn. The rifle fire comes over the hill, echoing in the valleys and back from the ships. Sometimes it is difficult to tell whether it is the sound of ripples on the beach or firing.

Monday, May 3rd. I was called up at 3 a.m. to examine three prisoners. Our attack had failed, and we have many casualties, probably not less than 1,000. The wounded have been crying on the beach horribly. A wounded Arab reported that our naval gun fire did much damage.

The complaint is old and bitter now. We insist that the Turks are Hottentots. We give them notice before we attack them. We tell them what we are going to do with their Capital. We attack them with an inadequate force of irregular troops, without adequate ammunition (we had one gun in our landing) in the most impregnable part of their Empire. Last night our own guns destroyed our position and the Turks swarmed in. They can bring any amount more men against us. This has been folly. We should have pretended we were going to have attacked Alexandretta or Syria instead of telling them where we were coming.

The *Goeben* is shelling the fleet and (11.30) has just struck a transport. The sea is gay and a fresh wind is blowing, and the beach is crowded but there is not a voice upon it except for an occasional order.

Thank heaven we haven't got any locusts; all the other plagues but that. 'Why do the heathen rage so furiously' and 'Shelter me with thy wing' were the appropriate psalms for yesterday. I saw the prisoners off and paid them the money that had been taken from them. The Turks are now expected to attack us. We suppose people realise what is happening here in London, though it isn't easy to see how troops and reinforcements can be sent to us in time; that is before the Turks have turned all this into a fortification. A good many men hit on the beach to-day. The mules cry like lost souls.

Tuesday, May 4th. The sea like a looking-glass, not a cloud in the sky, and Samothrace looking very clear and close. The moon is like a faint shadow of light in the clear sky over the smoke of the guns. Heavy fighting between us and Helles. A landing is being attempted. Pessimists say it is our men being taken off because their position is impossible. The boats coming back seem full of wounded. It may have been an attempt at a landing and entrenching, or simply a repetition of what we did the other day at Falcon Hill or Nebronesi, or whatever the place is.

Shaw wants me to find out about the Turkish spies who are said to call to our officers by name and the pigeons which are said to carry a post regularly every morning. I don't believe it. Men can't go about with pigeons crooning under their arms, and besides a carrier pigeon goes home, not to a Turkish commander who has been good to it.

The attack has failed this morning. Letter from George. Worsley wants me to go to Samothrace to start stories there. Perfect peace here except for rifles cracking on the hill. Smith and I wandered off up a valley through smilax, thyme, heath and myrtle to a high ridge. We went through the Indians and found a couple of very jolly officers, one of them since killed.

There are a good many bodies unburied. I thought we were going to be shot and so we should have if we had taken the short cut that I wanted to. Not many men hit. We helped to carry one wounded man back. I didn't realise what hard work it is. Another man was terribly wounded. The stretcher bearers are splendid fellows and have been awfully good too about the wounded Turks. On the way back we passed Birdwood; he is a dear. At one place we saw a horribly muddy little pond with a man standing in it in trousers shovelling out mud, but the water in a tin was clear and cool and very good. There is a horrible smell of death passing down the valley.

It is curious that the men seem to like the Turks much better now that they see what fighters they are. No one seems annoyed when I say they are good fellows, and they now realize that war isn't a one-sided affair like shooting rabbits. You've got to be killed as well as kill. A Company of the Auckland has got cut off but may be able to return. General Godley went further and to the left with Tahu this afternoon. Smith and I to the right. The General and Tahu got up to the Turkish trenches, quite close to them. The Turks threw hand-grenades and our supports broke. The General and Tahu rallied the men but a good many were killed, amongst them the General's orderly, a gentleman ranker and a first-rate fellow.

Wednesday, May 5th. Kaba Tepé. The other day, when our attack below failed, the Turks allowed us to bring off our wounded. This was after that unfortunate landing. Went on board the *Lutzow* to-day, and got some of my things off. Coming back the tow rope parted, and we thought that we should drift into captivity. It was rough and unpleasant.

I suggested to General Godley (1) to send for spies from Egypt (2) to have an armistice for the burial of the dead. I would go out and arrange it with the Turks, though one might get hit before one reached them. Smith has been sent for to the Arcadian. I use his dugout for writing. The *Lutzow* is in and I have got wine and a spoon and a clean shirt from her, also Christo Karalampa, the General's cook. I did not much care for being under fire on the sea, but the others minded more I think.

Thursday, May 6th. Very windy cold night. The dead are unburied and the wounded crying for water between the trenches. I have got the doctors to talk to Birdwood about an armistice. He thinks that the Germans would not allow the Turks to accept an armistice. Colonel Essen landed this morning. He has brought the rumour of 8,000 Turks killed lower down. We attacked Achi Baba at 10 a.m. There was an intermittent fire all night.

This morning I went up to the trenches with the General by Walker's Ridge the view was beautiful. The plain was covered with friendly olives that reminded me of Annah, I think, between Bagdad and Damascus. There was my General and Birdwood and Mercer. A perfect maze of trenches. As we went along the snipers followed Onslow's helmet, stinging us with dirt. Many dead. I saw no wounded. Here, on the beach the shrapnel has opened fire from a new direction. It is generally a few yards off the beach but near enough to ruffle it considerably. On the roof of this dugout it pipes to us swiftly and threateningly. I had always put the big Turkish attack for to-day, but it doesn't look as if it is going to come off. I suppose they are making light railways to bring their howitzers up and then rub us off this part of the Peninsula. This last shell that has just struck the beach has wounded two officers and killed and wounded several men, killed and wounded twenty-two mules. Many more mules are now reported hit. We wonder how the attack is getting on in the south, and if they are getting it as hot as we?

Friday, May 7th. A bitter night and morning. I have asked to be allowed to go and tell the Turks that if they surrender they will not be killed. It's taking advantage of old friendship but that can't be helped. The General doesn't want to say yes, but he has consented. I can get within twenty-five or thirty yards of them. Hay, who is a proper bully, tried to make Harold do this. If Harold is killed his wife won't get a single penny. I told Hay that if anyone did this it should be him, and he could do it to the Arabs. He shut up at once. Then General Birdwood wants the Arab officer prisoner to go and shout to them. I am not in love with the idea myself, but if he is sent Hay should go too. A shell just passed overhead and burst when I heard maniac peals and found the cook flying up. He had been hit in the boot and was laughing like mad. It is a nuisance one has to sit in the shade instead of sitting in the sun. They have got our exact range and are pounding one shell after another. I hope it means I may have a quieter walk this afternoon and that they will have a rest for this has been pretty bad. Am hoping to get letters again. Great battle at Helles now going on.

Yesterday one man among those killed on the beach had a bullet through his heart while he was sleeping. Not a bad way to end, without hate. A shell has just burst over our heads and has hit a lighter which it has set on fire.

The dead mules that have been towed out return to us. Two boats needed to take them away again. I have borrowed a megaphone from Commander Dix (wounded). Shellfire very good but the cases don't burst so most of the wounds are simple shrapnel wounds, not case wounds. I am getting quite deaf from the shelling. This is the twelfth day. It doesn't seem possible not to have been hit. Three cases of self-mutilation on N. Brigade. Commander Dix is a very fine fellow, a West Country man. He lays down the law on everything, has been everywhere and done everything. When he was hit in the head Turkish Charley told him that his brain was hanging out of his skull. He said he could see and feel it.

At 1.30 I went up the Monash Valley which the men often call the valley of death. I passed a stream of haggard, tragic figures, wounded and unwounded, coming down through the brilliant sunlight. I saw Monash[37] at his HQ and General Godley with him. General Godley said he wouldn't have standing-up shouting when I made my speech to the Turks. I must lie down etc. The shelling overhead was terrific, but it did no damage as the shells threw forward. I don't know how many burst a minute, but the smoke made a shadow between us and the sun. It was like the crash of a train going over the sleepers of a railway bridge. Old Monash, whom I had last seen on review days, an incongruous figure in the desert, tried to speak on the telephone and say I was coming, but

37.   General Sir John Monash GCMG KCB VD (1865–1931).

it was a difficult business made worse by the noise. Finally I went up the slope to Quinn's post, with an escort, running and taking cover, and panting up the very steep hill. It felt as if bullets rained, but the fact is that they came from three sides and have each got about five echoes. There is a *décolleté* place in the hill that they pass over. I got into the trench and found Quinn, tall and very open-faced, swearing like a trooper, much respected by his men. He sent for his officers but they slept, and it was difficult to get them. The trenches in Quinn's Post were narrow and low, full of exhausted men sleeping. I crawled over them and through tiny holes. There was the smell of death everywhere. I spoke in three places. In the first place my speech elicited a furious volley which, or part of which, came through the sandbags, but after that silence and amazement. I didn't lie down, it was no use doing that. I said: 'Comrades, keep your head down, lest while I speak an accident should befall you. I am an English Officer and do not lie. If you want to surrender throw down your arms, hold up your hands and come across in daylight. You will have good food and good water given you. This is a German business. Between us and you there is no quarrel. Eski dost dushman olmaz (An old friend cannot be an enemy.). Allaha ismarladuk (farewell). Then they shot again. The Australians were very interested and biddable. They said: 'Law, I wish I could do that.' I felt sorry for them. They are children who can only see their own side. They feel they are justly aggrieved when the Turks have shot their pals.

Going back the men in the valley were terrified at snipers, though I do not think there are many, but it is not good for morale when they lie in funk holes and shout to everybody 'Lie down, curl up, get out. There's a . . . sniper round the corner.' It isn't really worth while taking cover and it's very undignified. It's a good thing to make the men do it, but except in the case of shrapnel it's better not to oneself. It does help in the case of shrapnel. On getting back here we had a very heavy fire which broke up our dinner party, wounded Anderson, stung Johnny[38],

38.   Johnny Allan, AH's servant. Allan had travelled with AH on his journeys to Albania before the war.

and hit me. Jack is sick. Men digging all round now at night. I am writing by candlelight blown by the wind. I wonder what the Turks are thinking. They fairly buzzed their bullets at us when I said that the Germans are not good fellows. Eastwood dined. He had humorous stories to tell of the first day's fighting. I think the Australians must have got two miles beyond our present position. Brown has gone down with the Otagos to Helles. I hope that Cazalet and he are all right. The wounded have been left to die of thirst between the trenches. The Turkish wounded and ours too. It is a filthy shame and could be prevented.

Johnny and several others are ill. A good many have chills and stomach trouble. Dead mules come floating back to the beach and perfume the air. I discovered that Pirie Gordon and Hay had forged a letter signing the name of a Turkish prisoner to it. I objected to this most strongly. Saw Skeen and Villiers Stuart[39], and said though it was none of my business I thought it was a pity as it was not at all straight. I should have very much objected if the Germans had forged a letter in my name when I was a prisoner. They agreed. Letter suppressed. Goodbye Gordon, goodbye Hay. There are no clouds but the air is fresh, though the smoke from the steamers is rising straight up and the noise of rifle fire is no louder than cricket balls on the bat.

Here are the three things we have to fear:-

1. *Any attack that took the height. The Navy couldn't help them. We should soon be too much mixed.*
2. *The blessed big guns to lollop over Howitzers.*
3. *Disease. The Turks already have dysentery.*

There is an uncanny whistling overhead. It must come from the bullets and machine guns or Maxims a long way off. It sounds eldritch. 'T'. very sick after seeing some wounded on the beach, and yet his nerves are very good. Eastwood told me that he was sure to get through. I told him not to say such things. He had three bullets through his tunic the other day. I went on the

39.　　Major Charles Villiers-Stuart (1874–1915).

Lutzow to get the rest of my stuff off, and found Colonel Ryan ('Turkish Charlie')[40] full of awful descriptions of operations. Many wounded on the boat, all very quiet. Had a drink with a sailor, the gloomiest man that ever I met. He comes from Southampton, and thinks we cannot possibly win the war. It's become very cold.

Diary, Sunday May 9th. Came back last night on a picket boat with a big steam launch and 200 men of mixed units. The little Lieutenant in charge and an amazing little Welsh RN futile as a moth but kind. He said the whole organization was too hopeless. Old Colonel Patterson, fat old fool, thought you could embark or disembark 100 men in ten minutes. The sailors have to work sometimes 20 in the 24 hours. Sometimes no sleep at all. It seemed likely we would be left out all night, the men under no kind of cover from shrapnel and without food. If we were given food it would be by the kindness of the sailors giving us their own food. At last we got in. Old Patterson ought to be sent to an asylum. He is weak as a rabbit and obstinate as a mule. This morning is still and lovely. Yesterday while I was away they were shelled pretty badly here. It is begging now with the big guns. There is a rather fearful moaning and screaming, and then a crash and high columns of water shooting up. A fortnight ago we began this adventure. I wish we were the servants or victims of dreamers and not of gamblers. It's neck or nothing with the politicians now, so I don't suppose any compromise will be considered. When I went to wash in the sea this morning a dead mule stopped me. There are many along the beach. They charge you when they are alive and prevent you washing when they are dead. The other day one came at me open-mouthed and when luckily having my stick I whacked his head, he turned round and kicked. That was in Monash Valley, and that same afternoon I saw another methodically clear the narrow path on the beach, kicking first to the right then to the left. The firing was so hot yesterday that when the General and Tahu were waiting for twenty minutes to get past a

40.   Because he had been through the siege of Plevna and held a number of Turkish decorations.

74

point he actually smoked a cigarette. Worsley[41] says it's very hard to get work done on the beach; in fact it's almost impossible. They said that the gun which had been enfilading us was knocked out, but this is not true as it is enfilading us now and it looks as if we shall have a pretty heavy bill to pay. The beach is holding its breath, and between the sound of the shrapnel and the hiss there is only the noise of the waves and a few low voices. Harrison, who was slightly wounded a few days ago, was yesterday resting in his dugout when he was blown out of it by a shell. To-day he was sent to the *Lutzow*, and we watched him being shelled the whole way, his boat wriggling. It seems as if the shells know and love him. I am glad he won't be dining with us any more; a magnet like that is a bore, though he is a very good fellow. The land between us and the 29th is reported to be full of barbed wire entanglements. Tomorrow the General has decided to move HQ to a safer place. I shall however stay here if I can; then I can have a dugout to myself. Privacy is more important in war than is safety.

I wish I had the *Iliad*. I am reading the *Revolt of Islam* which I do not care about. Shakespeare and the Old Testament.

Monday, May 10*th*. Raining and cold. Jack better.

Colonel Braithwaite[42] woke me last night with the news of the sinking of the *Lusitania*. Last night we took three trenches, but lost them again this morning. We have been attacking in this way lately. I think you have got to hit the Turks or they will hit you, that is the same with every Eastern or Western Front too, but it is becoming expensive in life. The attackers lose. Nikolas, the interpreter, was anxious to bribe Essad Pasha (not the Albanian) who was reported to have sold Janina for 20,000. I doubt if he did, and I doubt if you could, and am rather a Pharisee about it, but it certainly would save a lot of lives. Have discussed this. I proposed to the General to go out with the Greek Nikolas at night towards Anafarta and there dig in or hide in a wood, while he got hold of Greek notables and then arrange for Greeks to come in every

41.   Supply officer of the New Zealand Division.
42.   Brigadier William Braithwaite CB CMG DSO (1870–1937). At the time a Staff Officer on Godley's staff.

night with information about enemy guns etc., these men to be paid by results. They jumped at this. They always do seem to jump at any chance of sacrificing an interpreter. (1) Will Balas, the guide, come out? (2) Are any Greeks left? (3) By boat or land? (4) In uniform or Mufti? (5) Payments on what scale to be promised?

(Major) Sam Butler came last night; I was glad to see him. S.B. had been a great friend of mine in Egypt and brought me and others letters, of which we were badly in need, and stores, which were very welcome. We met upon the beach, and decided to celebrate the occasion in the Intelligence dugout, for my friend had actually got some soda and a bottle of whisky, two very rare luxuries on the beach.

This morning dug new dugout. Felt very well. Shells coming back to HQ, one hit seven men and killed five – two of them asleep. The Turks get their wounded in by means of grapnels.

Diary. We went into the Intelligence dugout and sat there. Then a shell hit the top of the dugout. The next one buzzed a lot of bullets in through the door. The third ricochetted all over the place and one bullet grazed my head. I then said: 'We'd better put up a blanket to save us from the ricochets.' At the same time Johnny was shot next door and Onslow's war diary was destroyed. A pot of jam was shot in General Cunliffe Owen's hand, which made him very angry. Vyvian, the Beachmaster, dashed into our Intelligence dugout gasping while we held blankets in front of him. Two days ago a man was killed in his dugout next door, and another man again yesterday. Now two fuses had come straight through his roof and spun like a whipping-top on the floor, dancing a sort of sarabande before the hypnotized eyes of the sailors. Also Sam Butler's whisky was destroyed in the luncheon basket. He broke into furious swearing in Arabic. The naval people are now ultimating against shrapnel and against war. All this is a bore and rather a strain on some men's nerves in the end. I saw one man hit walking with the General the other day, dancing round him, in front and behind, and all over the place. I own to having lain down the first day myself. Time, men, money, ammunition are all being wasted here.

Wednesday, May 12*th.* Rain, mud, grease, temper all night, but we shall long for this coolness when it really gets hot. No bombardment this morning, but the Greek cook, Christo Karalampa (Christopher of the Black Lamp), came and gave two hours' notice, with the rain and tears running down his face. I am not surprised at his giving notice, but why he should give me notice and be so meticulous about the time I can't think. However I soothed him. Bored to death with the shelling. No one talks of anything else. Yet it must be worse for the Turks. I had a curious walk through the dark last night past Greeks, Indians and Australians, across a rainswept, windswept, bullet-swept hillside – one through my coat. The Indians and the Deal Battalion are on the left of the New Zealanders' position. The Imperial Officers on the Staff of some of the Colonels of colonial troops complain that their COs don't understand the functions of a Staff and give them perpetual little odd jobs, corporals' jobs. They have too to stand to arms at every burst of firing in the night. However, this is getting better. Many of these Colonels are business men, who never in their wildest dreams contemplated being in such a position, and they have really risen to the occasion splendidly. The Generals have at last been prevailed upon not to walk about on the beach in the daytime dangling their Staffs after them. Two German and one Austrian submarine expected here. The transports have been ordered to Mudros.

Thursday, May 13*th.* Very calm morning, the echoes of rifle fire on the sea. I went with Cunningham to take General Russell[43] up from Reserve Gully to Walker's Ridge. I like General Russell and dislike Cunningham. I wish it wasn't the 13th. I got rid of Cunningham and came back alone by the beach. It was as beautiful a morning as I have ever seen with the sky flaming softly, not a cloud anywhere and the sea perfectly still. I lay in the scrub with wild flowers all round and watched, and not even the dead mules could spoil it. Guns thundered in the distance like at Mons. The Turks are fighting very gallantly. The position is no clearer. It is very difficult to remedy the bungle. I think it would be better for

43.   Lieut.-General Sir A.H. Russell KCMG KCB (1868–1960).

our prestige at all costs to stay here even if we get wiped out or taken, than to leave.

After breakfast I examined an intelligent Greek prisoner from Taifir Keui. I was telephoned for by Colonel Monash in great haste and went off up his valley as quickly as possible. There I found all the men in a state of nerves and panic along the road because of snipers. The Turks had put up a white flag above their trenches opposite Quinn's post. I think this was an artillery flag and that they hoped to avoid the fire of the fleet by this means. I talked to one of them about twenty-five yards off through a hole. While I was there a captain was hit. I saw Quinn, who was going for a rest, looking very jolly. After that I came back and had a long talk with the General. The people at Helles aren't making headway, and it seems unlikely except at tremendous cost and possibly not then, that they will. We are pretty well hung up except on our left; why not try there? The Turks are not yet entrenched or dug in there as in other places. I am so deaf from the fire this morning that twice I did not hear a shell and therefore did not take cover and nearly got shot.

I had to bully Yanni of Ayo Strati till he sobbed on the cliff. I then threatened to dismiss him, after which he grew cheerful, for it was what he wanted. The General wanted to know if his wages had been paid. I told him no, they had only been docked. For the month he has been here he has lost five shillings which I fined him for detrimental cowardice.

The Turks have again got white flags out. Have been ordered to go up at dawn. Skeen[44] wanted Kyriakidis to come, I said it wasn't fair.

Friday, May 14*th*. 4 *a.m.* Last night at 9.15 a foolish order came to me from the General to take up the Greek with me to shout to the Turks that he was well-treated and well-fed. I found Villiers Stuart with difficulty and explained that the Greeks would have about as much influence with the Turks as an Italian organ grinder would with me. I got the order rescinded.

I walked up the valley. The crickets were singing in the bushes

44.   General Sir Andrew Skeen KCB KCIE CMG (1873–1935)

at the opening of the valley and the place was cool with the faint light of coming dawn. Then a line of stretcher-bearers with the wounded, some quiet, some groaning. Then came the dawn and the smell of death that infects one's hands and clothes and haunts one.

They weren't over-pleased to see me at first, as after my speech the other day they had had an awful time from hand-grenades, and their faces fell when I appeared. I spoke from the same place. Then I went to another, and lastly to a trench that communicated with the Turkish trench. The Greek who had surrendered last night came down this trench and the Turks were said to be five to ten yards off. It was partly roofed, and there were some sandbags, between two and three feet high, that separated us from them. Leading into this was a big circular dugout, open to heaven. I got the men cleared out of this before speaking. In the small trench there were two men facing the Turks and lying on the ground with revolvers pointed at the Turks. I moved one man back out of the way and lay on the other – there wasn't anything else to be done – and spoke for five minutes with some intervals. Once a couple of hand-grenades fell outside and the ground quivered, but that was all. I got the guard changed then left the trench, pleased that it was over, and began an argument with a Major, Glasgow, who had only just come, as to whether the Turks were good fellows. A lot of bullets were going over and past, but I thought we were under cover until one touched my hand. I said: 'Look at that.' The Major, to whom this was a new experience, bullets coming from three different ways each with a lot of different echoes jumped, and said: 'Well, probably you are right. They may be good fellows. Now I am going back.'

The loss of the *Goliath* is confirmed and the fleet has gone, leaving a considerable blank on the horizon and a depression on the sunlit beach. Four interpreters were arrested to-day and handed over to me. I put them on to dig me a new dugout, round which a colony of interpreters is growing: Kyriakidis, who is a fine boy, aristocratic-looking, but very soft, who I want to send away as soon as possible, and others. My dugout is in the middle of wild flowers, with the sea splashing round. Since the ships have all gone we are, as a consequence, short of water. The submarines have done in another way what so many men expected the Turkish Howitzers to accomplish. The *Queen Elizabeth* is to go home. The Turks have been shelling our barges hard for an hour. We are to make an attack to-night and destroy their trenches.

Saturday, May 15th. The attack on the trenches has failed. There are many of our wounded outside our lines. Have been asked if I will go out with white flag. Of course. Am to see Birdwood in half an hour, but I shall say that the order by us not to pay respect to white flag should be rescinded. Why should Turks respect it if we don't? Saw Skeen and suggested (1) that this order be enforced (2) that an arrangement be come to with regard to the wounded on both sides. He agreed to (1) but he said (2) was not possible. While I talked to Skeen a shell hit one man in the lungs and knocked Colonel Knox in the back without hurting him. General Birdwood was hit yesterday and General Trottman[45] the day before. While we talked water arrived. A message then came from Colonel Chauvel[46] to say there were not a lot of wounded, only two. I said I proposed to go straight up and nip out with a white flag and bring them in. Skeen said 'no'. A thing like that may lead to trouble and make any future arrangement impossible. Maxims are searching all the time, and though the Turks in front of you may respect the white flag, a Maxim two miles away won't see it and then there will be accusations of treachery. Meanwhile the two wounded had to be saved, and another scheme drawn up. This Skeen sat down to do. In a few minutes a telephone message arrived from the doctor in the trenches that the two wounded had died. I came back to HQ and heard General

45.   Brigadier C.N. Trottman CB. Commanding 3rd Royal Marines Brigade.
46.   General Sir Henry 'Harry' Chauvel GCMG KCB (1865–1945). At the time (Brigadier) Chauvel was commanding the 1st Light Horse Brigade but took over acting command of the New Zealand and Australian Division on the position becoming permanent on 2 October 1915. In November 1915, he became commander of the 1st Division, which he commanded through the final phase of the Gallipoli Campaign, the evacuation, and the reorganization in Egypt.

Bridges[47] asking the General if there was any objection to his going up the Monash Valley. In a few minutes he was shot through the thigh. The snipers are getting many of our men. If the Germans were running this show they would have had 200,000 men for it.

Last night Kyriakidis heard a nightingale. I notice that the cuckoo has changed his note, worried about the shrapnel. I don't blame the bird. My new dugout is built. It has a corridor and a patio, and is sort of Louis Quinze. I have got away from Jacky Hughes, who is a very good fellow but he, Tahu and I were too crowded in the last. Now in this I can give parties and look at the view. The food is good, but we are always hungry.

Went out with Colonel Bill Braithwaite. He is a very great man for his luxuries, and looks on cover as the first of these. He is very funny about shelling, and is huffy, like a man who has received an insult, if he gets hit by a spent bullet or covered with earth. They have got the range of our new Headquarters beautifully – two shells before lunch, one on either side of the kitchen range. The men and the mess table covered with dust and stones. The fact is our ships have gone; they can now do pretty much as they like. Most people here agree that the position is hopeless, unless we drive the Turks back on our left and get reinforcements from Helles, where they could quite well spare them.

Sunday, May 16th. A day made for Trojan heroes to fight. As a matter of fact there is some friction between the Generals. Poor General Bridges reported very bad. I went into Butler's dugout and a shell came, hitting five men. The beach atmosphere alters in the most extraordinary way. In the mornings they say the Generals are pawns, Winston is a knave and a murderer, things are going badly. In the evening they say everything is for the best, we are the greatest people on earth and shall win through even in this show if only the

47.   Major General Sir William Bridges KCB CMG (1861–1915). Commander 1st Australian Division. Bridges is one of only two Australian World War I soldiers who were killed in action or died of wounds who were buried in Australia. The other is The Unknown Soldier, disinterred from a French grave and buried at the Australian War Memorial in 1991.

things are done which we point out. A Greek of Butler's is to go out again. It is a risky business; I don't know if the information to be gained is in proportion to the risk run to life and also the chance of treachery.

I have been absolutely contented here all this time, and have been singularly happy. This sounds very selfish; but it is after all comparative. If one sits down to count the misery of this place or any other during the war, you are adding another mite of misery. When this place is a butcher's shop, as it often is, I loathe it; otherwise the sea and the sky are beautiful, and there are some very jolly fellows. I would not change this for anything else, short of having a say in the settlement of things, which isn't likely to come my way. They are pounding at us again and have just hit another interpreter and another man close by. My typewriter has come up. One bottle sweet wine, one bottle whisky and plenty of cigarettes. I saw Skeen. He said that Birdwood is making out a scheme which will be shown to me. He is going to ask me to go out with a flag of truce and a bugler. I said it would be a very great pleasure, which it will. I am enchanted with my new dugout. There is a very brave German Artillery officer. I haven't seen him but they say he is a huge man and walks about everywhere under fire, but I dare say it is one of the many legends.

Monday, May 17th. The anniversary of the relief of Mafeking to-day. The General wants to telegraph to Baden Powell. I walked out to the left with Sam Butler and bathed in the beautiful quiet sea. Others were bathing too, and sometimes shrapnel bathed also. There was the scent of thyme and the scent of death on the beach. Most of the graves were very hurriedly made. I got a touch of the sun and had to lie down, and couldn't walk straight for some time. When I got back I heard that poor Villiers Stuart had been killed that morning, instantaneously. I was just going down to thank him for his kindness of two days ago when instead of sending for me about some little thing he took the trouble to come up the hill. Bullets fell all round Tahu after I left him.

Tuesday, May 18th. Last night poor Villiers Stuart was buried. The funeral was to have been at sunset, but at that time we were savagely shelled and there was some delay. We formed up in as decent a kit as we could muster, and after the sun had set in a storm of red, and while the young moon was rising, the procession started. We stumbled over boulders, and met stretcher-bearers with dead and wounded; we passed Indians driving mules and shadowy Australians standing at attention, till we came to the graves by the sea. The prayers were very short and good, interrupted by the boom of our guns and the whining of Turkish bullets overhead. The semi-circle of officers joined in the prayers. Some were much moved as he had been a great friend of many of them. He was a very good fellow. His salute was fired above his head from both the trenches.

Butler told me that Birdwood had asked for him as GSO 3. He wanted to know if George Lloyd would want it. I said no; that it was Butler's profession, his job and his chance and George would see that.

We shelled the village of Anafarta yesterday, which I don't much care about. A good many here want to destroy the minaret of the mosque. I can see no difference in principle between this and the destruction of Rheims Cathedral. Kyriakidis told me a Greek cure for sunstroke. You fill the ears of the afflicted one with salt water; it makes a noise like thunder in his head, but the sunstroke passes. Christo thereupon got me salt water in a jug without telling me, and several thirsty people tried to drink it.

A German submarine seen here. 4 p.m. A day of almost perfect peace; the rifle fire ceased sometimes for several minutes together but 8-inch shells were fired into our trenches. I wrote a letter to the Commander-in-Chief of the Turks to be submitted to Birdwood before I go out. The people have begun to sing for the first time and there is something cheerful in the air. The enfilading gun is reported to be knocked out, but gunners are great optimists. No news from Helles. I am experimenting wearing no socks. Turkish reinforcements just seen coming up. Attack expected at 3 a.m. We stand to arms here.

Wednesday, May 19th. Work under heavy shellfire. This grew worse about 6.30. Several heavy shells hit within a few yards of this dugout and the neighbouring ones, but did not burst. A little farther off they did explode, or striking the sea, raised tall columns and high fountains of white water. Colonel Chaytor badly wounded in the shoulder. A great loss to us. He looks happy or rather elated under the influence of morphia. I have got leave to send away Ashjian, the Armenian boy; he is simply terrified. And this after all is a quarrel for those directly concerned. The Germans have brought up about twelve more field guns and four or five Jack Johnsons, and the shelling is very heavy. Saw a horrid sight: a barge full of wounded was being towed out to the hospital ship. Two great Jack Johnsons came, one just in front of them; then when they turned with a wriggle, one just behind them, sending up towers of water, and leaving two great white roses in the sea that turned muddy as the stuff from the bottom rose. They had shells round them again, and a miraculous escape. It's cruel hard on the nerves of wounded men, but of course that was bad luck, not wicked intentions, because the enemy couldn't see them.

I went down to the beach by the new cut-out. A Private happened to follow me in the thick of the shelling. I said 'Stop, I want to see if it can get into the cut-out.' As I spoke a shell burst just behind him against the side of the cut-out. He said: Now sir, you have seen; let us go on.' As we got out another shell hit just in front of my foot. This is worse than our first days because of the fierce attack on top with this here. If the Turks had done this earlier they might have had us out. Now we ought to be all right, but they cannot go on using ammunition like this. Their losses are said to be very great. If the Kaiser is a man of blood, what about Winston? His vanity primarily the cause for us getting killed and the Turks too; for even if this campaign was right, all agree its strategy was all wrong. These Turkish reinforcements are said to be from Helles. They have done what we ought to have done. Now they are sending 11-inch at us. It's too bad. I saw Skeen. He said to me: 'You had better be ready to go out this afternoon; we have just shot a Turk with a white flag. That will give us an excuse for apologizing.' I suppose it will. It seems to me it will also give the Turks an excuse for retaliating.

Wind is very fresh. I had two narrow misses. A Turkish officer just brought in says the real attack is to be this afternoon, now at 1.30. I spent an hour in the hospital, interpreting for the Turkish wounded. The Australians are very good indeed to them. As I came back the pause in the shelling ended. I found the General's dugout had been hit hard. He is vexed and says he doesn't know where to go. Nothing to be done but to dig deeper. It really isn't worse than it has been before. I suppose we have to thank the German aeroplane of this morning for some of it. Chaytor has gone light-headed, asking me not to go out with the party I wanted to. Ian Hamilton[48] has refused the Turks, request for an Armistice. I saw Birdwood, he told me so. I said: 'Would there be any objection to my going to General Hamilton and seeing him, or rather that I wanted to go there, might I see him if I went?' He said certainly.

From the third week of May to the third week in June was the kernel of our time in Anzac. We had grown accustomed to think of the place as home, and of the conditions of our life as natural and permanent. The monotony of the details of shelling and the worry of the flies are of interest only to those who endured them, and have been eliminated, here and there, from this diary.

During this month we were not greatly troubled. The men continued to make the trenches impregnable, and were contented. It was in some ways a curiously happy time.

The New Zealanders and the Australians were generally clothed by the sunlight, which fitted them, better than any tailor, with a red-brown skin, and only on ceremonial occasions did they wear their belts and accoutrements.

Our sport was bathing, and the Brotherhood of the Bath was rudely democratic. There was at Anzac a singularly benevolent officer, but for all his geniality a strong disciplinarian, devoted to military observances. He was kind to all the world, not forgetting himself, and he had developed a kindly figure. No insect could resist his contours. Fleas and bugs made passionate love to him, inlaying his white skin with a wonderful red mosaic. One day he undressed and, leaving nothing of his dignity with his uniform, he mingled superbly with the crowd of bathers. Instantly he

48.   General Sir Ian Hamilton GCB GCMG DSO TD (1853–1947). Commander-in-Chief of the Mediterranean Expeditionary Force March–October 1915.

received a hearty blow upon his tender, red and white shoulder, and a cordial greeting from some democrat of Sydney or of Wellington: 'Old man, you've been amongst the biscuits!' He drew himself up to rebuke this presumption, then dived for the sea, for, as he said, 'What's the good of telling one naked man to salute another naked man, especially when neither have got their caps?'

This month was marked by a feature that is rare in modern warfare. We had an armistice for the burial of the dead, which is described in the diary. On the Peninsula we were extremely anxious for an armistice for many reasons. We wished, on all occasions, to be able to get our wounded in after a fight, and we believed, or at least the writer was confident, that an arrangement could be come to. We were also very anxious to bury the dead. Rightly or wrongly, we thought that GHQ, living on its perfumed island, did not consider how great was the abomination of life upon the cramped and stinking battlefield that was our encampment, though this was not a charge that any man would have dreamed of bringing against Sir Ian Hamilton[49].

Diary. Wednesday, May 19th, 1915. Kaba Tepé. General Birdwood told me to go to Imbros to talk to Sir Ian Hamilton about an armistice, if General Godley would give me leave.

Thursday, May 20th, 1915. Kaba Tepé. Have been waiting for four hours in Colonel Knox's boat, which was supposed to go to Imbros. Turkish guns very quiet. I hear that Ock Asquith and Wedgwood are wounded. A liaison officer down south says: 'When the Senegalese fly, and the French troops stream forward twenty yards and then stream back twenty-five yards, we know that we are making excellent progress.' There is a Coalition Government at

---

49.   AH being both extremely diplomatic and 'tongue in cheek'. His real views were expressed in a letter to his wife Mary, written in June 1915, in which he wrote 'Ian Hamilton has been here twice, I think for a quarter of an hour each time and has never been around the positions at all. GHQ are loathed.' His view of Hamilton was further expanded in another letter in July 1915 in which he stated 'Hamilton has the obstinacy of weak men. I have had one or two instances when I have seen how he and his staff believe what they want to believe in the face of all sense and evidence.'

home. We think that we are the reason of that; we think the Government cannot face the blunder of the Dardanelles without asking for support from the Conservatives.

6 p.m. Arcadian. I came on to the *Arcadian* finally with George Lloyd. Have been talking to Sir Ian Hamilton with regard to the armistice. Hamilton said: 'I agree with you in principle. I have telegraphed to Kitchener with regard to Birdwood's desire for an armistice and the question of sending you out, but it is largely a political business. Greece is out. Bulgaria and Italy may come in, but they won't if it can be made out that we are suing for an armistice'. I agreed with that. I said that if the political situation admits it I think an armistice would be good for these reasons:

(1) *It is not decent to let the wounded die unnecessarily of thirst*
(2) *We have now knocked the Turks. It is for us to grant them favours. Later we shall want to advance, it will then be our turn to lose. If we give an armistice now, we can ask for one then*
(3) *Sanitation demands it*
(4) *It will show the Turks we are not the brutes the Germans make us out and produce a good impression all over the East.*

Having knocked the Turks, said I, why can't we tell them to bury their own dead, and look after their wounded. He acquiesced but said it must be unofficial. I didn't say this must almost inevitably give rise to accusation of bad faith etc. He said: 'I should like to do the decent thing.' He looked very worried and asked me to tea which I refused.

I saw Compton MacKenzie, private novelist to Sir Ian Hamilton and Clive Bigham[50] was also there, looking I suppose for orders, but kindly lending me Shakespeares.

Friday, May 21st, 1915. Kaba Tepé. I had to sleep the night as

---

50.   Lieutenant-Colonel the Hon Charles Bigham, Viscount Mersey CMG CBE PC (1872–1956).

I could not get off, though I was reluctant to stay fearing there might be an attack which I should miss. As I waited after breakfast Sir Ian Hamilton came up in a fussy rage and asked vehemently 'What do you think of it now?' I didn't know what he was talking about. He said: 'Last night the Turks put up a white flag and massed behind it in their trenches. They meant to rush us and used a ruse. If you had had your way, our fellows on the beach would now all have had their throats cut or be swimming about in the sea. It was very difficult for me to say no to B. after the very nice way in which he asked me.' I said I knew nothing of all this. That it wasn't a question of sentiment, as he said, but of sanitation, and that even if the Turks were treacherous every day in the week (and Skeen's programme was drawn to prevent that) it was no reason why we should share Asiatic cholera with them. He repeated 'I am very glad I had the strength of mind to refuse.' A vain weak man, whose proper headquarters are the *Arcadian*.

I came back with four 'Arcadians'. A shell came a long way off but they all bobbed and lay down and got in the cabin. Yesterday as we started a German aeroplane dropped a bomb near us. I thought it was an ordinary shell. While I had been away there had been a parley, but it was not a case of bad faith as the 'Arcadians' believed; the Turks had put up white flags, as Sir Ian had said, but everyone admitted there was no case of bad faith. It was said we had shot one Red Crescent man by mistake. General Walker[51] had gone out and talked to the Turks, just like that. Both sides had, apparently, been frightened. The General was sorry I had missed it. I walked up with him to Reserve Gully to see the new brigade. The evening sun was shining on the myrtle in the gully, and all the splendid fellows were half-stripped and singing and whistling while little fires crackled everywhere.

Saturday, May 22nd, 1915. Kaba Tepé. Sam Butler was sent out yesterday to talk to the Turks, but he did not take a white flag with him, and was sniped and bruised. I saw Birdwood; he said Ian

---

51.   Lieutenant-General Sir Harold Walker KCMG KCB DSO (1862–1934). At that stage Chief of Staff to General Birdwood (although much of the actual planning was left to Colonel Skeen who succeeded him).

Hamilton was very angry and had written him a letter beginning 'My Dear Birdwood, I am frankly horrified'. Birdwood told me to talk to the Turks first opportunity and say nice things to them.

Diary. I went out with Butler, we hurried along the beach, crossed the barbed wire entanglements and met a fierce Arab and a wandery-looking Turkish Lieutenant. Then came Kemal Bey[52]. Sam and Kemal Bey, as they came, provided the Australian escort with much innocent laughter. Our barbed wire down to the sea consisted only of a few light strands, over which the Turk was helped by having his legs raised high for him. Sam, however, wished him, as he was blindfolded, to believe that this defence went on for at least twenty yards. So the Turk was made to do an enormously high, stiff goose-step over the empty air for that space, as absurd a spectacle to our men as I was to be, later, to the Turks. The Australians were almost sick from internal laughter.

Diary. Kemal Bey asked for a hostage and I said I was ready to go. They bandaged my eyes and I mounted a horse and rode off with Sahib Bey and spent four or five comfortable hours with him. At one moment the soldier who was supposed to be leading my horse had apparently let go and had fallen behind to light a cigarette or pick flowers. Sahib Bey called out: 'You fool, can't you see he is riding straight over the cliff?' I protested that this negligence was an infringement of the Hague Convention. We left the smell of death behind and rode along by the sea for some way, for I could hear the waves. Then we went round and round, I think to puzzle me, and we ended up in a tent in a grove where they took the handkerchief off, and Sahib Bey said: 'This is the beginning of a life-long friendship.' We had cheese and tea and coffee. He ate first to show me it was all right, though I said it was an insult to me. He tried to impress me with their well-being. He said it may not be political economy, but it is very comfortable having no exports, such lots of everything and all so cheap too; he hated all politicians and had sworn a vow never to read the papers. He knew my name and thought we had met. Later the

52.   Major Kemal Bey (from) Ohri (Binbasi Ohrili Kemal Bey). The commander of the Operations Group of the 3rd Army Corps.

other officer in the tent, a charming fellow, cleared out and left us alone. I then said: 'Why ever did you do this, my dear? Could you win the Caucasus or Egypt? What was there to gain? You had all to lose. Germany has made a victim of you like Belgium. She wanted to hold our troops up, and that she accomplished. She wanted to make trouble in India and Egypt. There she failed.' 'Yes,' he said, 'there are many of us who think like you but we must obey. We know you are just, and that Moslems thrive under you, but you have made cruel mistakes by us, the taking of those two ships and the way in which you took them.' He asked me a few questions which I put aside. He had had a conversation with 'Dash' Blamey the day before. Blamey is the Australian Intelligence Officer. He had apparently told him where Hamilton was and what a bore he had been about the armistice, also the number of Turkish prisoners we had taken.

In the end I said '*Salute my friends. If I am not killed and can help your countrymen later I will do so to the best of my power*'. We parted great friends. It was a picturesque day, the walk through the rain, and then Sam and I sitting with the fierce Arab, smoking, in fields of glorious poppies, with the sea glittering by us, and later the long slow eastern talk with Sahib Bey, and the ride blindfolded to and from Kaba Tepé. We got very wet, and I rubbed my feet with shingle for I was not wearing socks.

Sunday, May 23rd, 1915. Kaba Tepé. We landed a month ago. We now hold a smaller front than then, also the *Albion* has gone ashore. The rest of the fleet has left us. She remains a fixture. All the possible boats are rushing up to the *Albion* to tow her off.

The Turks are sending in a hail of shrapnel. There is the deuce of a fight on. It will be an awful business if they don't get her off. They have got her off thank goodness, everyone here breathes a sigh of relief.

We wonder if all the places with the funny accidental names will one day be historical, Johnson's Jolly, Dead Man's Ridge, Quinn's Post, the Valley of Death? Plugge's Plateau and Walker's Ridge. Poor Plugge. A brave and good man, twice wounded, paid no attention the first time. I didn't think that a schoolmaster would fight like that. The New Zealanders are most gallant fellows.

The big fight ought to come off, after the armistice. Two more divisions have come up against us. They will probably be en masse at one point. All was quiet last night but a shell came into the New Zealand hospital on the beach which is the safest place and killed four wounded men and one dresser and some more outside. It is these new guns whose position we still have not learnt.

Tuesday, May 25th, 1915. *Kaba Tepé.* We had the truce yesterday. I was afraid something might go wrong, but it went off all right. Skeen, Blamey[53] and Howse VC[54] and I started early. Skeen offered me breakfast but, like a fool, I refused. He put some creosote on my handkerchief. We were at the rendezvous on the beach at 6.30. Heavy rain soaked us to the skin. At 7.30 we met the Turks, Miralai Izzedin, a pleasant, rather sharp, little man; Arif, the son of Achmet Pasha, who gave me a card, 'Sculpteur et Peintre,' and 'Etudiant de Poésie.' I saw Sahib and had a few words with him but he did not come with us. Fahreddin Bey came later.

We walked from the sea and passed immediately up the hill, through a field of tall corn filled with poppies, then another corn-field; then the fearful smell of death began as we came upon scattered bodies. We mounted over a plateau and down through gullies filled with thyme, where there lay about 4,000 Turkish dead. It was indescribable. One was grateful for the rain and the grey sky. A Turkish Red Crescent man came and gave me some antiseptic wool with scent on it, and this they renewed frequently. There were two wounded crying in that multitude of silence. The Turks were distressed, and Skeen strained a point to let them send water to the first wounded man, who must have been a sniper crawling home. I walked over to the second, who lay with a high circle of dead that made a mound round him, and gave him a drink from my water-bottle, but Skeen called me to come on and I had to leave the bottle. Later a Turk gave it back to me. Nazim,

---

53.   Field Marshal Sir Thomas Blamey GBE KCB CMG DSO ED (1884–1951).
54.   Major General Neville Howse VC KCB KCMG (1863–1930). Director of the Australian Medical Service.

the Turkish captain with me said: 'At this spectacle even the most gentle must feel savage, and the most savage must weep.' The dead fill acres of ground, mostly killed in the one big attack, but some recently. They fill the myrtle-grown gullies. One saw the result of machine-gun fire very clearly; entire companies annihilated – not wounded, but killed, their heads doubled under them with the impetus of their rush and both hands clasping their bayonets. It was as if God had breathed in their faces, as 'the Assyrian came down like the wolf on the fold.'

The line was not easy to settle. Neither side wanted to give its position or its trenches away. At the end Skeen agreed that the Turks had been fair. We had not been going very long when we had a message to say that the Turks were entrenching at Johnson's Jolly. Skeen had, however, just been there and seen that they were doing nothing at all. He left me at Quinn's Post, looking at the communication trench through which I had spoken to the Turks. Corpses and dead men blown to bits everywhere. Blamey was with me part of the time: easy to get on with; also a gentleman called indifferently by the men Mr. or Major Potts. A good deal of friction at first. The trenches were 10 to 15 yards apart. Each side was on the *qui vive* for treachery. In one gully the dead had got to be left unburied. It was impossible to bury them without one side seeing the position of the other. In the Turkish parapet there were many bodies buried. Fahreddin told Skeen he wanted to bury them, 'but,' he said, 'we cannot take them out without putting something in their place'. Skeen agreed, but said that this concession was not to be taken advantage of to repair the trench. This was a difficult business.

When our people complained that the Turks were making loopholes, they invited me into their trench to look. Then the Turks said that we were stealing their rifles; this came from the dead land where we could not let them go. I went down, and when I got back, very hot, they took my word for it that we were not. There was some trouble because we were always crossing each other's lines. I talked to the Turks, one of whom pointed to the graves. 'That's politics,' he said. Then he pointed to the dead bodies and said: 'That's diplomacy. God pity all of us poor soldiers.'

Much of this business was ghastly to the point of nightmare. I found a hardened old Albanian *chaoush* and got him to do anything I wanted. Then a lot of other Albanians came up, and I said: 'Tunya tyeta.'[55] I had met some of them in Janina. They began clapping me on the back and cheering while half a dozen funeral services were going on all round, conducted by the chaplains. It was unseemly and I stopped it. I asked them if they didn't want an Imam for a service over their martyrs, but the old Albanian roared with laughter like the pagan he was, and said that their souls were all right. I didn't see many signs of fanaticism; one huge savage-looking Anatolian refused cigarettes and cursed; Greeks came up and tried to surrender to me, and were ordered back pretty roughly, but considering the amount of men we had killed, they remained unmoved and polite. I might have been able to do the same vis a vis to the Turks. I couldn't have vis a vis to the Germans. Probably they couldn't have with Russians.

Blamey came to say that Skeen had lost Hough and wanted me, so he, Arif and I walked to the sea. The burying had not been so well done in places, and Vassif took exception to it. Some bodies had been blown to pieces. As we went along we took our own rifles from the Turkish side minus their bolts, and gave up to the Turks their rifles in the same condition. When there was a doubt we gave them its benefit.

Our men gave cigarettes to the Turks, and beyond the storm-centre at Quinn's Post the feeling was all right. We sat down and sent men to look for Skeen. Arif was nervous and almost rude. Then Skeen came. He told me to get back as quickly as possible to Quinn's Post, as I said I was nervous at being away, and to retire the troops at 4 and the white-flag men at 4.15. I said to Arif: 'Everybody's behaved very well. Now we must take care that nobody loses his head. Your men won't shoot you and my men won't shoot me, so we must walk about, otherwise a gun will go off and everybody will get shot.' But Arif faded away. I got back as quickly as possible. Blamey went away on the left. I then found that the Turks' time was eight minutes ahead of ours, and put on

55.   The usual Albanian greeting.

our watches. The Turks asked me to witness their taking the money from their dead, as they had no officer there. They were very worried by having no officer, and asked me if anyone were coming. I, of course, had no idea, but I told them I would see that they were all right. They were very patient. . . .

The burying was finished some time before the end. There were certain tricks on both sides I think. One of our Padres got the communication trench which had bothered us so much filled in by burying the dead there. Both sides did a bit of spying. Later a prisoner told us that the Turkish GHQ came out dressed up as Red Crescent men, and our Generals were looking round too, disguised, not by putting on clothes but by taking off their coats. The same thing in principle.

All the Turks cursed politicians and their work. I made our men and the Turks talk together. They exchanged money and badges. At 4.00 the Turks came to me for orders. This couldn't happen anywhere else. I retired their troops and Potts and I retired ours. At 4.07 I retired the white-flag men, making them shake hands. I came to the upper end. There about a dozen Turks came out. I told them how good their people had been to me in the past, giving me food and hospitality when they lacked food themselves, and said I looked forward to being friends again when this was over, if they didn't shoot me the next day. They said, in a horrified chorus: 'God forbid!' The Albanians laughed and cheered, and said: 'We will never shoot you.' Then the Australians began coming up, and said: 'Good-bye old chap; good luck!' And the Turks said: 'Oghur Ola gule gule gedejekseniz, gule gule gele-jekseniz' (Smiling may you go and smiling come again)[56]. Then I told them all to get into their trenches, and unthinkingly went up to the Turkish trench and got a deep salaam from it. I told them that neither side would fire for twenty-five minutes after they had got into the trenches. One Turk was seen out away on our left, but there was nothing to be done, and I think he was all right. A couple of rifles had gone off about twenty minutes before the end but Potts and I went hurriedly to and fro seeing it was all right. At

56. Or 'Good luck, go safely and safely return.'

last we dropped into our trenches, glad that the strain was over. I walked back with Temperley[57] whom I met, and got some whisky for the infection in my throat and iodine where the barbed wire entanglement had cut my legs. I am glad that I worried about this Truce though it would probably have come about anyhow. The Turks have seen their dead in thousands, they have also seen that we aren't bad fellows, and the infection is less. All that is to the good.

There was a hush over the Peninsula. . . .

Wednesday, May 26th, 1915. *Kaba Tepé*. This morning all of us who were there still feel the infection in our throats and noses and shall for some days. I was sitting talking to Dix and asked him if he really believed there were submarines. 'Yes,' he said, 'unfortunately', and came to the door of the dugout and swore, and said: 'There is the *Triumph* sinking'. Every picket boat dashed off to pick up the survivors. The Turks were good and never shelled them at all. There was fury, panic, impotent rage on the beach and on the hill. I heard Colonel 'Uncle Bill' Ball half off his head saying 'you should kill all enemies: Like a wounded bird, she is. Give them cigarettes. The swine!' He shook his fist. Men were crying and cursing. Very different to last night when we were all wishing each other luck.

In the afternoon I went round past Monash Gully towards Kaba Tepé and bathed; one shell landed in the sea, one on the beach. I came back over the ridges having a beastly time from the shrapnel which tumbled round me. We have now undermined Quinn's Post with a sap. We are worried by flies and ants past endurance.

Thursday, May 27th, 1915. *Kaba Tepé*. A very wet night. This morning there was no fleet and only one destroyer, we therefore await a great bombardment. I do wish that the Turks would forget how to shoot. We are to be shot at now for an indefinite period without the power of replying effectively, and the knowledge that we are firmly locked outside the back door of a side-show, besieged by more submarines at sea and Turks on the land.

---

57.   Harold Temperley (1879 –1939), an Intelligence Officer. Towards the end of his life Temperley became Master of Peterhouse, Cambridge.

Went with the General to General Russell's trenches. They are very much improved. The men call an ideal trench a Godley-Braithwaite trench; that is, tall enough for General Godley and broad enough for Colonel Braithwaite. Bathed. Charlie Bentinck[58] arrived. His destroyer lay just off the beach and was shelled. Some sailors and five soldiers killed. Forty-five wounded. Very unfortunate. If they had come yesterday, it would have been all right – a quiet day, though we had thirty men sniped. The *Majestic* reported sunk off Helles. Off to Mudros to get stores.

Friday, May 28th, 1915. Mudros. Left after many delays, and slept on deck. Very cold. The Greeks are now intriguing against us. The Greek military attaché has been here communicating with the Queen of Greece. Mudros almost entirely French Algerian and Senegalese. I think it is a pretty tall order to put a black Senegalese cannibal into Red Cross uniform. A reward has been published for information re. submarine depots. Have felt much could be done, but doubted if Admiralty was doing it.

Saturday, May 29th, 1915. Lemnos. Drove across the island to Castro. There was a delightful spring half a mile from Castro and a café kept by a Greek. His wife had been killed by the Turks. Great fig-trees and gardens. I met two naval officers, who told me Wedgwood[59] had died of wounds. I am very sorry; he was a lion of peace, I admired him a lot. Castro is beautiful, with balconies over the narrow streets, half Turk and half Greek, and shady gardens. I bathed in a transparent sea, facing Athos, which was gleaming like a diamond. I watched its shadow come across the eighty miles of sea at sunset, as Homer said it did. I found a Greek, who had been Cromer's cook. He said he would come back and cook for me, if there was no danger. He said he knew that GHQ cooks were safe, but his wife would not let him go on to the Peninsula. He said her idea of warfare was wrong. She always thought of men and bullets skipping about together on a hillside.

58.   Lieutenant-Colonel Lord Charles Cavendish-Bentinck DSO (1868–1956).
59.   AH was misinformed. Lieutenant Commander (later Colonel) Josiah Wedgwood MP (1872–1943). Later Baron Wedgwood of Barlaston.

Sunday, May 30th, 1915. *Mudros*. I bathed before dawn and went back to Mudros with masses of mosquito-netting, etc. Turkish prisoners of the French were being guarded by Greeks. It was rather like monkeys looking after bears. They were uniforms that were a cross between Ali Pasha of Janina and Little Lord Fauntleroy. I saw Hoyland, who had been on the *River Clyde*. I was right to call the *River Clyde* the death ship. Hoyland looked as if he was still watching the sea turn red with blood as he described the landing on Gallipoli. Jack was sick, and I had to leave him with my coat. Went and saw my friend the Papas of the little Greek church on the hill.

Monday, May 31st, 1915. *Anzac*. I saw Hutton this morning, slightly wounded. Bathed at the farthest point towards Kaba Tepé, but had to fly with my clothes in my hand, leaving my cigarettes. Hid in gully, shelled again and crossing the ridge, very dangerous indeed. I had almost forgotten the war. Today is a Greek day, hot and lovely.

Wednesday, June 2nd, 1915. *Kaba Tepé*. I went out last night to the outposts where a Greek had been taken. His examination this morning would have made a wonderful picture with the setting of the fresh blue sea and mountain, the man himself biblical and full of gestures, surrounded by tall English officers and a number of half-naked soldiers.

Last night we sent up two bombs from Japanese mortars over by Quinns. It sounded beastly. This morning I went to Reserve Gully where the Monash Brigade is resting for the first time for five weeks. The General, looking like a hero, made them a speech from a kind of throne in the middle of the sunlit amphitheatre in which they sat. It was an odd sight, tier after tier of clean-shaven athletes, very handsome and brown as Indians. Bullets swept over all the time, sometimes drowning his voice. Quinn is killed, I am sorry. He was a brave, strong, jolly, coarse fellow. Screaton[60] also is killed, he was quiet and shy. He died at Helles. Curious the different types I have known killed here – Rupert Brooke, Doughty and Wedgwood.

60.   Lieutenant Thomas Screaton (1892–1915). 15th North Auckland Company, Auckland Infantry Battalion.

Friday, June 4th, 1915. Anzac. Nothing much doing. I feel we still might compromise about Constantinople:

> (1) *Our first essential is as an Eastern Empire not to have an unsuccessful Eastern Campaign*
> (2) *To open the Dardanelles*
> (3) *To occupy, if only nominally, Constantinople. Don't know if the Turks would as yet agree to any of these things, or how far our old engagements with the Russians bind us.*

George Lloyd came over. Very glad to see him. This morning I went with Shaw to the extreme left, through fields of poppies, thyme, and lavender. We saw a vulture high overhead, and the air was full of the song of larks. At Helles there was a savage attack going on. There was very bad sniping. In some places the trenches are only knee-high; in other places there are no trenches and the Turks are anything from four to eight hundred yards off. Yesterday seventeen men were hit at one place, they said, by one sniper. At one place on the way, we ran like deer, dodging. The General, when he had had a number of bullets at him, also ran. Sniping is better fun than shrapnel; it's more human. You pit your wits against the enemy in a rather friendly sort of way. A lot of vultures collecting.

Saturday, June 5th, 1915. Anzac. Examined sixteen prisoners. Food good, munitions plentiful, morale all right. The individuals fed up with the war, but the mass obedient and pretty willing. No idea of surrendering. They think they are going to win. There was one Greek, a Karamanly, who only talked Turkish. He did not say until to-night that he was wounded. The flies are bad.

Sunday, June 6th, 1915. Anzac. A sergeant called to Turks this morning to surrender, one put his head up and was instantly shot. Two Turks, by Birdwood's orders, to go and call on others to surrender to-night. Very hot, flies bad, have filled my dugout with kerosene. Helles fight indecisive. The French let us down. The Generals all being criticised. I think the end must be compromise;

with Ian Hamilton I doubt his being man enough to carry it through.

Went to the service this morning with the General, in the amphitheatre. The sermon was mainly against America for not coming into the war, and also against bad language. The chaplain said he could not understand the meaning of it. The men laughed. So did I.

Monday, June 7th, 1915. *Kaba Tepé*. This morning the land was sweet as Eden and there was the calm of the first creation. I wanted to gallop on the Turkish officer's horse to Nebronesi point but could not find the officer in charge, and later was prevented. Hough has been stellen bosched to the firing line, half stellenbosched, half Uriah the Hittite by Blamey, not because of Mrs. Hough. Tremendous shelling going on round the dugout; if this keeps up it will be knocked down and I shall be hit. In the night I was invaded by mice. This afternoon Butler, Onslow and I climbed the hill and had a beautiful view. Everyone rather ill and feverish. The Intelligence Office of Harold Pirie-Gordon[61], poor chap, who went sick a long time ago, and Hay whom we call Kru Ot (dry grass in Turkish equals Hay) when we don't want him to understand, has been moved higher and safer. I rather liked the stuffy old place which was called 'The Mountain Path to the Jackal's Cave.'

The attack last night failed, but the drone of the rifles went on unceasingly, like the drone of a dry waterfall. We shall not get to Constantinople unless the flat-faced Bulgars come in.

Yesterday I lunched with Temperley at the HQ of Monash Valley. Times have changed: it's fairly safe going there through a long sap they have dug, and the noise is less bad.

Colonel Infantry Johnston who is the Brigadier had seen a lot of the Crown Prince in India, and said he was a very good fellow. Dined with Woods, Dix, Sam Butler and Edwards. Champagne galore for once, political stories and a great dinner.

Went off this morning to No. 2 with the General. Sap all the way now, much safer, only one snipe at all of us together instead of, as last time, each one having several shots at him alone. The

61.   Lt Harry Pirie-Gordon RNVR. An Intelligence officer.

Turkish birds were singing beautifully as we went. There was also a Turkish snake, which I believe was quite harmless, but Tahu killed it. One can see the men are growing pretty weary. They aren't as resigned as the 10,000 brother monks of Mt. Athos. It was the proper name to give this cover, the name of ANZAC, for Anjak in Turkish means only just or barely.

Friday, June 11th, 1915. Kaba Tepé. I have been considering if it would be of any use to be made prisoner. If one got taken one would have to get taken very plausibly and it would have to appear an unwise reconnaissance. I will talk to the General about it. I wonder if it came off if I would have the chance of seeing and talking with Talaat. Nearly all the Australians on the beach are half or quite naked. Many of the New Zealanders too. This is pretty well the same. They lie about and bathe and become darker than Indians. It's an extraordinary thing that if the sun gets at a naked white man it does make him darker than a native. A more delicate skin I suppose. The General objects to this. 'I suppose,' he says, 'we shall have our servants waiting on us like that.' His stud groom Douglas who looks after the donkeys is never dressed. The flies are very bad, and so are the mice but they fear that my typewriter is a trap and leave me a little alone. The shelling also is bad and I thought I saw lice this morning.

This morning I saw five men hit and there were a lot more. Edwardes is very pessimistic. He is one of the nicest fellows I have ever met. The only compensation that this war gives us is friendships that one would never have made otherwise, but it doesn't make amends for those friends one has lost.

Saturday June 12th, 1915. Kaba Tepé. Two months ago to-day we left Alexandria. I told General Godley I was ready to be made prisoner, mainly for these reasons. It is very important for us to get through, and it is very important for the Turks to survive, but if we make it evident that we want to begin negotiations we court a rebuff, and if they, on the other hand, make démarches which we don't accept they have put themselves wrong with the Germans and probably their own countrymen too. Therefore what you want if you can get it is a telephone that won't compromise either party. I could talk to the Young Turks whom I have known and helped and,

100

with their winking at it, pass on their views. I said it was no use putting it before GHQ. They would take no idea that was not their own, and they never had any, and anyway becoming prisoner would be quite the last to occur to them. The General agreed with me. He said if he was Hamilton he would certainly have encouraged a number of things of that kind, and was kind enough to say pleasant things. He said he would speak to Birdwood, meanwhile I had better think out details. The General has gone sick, worse luck.

Sunday, June 13th, 1915. *Kaba Tepé*. A lot of mules and several men hit yesterday. Last night, Sam and I were on the beach, when a man on a stretcher went by, groaning rhythmically. I thought he had been shot through the brain. Later on I went into the hospital to find a wounded Turk, and found that this man had never been hit at all. He had been doing very good work till a shell exploded near him and gave him a shock. Then he went on imitating a machine gun. Some men in a sap up at Quinn's have been going off their heads. Birdwood is a very good fellow but he won't hear of the prisoner business.

Awful accounts of Mudros: flies, heat, sand, no water, typhoid. To-day are the Greek elections.

Am dining with Harold Woods. 'The beach' now says that It has been poisoned by the Greek guides, whom he illtreats and uses as cooks. I shouldn't wonder. The shelling is bad. I am going to make a new dugout to get away from the flies and mice. The Turkish prisoners will do this. I pay them a small sum.

Tuesday, June 15th, 1915. *Kaba Tepé*. Colonel Chauvel has pleurisy, Colonel Johnston[63] enteric. The sea's high and the Navy depressed. There is a perpetual row between the Navy and the Army. One man and two mules killed in our gully this morning; the body of one mule blown about 50 yards both ways.

Wednesday, June 16th, 1915. *Kaba Tepé*. Rain. I was to have gone to Helles with Woods to see Deedes[64], but no boats went; it

---

63.　　Commanding New Zealand Infantry Brigade. Afterwards killed at battle of Messines in 1917.
64.　　Brigadier Sir Wyndham Deedes (1883–1956).

was too rough. I was going down from HQ to see Butler about spies when General Cunliffe Owen said to me.:'Wait a bit, the shelling is too bad now and I will come with you,' but I couldn't wait. A shell fell in the gully as I crossed a few yards from me. Woods came out to see where it had hit. It went into Maconochie's dugout where Hough was and sent him out, dizzy, black and shaken, his furniture destroyed. Hay tried to turn him out of the Intelligence dugout but we protested. He isn't a pleasant fellow, but I felt sorry for him. The General has come back with the last casualty lists from France. One feels ashamed of being alive. I wish I hadn't written to some people whose sons have since been killed. One couldn't guess that all these men were going to be killed.

Thursday, June 17th, 1915. *Helles*. Thirty men killed and wounded on the beach to-day. This morning I came to Helles with Woods. As we got there a submarine had two shots at one of our transports by us. I was to have seen Deedes, but he had gone off to see Gouraud. George Peel walked in and took me round the beach, two miles on. We climbed on to the headland, in what he called 'the quiet track of the Black Marias.' He talked of every mortal thing – the future Liberal and Socialist, the possibility of touching the heart of the people, the collapse of Christianity, our past and our policy. I left him and walked back across thyme and asphodel, Asia glowing like a jewel across the Dardanelles in the sunset. At night I talked late and long with Dash. Every Department is jealous, everyone is at cross-purposes, no co-operation between the War Office and the Foreign Office.

Walked in the morning to the HQ of the Royal Naval Division with Whittall. We were shelled most of the way in the open landscape. There was no cover anywhere. It felt unfamiliar. I was unfavourably impressed with the insecurity of life in this part of the world, and wished for Anzac. In the evening we drank *mavrodaphne* and tried to get rid of Hough.

Friday, June 18th, 1915. *Kaba Tepé*. I left Helles in the middle of very heavy shelling, a star performance. A lot of horses killed this morning. A submarine popped up last night. As we came back to Anzac the Turks shelled our trawler and hit her twice, but without doing any damage.

Shelling grew worse at Anzac, and sickness began to make itself felt. Men were sent across to Imbros when it was possible to rest.

Diary. On June 25th I went across to Imbros with Harold Woods and the Greek miller, Nikolas. Hawker was there and mad Elliot of Macedonia whom I did not see. If Elliot took a dislike to any man he dug him out of his dugout. We slept uncomfortably with flies to keep us warm on the ground. As I wrote this Johnny was hit outside, and another shrapnel came through my dugout, one bullet glancing off my typewriter. Johnny not bad; carried him down at once with Conolly under very heavy fire, and got him special attention. Luck for the General – his blankets were riddled with bullets. Johnny hit through the calf of the leg. Thousands of flies on the wounded. Many men hit on the beach. They have our range completely. Two days ago Colonel Parker had his chair and table smashed while he was in his dugout. He left it and went to have tea with Wagstaffe. There he was reading and another bullet came and tore the paper in his hand in two. I have been covered twice with dirt by a shell, not counting this afternoon, in the last three days. L.S. Amery[65] came with Kelly. I only saw him for a minute, worse luck, but he is coming back to-morrow, I hope, when we can have a talk. GHQ turned up in force, and walked about like wooden images.

We have a foolish sergeant MacAlister, a clerk. He has got tired of writing, and, wanting to change the pen for the sword, borrowed a rifle and walked up to the front line at Quinn's Post. There he popped his head in and said: 'Excuse me, is this a private trench, or may anyone fire out of it?'

The sound of battle has ended. Men are bathing. The clouds that the cannonade had called up are gone, and the sea is still and crimson in the sunset to Imbros and Samothrace.

Tuesday, June 29th, 1915. *Anzac.* When I went down Johnny had already gone. Shall go to the hospital ship to-morrow, inshallah. We have advanced 1,000 yards down at Helles but no details yet. Many men shot here yesterday by the Anafarta gun. This gun has as good a tale of killed and wounded as, I should

65.   Lieutenant-Colonel Leopold Amery (1873–1955).

think, any gun of the war. Every day it gets its twenty odd. On my roof again to-day but not inside. The Australians attacked on the right flank yesterday; about fifty killed and wounded. They think the Turks suffered more heavily. I went for a walk to the extreme left with the General. Terrific heat. We came to a beautiful little valley filled with thyme and wild lavender which the Maoris are to inhabit. The men were bathing beyond the shrapnel point. They said the Turks were very good and let them. It is extraordinary to remember that the Army Corps order was pretty close to NO QUARTER when we started this campaign. Men are practising bomb-throwing everywhere. Had two letters two months old; also the whisky sent me from Alexandria was all looted. Mrs. Luscombe, the ex-Lady of the ex-Grand Vizier of Afghanistan who is in prison because he, the Ex-Grand Vizier, was a progressive man, wants me to get her boy a place as a saddler. Lots of men here would like that job. It's a day of blessed peace, but there's a lot of feeling about the Anafarta gun, and bathing is stopped on the beach till night. The men are now darker than Red Indians.

Wednesday, June 30th, 1915. Anzac. Last night I went down to the hospital and was inoculated for cholera by Corbyn, a witty man. A trench had been blown in, and men were lying groaning on the floor, most of them suffering from shell shock, not wounds. Corbyn said many of the doctors had not been able to face the work. The wounds and mutilations were too horrible. I remember the same in France. I asked him why the wounded were not sent to Cyprus instead of Mudros. He said because it's a splendid climate and there is heaps of water. The first doctor at Mudros is useless, the second a drunkard so I hear. Anyway, what is certain is that the condition of the sick and wounded is awful. That they can tell one.

There was a fight here last night and bullets all over the place. This morning it is very rough and I can't yet get to the hospital ship. Prisoners coming in. The General had a row with the Staff because he said he got no information and told me to examine the prisoners. This I wouldn't do, as it's no use for an outsider to quarrel with the regular soldiers.

July 1st, 1915. *Anzac*. I examined the prisoners, amongst them a tall Armenian lawyer, who talked some English. I asked him how he had surrendered. He said: 'I saw two gentlemen with their looking-glasses, and came over to them.' By this he meant two officers with periscopes. He said that the psychology of the Turks is a curious thing. They do not fear death, yet are not brave. They attack a man-of-war vessel with rifles yet are not brave. No water came in yesterday. The storm wrecked the barges and the beach is covered with lighters. We got brackish water from the hill. I could not get to Jack for work.

At lunch I heard there were wounded crying on Walker's Ridge, and went up there with Zachariades. We found a very nice Australian, Major Reynell. We went through the trenches, dripping with sweat. It was a boiling day and my head reeled from the inoculation; then we had to crawl through a sap over dead Turks, some of whom were in a ghastly condition, headless and covered with flies; then out from the darkness into another sap with another dead Turk to walk over. The Turkish trenches were thirty yards off and the dead lay between the two lines when I called. I was answered at once by a Turk. He said he couldn't move, and I went out to him with a rope and a water-bottle. I gave him a drink but could not carry him for fear of hurting him and there was a heap of dead in the way. He was a big man, badly wounded. Reynell came out and we got him in, stumbling over the dead amongst whom he lay. I went back for the water-bottle but they began shooting to warn me and I picked up a bayonet and ran back into the trench. A dreadful time getting the Turk out through the very narrow trench. I got one other, unwounded, shamming dead. We threw him a rope and in he came[66]. After that I went to Monash Valley and jumped out of a sap there and shouted into the scrub but got no answer.

The taking of the second Turk was a curious episode that perhaps deserves a little more description than is given by the diary. The process of catching Turks fascinated the Australians,

66.   In a letter to Mary Herbert, AH's wife, Major General Godley described this incident as '*a VC action in reverse*'.

and amongst them an RAMC doctor who came round on that occasion. This officer prided himself upon neatness and a smart appearance, when the dust and heat of the Dardanelles had turned everyone else into scallywags. After he had attended to the first wounded man, he pointed out the second Turk lying between our trenches and the Turks' and only a few yards from either. 'You go out again, sir,' said the Australians; 'it's as good as a show.' I, however, took another view. I called out to the Turk: 'Do you want any water?' 'By God,' he whispered back, 'I do, but I am afraid of my people.' We then threw him a rope and pulled him in. He told us that the night before he had lost direction in the attack. Fire seemed to be coming every way, and it had seemed to him the best plan to fall and lie still amongst his dead comrades. The doctor gave him some water, with which he rinsed his mouth, and I left him under the charge of the RAMC doctor. This is what happened subsequently. They had to crawl back through the secret sap, from which the bodies of the dead Turks had by that time been removed and left at the entrance. The Turk was blind-folded, but when he saw his dead comrades, over whose bodies he had to step, he leapt to the conclusion that it was our habit to bring our prisoners to one place and there to kill them. He gave one panic-stricken yell; he threw his arms round the neck of the well-dressed officer; they fell and rolled upon the corpses together, the Turk in convulsions of fear clinging to the neck of the doctor, pressing his face to the faces of the dead till he was covered with blood and dust and the ghastly remains of death, while the soldiers stood round saying to the Turk: 'Now, don't you carry on so.'

Diary. Friday, July 2nd, 1915. *Anzac.* At night a great storm blew up. The lightning played in splendid glares over Imbros and Samothrace, the sea roared, the thunder crashed and the rain spouted down. After a time that stopped and looking out I saw a cloud, black as ink, coming down like a pall just overhead. I went to the General whom I found out and asked him if he thought it was gas; he thought it was a water spout, but it left him pretty cold. Had a divine bathe this morning with Birdwood but am feeling rather ill.

106

Yesterday morning I found the two Whittalls en route for Helles. They had come with General de Lotbinière[67] and his periscopes. I went off to the *Sicilia* to see Jack, and had a lot of trouble about a pass. I saw Jack. He said they had re-bound his leg on the beach, but that it had not been looked at for eighteen hours on the boat. It had swelled to double its size. Then a doctor came and said the bandage had been done too tight, and there was a chance of his losing his leg. I felt absolutely savage. Saw General Howse VC on shore whom I loathe, but who is going on board and bosses the show, and I got him to promise to do what he could. We had a bad time going home. We were slung off the ship in wooden cases. It was very rough indeed, and when the wooden case hit the flat barge it bounced like anything. Then we were towed out on this flat barge, open to the great waves and shrapnel, to a lighter, and left off Anzac for a couple of hours. The Turks sent a few shells, absent-mindedly. Finally, a trawler brought us off, very angry.

Skeen dined, a scholarly fanatic, interesting about the next war, which he thinks will be with Russia, in fifteen years. A lot of people going sick.

I saw Cox to-night, who said that this is the worst storm we have had. We have only one day's water supply. We could have had as much as we had wanted, but many of the cans stored on the beach are useless, as they have had holes knocked in them by the shrapnel. We are not as abstemious as the Turks, who had been lying for so many hours under the sun, and shall suffer from thirst badly.

Saturday, July 3rd, 1915. *Anzac.* Macaulay has come as our artillery officer. I dined with him and H. Woods last night. Yesterday it rained. Jack's boat has gone. We are being badly shelled here. I shall have to change my dugout, if this goes on. The guide Katzangaris has been hit in the mouth.

67.   Brigadier-General Alain Joly de Lotbinière (1862–1944) was a French Canadian who served as Chief Engineer of the Anzac Corps. Joly de Lotbinière did much to improve the appalling water supply on Gallipoli, where he was Director of Works and Engineer-in-Chief during the evacuation of the peninsula.

Sunday, July 4th, 1915. Yesterday I went with the General and Ross to see the Maoris who have just landed. Saw one of Huias tribe and Dr. Buck the MP. The General made them a speech and they danced a very fine Haka with tremendous enthusiasm when he had finished. They loved digging their dugouts and even seemed pleased when they came upon the poor fellows who had been killed in or after the landing. Ian Hamilton wrote officially to ask if they required a special diet. General G. replied officially that he hoped to have sufficient stock of Turkish prisoners going to keep them fat. More people going sick. Doctor Fyfe told me that he and another doctor had asked to be allowed to help on board the hospital ships where they have more wounded than they can deal with, short-handed as they are, but have been refused permission by the RAMC.

Last night Smyth VC[68] dined with us, a cold man of theories. He got rather a feeble VC by shooting the last fanatical Dervish. There has been a great explosion at Achi Baba. Macaulay saw a transport of ours sunk this afternoon. . . George Lloyd came ashore with depressing accounts of Russia. He is probably going to come on this beach. Hope he does. Went off and bathed with Macaulay. Saw Colonel Bauchop, who promised me a present of some fresh drinking-water to-morrow. Christo's nerves are becoming bad and he will not get water when the shrapnel is falling. I am quite King David and send him down inexorably.

Monday, July 5th, 1915. *Kaba Tepé*. A breathless, panting morning, still and blue and fiery hot, with not a ripple on the sea. Colonel Bauchop, commanding the Otago Mounted Rifles, was shot in the shoulder last night. This morning we have had an exhib-tion of 'frightfulness' in the shape of vast shells. They burst with a tremendous roar that echoes to the sky and across the sea for more than a minute; their case or bullets fall over a great area. They started by striking the sea and raising great columns of water; now they burst and fall on land and sea for a minute of the burst. It has, however, had the effect of getting rid of Mr. Fox, a Socialist Czech,

68.   Maj.-Gen. Sir Nevill Smyth VC KCB (1868–1941). Commanding 1st Australian Infantry Brigade.

1. Lieutenant Colonel The Hon Aubrey Herbert MP. *Mrs M Melotte*

2. Irish Guards officers in Wellington Barracks on the morning they marched off to War. Included in the group are Lieutenant The Hon T E Vesey (Aubrey Herbert's cousin by marriage), standing, 3rd from left and Lieutenant H R Alexander (later Field Marshal Earl Alexander of Tunis) standing, 2nd from right. *Regimental Headquarters Irish Guards*

3. Irish Guardsmen preparing to leave Wellington Barracks en route to France, 12th August 1914. Aubrey Herbert stepped into the Battalion's ranks as they marched out of the barracks, having had an Irish Guards' uniform tailored for himself. *Regimental Headquarters Irish Guards*

4. On the move. France, August 1914. *Taylor Library*

5. Covering a flank. France 1914. *Taylor Library*

6. Royal Artillery in action, France 1914. Aubrey Herbert describes the passage of guns passing them at night "...with the sound of a great cataract." *Taylor Library*

7. Lancers, France 1914. Aubrey Herbert's future son-in-law, Capt A E Grant served with the 9th Lancers during the Great War and was awarded a Military Cross and bar. *Taylor Library*

8. Irish Guardsmen in France. When Aubrey Herbert went in search of billets for the Guardsmen on arrival in France, the Quartermaster Lieutenant H Hickie commandeered a bicycle ..... Aubrey Herbert used a horse! *Regimental Headquarters Irish Guards*

9. Stores on the beach at Anzac Cove. Until North Beach was developed, the Cove was the main 'port' of Anzac. All supplies, including water, were brought in using lighters and small fishing trawlers. *Aubrey Herbert*

10. A brief reprieve. ANZACs swimming at Anzac Cove. The beach was under regular fire from Turkish artillery and it is estimated that over 1000 men were killed or wounded on it (or in the water) during course of the Campaign. *Aubrey Herbert*

11. Stores coming ashore at Anzac Cove. One has to question how much use there was for bicycles? *Aubrey Herbert*

12. Unknown Colonel on a tour of the trenches at Gallipoli. *Aubrey Herbert*

13. Aubrey Herbert captures a relaxed moment at Gallipoli. *Aubrey Herbert*

14. A stark illustration of hardship of life in the trenches, Gallipoli 1915. *Aubrey Herbert*

15. ANZACs dining al fresco. In the background is the feature known as the Sphinx, an outcrop of the Sari Bair (Yellow Ridge range) that runs from the beach south of Anzac Cove to Koja Temen Tepe the highest point on that part of the Gallipoli Peninsula. *Aubrey Herbert*

from the doorway of my dugout. He was Labour candidate for Reading, and an undergraduate at Queen's and he will talk to me like a brother. He is a rich Czech who has been naturalized in New Zealand and is now Colonel Pridham's cook. Macaulay dined last night, came an hour late, he was looking at the sea and dreaming. The transport that went down was French; six lives lost, and the explosion was a French ammunition store. I am afraid this shelling is going to be demoralizing. It makes one's head ache. It is certainly worse than any of the 26 guns we have had against us up to now. Nothing can resist this thing.

Tuesday, July 6th, 1915. *Kaba Tepé*. Yesterday I went to Quinn's Post with General Godley in the morning. There was a fair amount of shelling. They had just hit thirteen men in Courtney's before we got there. We went into a mine that was being dug towards and under the Turkish trenches. At the end of the sap the Turks were only six to eight feet away. We could hear them picking. The time for blowing in had very nearly come. These underground people take it all as a matter of course. I should hate fighting on my stomach in a passage two feet high, yards under the ground. The Turks were throwing bombs from the trenches, and these hit the ground over us, three of them, making it shudder. Down below they talk in whispers. We went round the trenches. Saw none so fine as last time, when we came to the Millionaires' Sap, so called because it was made by six Australians, each the son of a millionaire.

In the afternoon I tried to sleep, but there was too much shelling. Kyumjiyan was hit, and has gone; Sam Butler was grazed. It was 11.2 shells filled with all kinds of stuff. We answered with a monitor whose terrific percussions shook my dugout, bringing down dust and stones. A submarine appeared, and all the destroyers were after her. Then two aeroplanes started a fight as the sun set down towards Helles, appearing and vanishing behind crimson clouds. Captain Buck, the Maori doctor and MP, dined with us, to wind up an exciting day.

This morning is like yesterday. No breath of air, but the day is more clear, and Samothrace and Imbros look very peaceful. Early again the shelling began. As I was shaving outside three shells hit the beach just in front. I wasn't watching the third, but suddenly heard a great burst of laughter. At the first shell a bather had rushed back to his dugout; the shell had come and knocked it in on the top of him, and he was dug out, naked and black, but smiling and none the worse. 'Another blasted sniper,' he said, which made the men laugh.

Active preparations are being made to fight the gas, as Intelligence says it is going to be used. Am going out with the General at 9.30. Was sent to get Colonel Parker but found him sick, and under pretty heavy fire, having a new dugout built. Came back and stood with the General, Thoms and others outside HQ. A shell burst just by us, bruised the General in the ribs and filled his eyes with dirt. A couple of spent bullets hit me in the shoulder. We went to No. 2 with Smyth VC, a soldierly prig or perhaps only diffident, Colonel Anthill and Poles. Anthill and Poles wanted me to arrange a truce to bury the Turkish dead on our parapet. They said they must or otherwise our men must get cholera; the heat and sand and flies and smell is awful. It's curious I smelt it when they spoke, though we were in a gully with nothing but thyme and lavender. It's the force of suggestion and the loathing I have of it. I said I would willingly walk out and tell the Turks they could bury their dead at an appointed hour. Smith said they would want to turn them to Mecca etc. I said: 'Nonsense; they hadn't last time', but the General said that GHQ wouldn't allow it. He would do what he could. We met Bauchop with an arm in a sling, but the bullet out of his shoulder, and Colonel White with his head still bandaged. Many cheerful Australians. I have got fond of them. They suffer from the worst element, and from political officers.

Wednesday, July 7th, 1915. *Kaba Tepé.* A fierce, expectant dawn. We shelled furiously at 4.30 a.m. Now absolute peace on a glassy sea. Last night Bentinck, Jack Anderson and I bathed. I was at the end of the pier; as I was beginning to dress a shell burst very close, the smoke and powder in my face. I fled half dressed; Colonel P. rose like Venus from the sea and followed with nothing. A calm Marine gave me my cigarette-holder.

Zachariades has returned from Imbros with stores. Butler very

angry as he is overdue. Birdwood would not grant a white flag for
burying the dead. This is because one of the prisoners on the
occasion of the Armistice reported that the Turkish staff officers
had put on Red Crescent clothes in order to have a look at our
trenches. They apparently, if this is true, went one better than
our Generals who disguised themselves by taking off their coats
and looking at the Turkish trenches, but Skeen and the rest pull
very long faces over it.

The Turks put up five crosses yesterday, all of which we shot
down. I first of all thought it was probably Greeks or Armenians
who wanted to show that they were Christians, wishing to
surrender, and telephoned up to Courtney's post to see if I could
go out and talk to them, but I now think the Turks were only
anxious to make us shoot at the sign of our religion. In this they
succeeded. Colonel Artillery Johnson has gone sick. I persuaded
the General to be inoculated. He and the others will be done for
cholera to-night. Saw George who said I could be liaison officer
with GHQ if I wanted to, but I do not think I will. A pretty cross-
fire going on now between Kaba Tepé with Anafarta, hitting the
beach between me and the sea.

Last night I dined with Harold and Macaulay. They told long
Eastern stories, and we had a very contented time, drinking light
white wine and also *mavrodaphne*, smoking and looking at the sea.
The Turks shelled a little after eight for the first time, answering our
tiresome and ineffective but provocative monitor fire. This morning
Tahu and East arrived with letters from home, and sherry. There is
not a sound upon the beach and not a ripple in the sea. The Turks
have settled down to business this morning and are bombarding
something cruel from Kaba Tepé. Most of the shells are twenty
yards beyond my dugout. Tahu has brought back a rumour that this
Division is to go on to England and refit there. Such bad shelling
and men are developing nerves. The sight is rather beautiful, a sea
like lapis lazuli and a burning sun, with columns of water like
geysers where the shells hit. I hear a good many men hit round here
to-day, though I didn't see anyone wounded.

Saturday, July 10*th*, 1915. *Kaba Tepé.* I went down to get the
General's things on board the picket boat, but just as I got there a

shell struck her and knocked a hole in her. There was another one and we sat and waited uncomfortably in this until he came. Then we pushed off, went on to the trawler *Ghelmer* and arrived for dinner on the *Triad*. I was still feeling pretty bad, but got better. The Admiral (de Robeck) talked after dinner. He said they had no knowledge of the intentions of our Government politically. The Greeks have been working hard against us. He had intercepted a telegram from the Queen of Greece, signed by Sophie to Kreizi the Greek Naval Attaché. Every kind of difficulty was thrown in his way when he wished to hold up boats carrying contraband. He is a simple and delightful person.

Afterwards I talked to Alec Ramsay[69], Dalhousie's brother. I slept in Commodore Roger Keyes[70]' cabin very comfortably indeed. He talked of lack of co-operation. I told him I had great opportunities of hearing the complaints of Army against Navy and vice versa. He was tolerant but sad.

Sunday, July 11th, 1915. Felt much better. Went ashore and saw Colonel Hawker and the Turkish prisoners. . . .Came back late at night, after some very jolly days. Best week-end I ever spent. The Turks have asked for another armistice in the south. This has been refused. If they attack, they will have to do it across their own dead, piled high, and this is not good for morale.

By this time the persecutions of the interpreters had greatly diminished. They were still badly treated by Ot, but to a large extent they had won the respect of the troops by their behaviour. The chief interpreter was an old Greek of some sixty-two or sixty-three years, Mr. Kyriakidis, who was given a medal for conspicuous gallantry at the bombardment of Alexandria and had served with General Stuart's unfortunate expedition. He was a gentleman, and one of the straightest men I have met. His

69.   Admiral Sir Alexander Ramsay GCVO KCB DSO (1881–1972).
70.   Admiral of the Fleet Lord Keyes of Zeebrugge and Dover GCB KCVO CMG DSO CF (1872–1945). Initially Naval Chief of Staff to Vice-Admiral Sackville Carden, commander of the Royal Navy squadron off the Dardanelles during the early part of 1915, Keyes subsequently took over the Dardanelles Minesweeping Force.

simplicity, courtesy, and unfailing courage had gained him many friends. He was also endowed with considerable humour.

He apparently went down and played poker and put on the respirator as a sort of mask with a lot of swagger; this has put the fear of death into the other interpreters who have had a deputation to Harold insisting that they too should be provided with masks.

Monday, July 12*th*, 1915. *Kaba Tepé*. One poor shadow was shot yesterday – an interpreter of whom we none of us knew anything, and who was on no list. Things aren't very comfortable. The General and the Staff hit it off about as badly as is possible. There are faults on both sides. A tremendous fire is going on, artillery and rifle. As I walked round here a lot of rife bullets or possibly machine-gun bullets whizzed round. All the air is full of thudding and broken echoes. Here no one minds anything much but high explosive. It's the look of the beastly thing and the wounds it makes that give one the loathing. The hospitals have been moved. They had too many casualties where they were before. An extraordinary American filibuster came and bothered me yesterday for hours, Captain Littler. A beard and a brain and an accent.

Tuesday, July 13*th*, 1915. *Kaba Tepé*. Tremendous fire around Achi Baba yesterday. French advanced 150 and we 200 yards. Don't know what the losses were. In the evening Macaulay and I took Harold Woods to No. 3. He had promised his wife not to go walking with me. Macaulay stopped to do a sketch and we walked on. Later I rested and smoked in an open place. I said to Harold this is all right. We hold all these ridges. Macaulay came along and said 'Good heavens, don't sit there, the Turks are only 300 yards away and you have no cover.' H. leapt as if he had been stung and we only got him on with great difficulty. We went to Bauchop's Fountain. Close by, two yards off there is an olive tree; a man resting under it three days ago was killed by a sniper, and his mate wounded but crawled back into the sandy way. On both sides there is tall wild lavender and what Macaulay calls pig's parsley. We crawled down the sandy track to the sea. He is rather sick. I met the General who asked Macaulay and me not to bathe going home. In the evening Tahu got out his gramophone and we had some songs which rested us all a great deal. The noise of the shooting drowned the singing sometimes. Today Ramadan begins. George Lloyd arrived this afternoon. He told me that they were going to apply for me to go to Tenedos. I told him I didn't want to go. He said they wanted me. I said I had been sick when I had trouble with Cunningham and was then ready to go, until I saw my General wanted me, but I was now again very happy here. He said it was a question of work. Perhaps I may get off. Anyway, I will wait and see what happens.

Yesterday evening General Godley went to Courtney's Post. As he got there the Turks shelled with heavy stuff, killing and wounding about twenty men. The General saw some bad sights and he hates those I think as much as I do. Reynell came to see me. I like him very much indeed.

Diary. Sunday, July 18th, 1915. Kaba Tepé. They are now shelling the pier, and killed a doctor, cutting off both his legs, and several other people, when I was bathing from the pier. Everybody is again going sick. The situation is changing. Every night we are landing guns. The moon is young now and growing. It seems, therefore, reasonable to expect that we cannot land forces of men that take time before the nights are moonless; that is, in about a month's time the preparations ought to be ready.

A few days ago we had an attack on Achi Baba, won about 400 yards and lost about 5,000 men. Two battalions got out of touch and were lost for a considerable time. The 'Imbros Journal,' 'Dardanelles Driveller,' or whatever it's called, said 'their return was as surprising as that of Jonah from the belly of the whale.' Good, happy author!

A German Taube over us throwing bombs and also heavy stuff, but not much damage lately. George Lloyd was here this afternoon, and while we talked a shell burst and hit four men.

Monday, July 19th, 1915. Kaba Tepé. My dugout has now become a centre for Australian and New Zealand officers, all good fellows. I had it made small on purpose, so that no one would offer to share it with me, and that makes it less convenient for the crowd that now sit in it. Two old friends come when the day's work is over, and grow sentimental by moonlight; both ill and, I am afraid, getting worse. All the talk is now about gassing. It is thought that they will do it to us here. As usual, new troops are reported to be coming against us.

Tuesday, July 20th, 1915. *Kaba Tepé*. There is always something fresh here. Now a lot of sharks are supposed to have come in. During the last two days there has been absolute silence, no shelling at all, nothing but the sound of crickets and at night a singsong chorus as the men drag up the great tanks prepared for water. Butler yesterday worked out a theory to prove that the Turks were to attack us last night. (1) No gunfire yesterday; the reason being they (the Turks) were moving troops. They didn't want us to fire at their troops, therefore didn't draw fire by shooting at us. (2) Ulemas have come down. There must be a special reason for this. (3) 10,000 coming up. Gas being prepared. All this means an attack on Anzac. To wipe us out would be a great feather in their cap. I am inclined to doubt another great attack. . . .Tempers all a bit ruffled. General Birdwood is sick. The heat is fierce and the stillness absolute. This afternoon I heard from Deedes, who asked me to go to Tenedos for a time . . .

Wednesday, July 21st, 1915. *Imbros*. On Wednesday I went over to GHQ and met old friends among the war correspondents. Met some of the New Zealanders who had come over for a rest, but were coming back for the expected attack. Meanwhile, they had been kept on fatigues most of the time, and were unutterably weary. At Imbros I was ordered to go to Tenedos and Mytilene.

Thursday, July 22nd, 1915. Came back to Anzac in the same boat with Ashmead Bartlett[71] and Nevinson,[72] and got leave to take them round in the afternoon. Later on, during one of the worst days of the Suvla fighting, I met my friend Nevinson picking his way amongst the wounded on their stretchers under fire. 'After this,' he said, decisively, 'I shall confine myself strictly to revolutions.'

Diary. July 23rd. Started for Imbros and went in the *Bacchante* pinnace, which was leaking badly from a shell hole. There were six

71.　　Ellis Ashmead-Bartlett (1881–1931). War Correspondent. His outspoken criticism of the conduct of the campaign played a major part in bringing about the dismissal of the General Sir Ian Hamilton.
72.　　Henry Nevinson (1856–1941). War Correspondent.

115

of us on deck, and one man was hit when we were about a hundred yards out. We put back and left him on shore.

Saturday, July 24th. Imbros. Went for a ride on a mule, and had a bathe.

At this point in the campaign, though the morale was excellent, depression began to grow. There was a great deal of sickness, from which practically no one escaped, though it was less virulent in its form than later in the summer. I had been ill for some time, and was very anxious to avoid being invalided to Egypt, and was grateful for the chance of going to the islands for a change of climate and light work, for the few days that were sufficient to give another lease of health.

The feeling that invades almost every side-show, sooner or later, that the home authorities cared nothing and knew nothing about the Dardanelles, was abroad. The policy and the strategy of the expedition were bitterly criticized. I remember a friend of mine saying to me: 'All this expedition is like one of Walter Scott's novels, upside down.' Walter Scott generally put his hero at the top of a winding stair, where he comfortably disposed, one by one, of a hundred of his enemies. 'Now,' he said, 'what we have done was, first of all to warn the Turks that we were going to attack by having a naval bombardment. That made them fortify the Dardanelles, but still they were not completely ready. We then send a small force to attack, to tell them that we really are in earnest, and to ask them if they are quite ready. In fact, we have put the man who ought to be, not the hero, but the villain of the piece, at the top of the corkscrew stair, and we have given him so much notice that when the hero attacks the villain has more men at the top of the circular stair than the hero has at the bottom. It's like throwing pebbles at a stone wall,' he said, mixing his metaphors.

Diary. Sunday, July 25th, 1915. On the Sea. I left for Tenedos; a most beautiful day. We have just been to Anzac, very burnt and wounded amongst the surrounding greenery. Pretty peaceful there, only a few bullets coming over.

Perhaps the record of a sojourn in the Greek Islands on what was really sick-leave, as the work was of the lightest, should not

116

be included in a war diary, but the writer looks back with amusement and pleasure to days that were not uneventful. They were passed with friends who were playing a difficult and most arduous part, and whose services, in many cases, have not received the recognition that was their due.

It was pleasant once again to be lord of the horizon, to have space through which to roam, and lovely hills and valleys to ride across in the careless, scented air of the Mediterranean summer, with the sea shining a peacock-blue through the pines. It is this space and liberty that men cramped in a siege desire, more than the freedom from the shelling of the enemy's guns. There was much, too, that was *opéra bouffe* in the Islands, that made a not unpleasant contrast to the general life at Anzac.

If there was spy mania on the Peninsula, it was multiplied tenfold, and quite reasonably, on the Islands, where part of the population were strongly pro-Ally, another part pro-German, while others were anti-British by the accidental kind of ricochet. These were the royalist followers of King Constantine, who hated Venizelos, and consequently the friends of Venizelos, Great Britain and France.

The situation on the Islands was one with which it was extremely hard to cope. We were very anxious to safeguard the lives of our men, and to prevent information going to the enemy, and, at the same time, not to pursue German methods. It was unceasing work, with a great strain of responsibility. There was an inevitable *va et vient* between the Peninsula and Imbros. From Imbros boats could slip across to Tenedos, Mytilene or the mainland. The native caïques would drop in at evening, report, be ordered to stay till further notice, and would drift away like ghosts in the night. Men, and women, performed remarkable feats, in appearing and disappearing. They were like pictures on a film in their coming and their going. Watchers and watched, they thrust and parried, discovered and concealed, glowed on the picture and darkened.

Anatasio, a Serbian by birth, was one of our workers, conspicuous for his quickness and intelligence. At the outbreak of the war he had already been five months in an Austrian prison at Cattaro, but the prospect of battle stimulated his faculties, and he escaped. One day at luncheon, I asked him where it was that he had learned Italian, which he did not talk very well. 'While I was in prison at Smyrna,' said he. 'What for?' said I. 'For stabbing a Cretan,' said he, and added that he would rather be five years in prison in Turkey than one in Austria. Then there was Avani, one of the most vivid personalities that I have ever met. He was a poet and a clairvoyant, a mesmerist and a masseur, a specialist in rheumatism and the science of detection, once a member of General Chermside's gendarmerie in Crete, and ex-chief of the Smyrna fire brigade. The stories of him are too many, and too flamboyant, to tell.

Diary. Avani mesmerized the wife of the Armenian dragoman. Unfortunately it went wrong. Her obedience to his volition was delayed and she only obeyed his commands in the wrong company some hours after.

He had given proof of rare courage, and also considerable indescretion. On one occasion, armed to the teeth, he burst into a perfectly innocent house at night, and, revolver in hand, hunted a terrified inhabitant. His only evidence against this man was, that when he had been caught and hurled to the ground and sat upon, his heart had beaten very fast, which would not happen, insisted Avani, if he had not been guilty of some crime.

Amongst our opponents were the romantic but sinister Vassilaki family, two brothers and three lovely sisters. Talk about them in the Islands was almost as incessant as was talk about shelling on the Peninsula.

Diary. Monday, July 26th, 1915. Tenedos. Yesterday I was very ill, and again to-day, but was injected with something or other and feel better, but weak. Tried to sleep yesterday, but one of our monitors at Rabbit Island bombarded hugely, shaking the bugs down on me. This place is clean, but there are bugs and some lice. Last night I dined with the Governor, Colonel Mullins, and a jolly French doctor, and Thompson, who has fallen ill. Am carrying on for him at the moment.

Tuesday, July 27th, 1915. Tenedos. Went to the trenches at Tenedos. They face the enemy. That is the most military thing

118

about them. Thompson went out to see the inhabitants. I was going with him, but felt worse and went to rest. The Turks here are in a very bad way. We do not allow them to work. It is inevitable. They mayn't fish or work at the aerodrome.

Wednesday, July 28th, 1915. *Tenedos*. Interpreted for the Governor of Tenedos, who, like Jupiter, rules with might, in the afternoon. In the evening I saw the Mufti, who had a list of starving, widows and indigent. . . .Last night the Cretan soldiers started ragging the Turks and singing, till I stopped them. They were quite good.

Still ill, but better. Had a beautiful walk in the evening, and a long talk with the Greek refugees working in the vines by the edge of the sea. The old patriarch addressed me all the time as 'chor-baji' – that is, Possessor of the Soup, the Headman of the village.

Thursday, July 29th, 1915. *Tenedos*. Yesterday morning I took a donkey and a boy and rode out to the French aerodrome, coming late for luncheon, but had coffee with about twenty French officers, all very jolly. Promised to let me fly over the Dardanelles. I went on to the Cretans in a pinewood. Their officer, a Frenchman, very keen on a show in Asia Minor. . . .The elder Vassilaki has been arrested. His brother saw him go by in a trawler. Am going to Mytilene, then return after three days, and leave here on Tuesday for Anzac. No news of anything happening. Tenedos is a beautiful town in its way, surrounded by windmills, with Mount Elias in the background. Its streets are narrow, picturesque, and hung with vines that make them cool and shady. At the end of the town there is a very fine old Venetian fortress, but its magnificence is outside; inside it is furnished with round stone cannon-balls, ammunition for catapults. In the last war the Greeks took the island, but one day a Turkish destroyer popped her nose in. All the Greeks fled, and the Mufti and the Moslems went and pulled the Greek flag down. Then in came a Greek destroyer, and the Turkish one departed. The Mufti and the Turks were taken off to Mudros, where he and they were beaten. He narrowly missed being killed.

Friday, July 30th, 1915. *Tenedos*. Slept very badly again. Had a letter from the OC. Poor Onslow killed, lying on his bed by his dugout. A good fellow and a fine soldier. Aden nearly captured.

I prophesied its capture in Egypt. I shall be recalled before anything happens.

The radiant air of Tenedos gave health as it did in Homeric times, and I left with the desire that others should have the same chance as myself of using that beautiful island as a hospital; but all the pictures there were not bright. Under the windmills above the shining sea there were the motionless, dark-clad, desolate Moslem women, sitting without food or shelter. Their case, it is true, was no harder than that of the thousands of Greek refugees who had been driven from their homes, but these at any rate were living amongst kindred, while the unfortunate Moslems were without help or sympathy, except that which came from their enemies, the British.

Diary. Friday, July 30th, 1915. Mytilene. I left by the Greek boat yesterday. On the boat I met a man who might be useful as an interpreter, Anibal Miscu, Entrepreneur de Travaux Publiques, black as my hat, but talks English, French, German, Italian, Spanish, Turkish, Greek, Arabic, Bulgar, Russian, and something else. The boat was stopped by our trawler, No. 48, and searched for contraband of war. The Greeks were furious. I landed at Mytilene, not having slept much and felling bad. Avani said they had tried to bribe him to allow some raisins through, and kicked up the devil of a row. He seemed to think that the raisins were dynamite. He was left guarding the raisins, all night, I believe, with his revolver.

I was given a warm welcome by Compton Mackenzie at Mytilene. He, fortunately for me, had been sent there by GHQ. I found several old friends – Heathcote-Smith, the Consul, whose work it would be impertinent for me to praise, and Hadkinson, whom I had last seen at my own house in England, where he was staying with me when the Archduke Franz Ferdinand had been murdered. Hadkinson had passed most of his life on his property in Macedonia. Of the Eastern and Southern languages he talked Greek, Italian, Turkish, Bulgarian, Serbian, and Albanian. His voice was as delightful as his knowledge of Balkan ballads was wide, and his friends made him sing the endless songs of the mountaineers. His personality had carried him through experiences that would have been disastrous to most men; battles, decisive in Europeans' history had raged in front of his doors, while his house had remained untouched; brigands of most of the Balkan races had crossed his farm, rarely driving off his stock, and most of the local peasantry in their misfortunes had come to him for help, for advice, doctoring or intercession. Until the European war had crashed upon the world, Hadkinson had been a good example of the fact that minorities, even when they are a minority of one, do not always suffer.

The people of Mytilene, at that time, were very pro-English, though the officials were of the faction of King Constantine. The desire I frequently heard expressed was that Great Britain should take over Mytilene, as she did the Ionian Islands, and that when Mytilene had been put in order it should be restored to Greece.

Diary. Friday, July 30th, 1915. *Mytilene*. H. Smith and Hadkinson have gone out with a motor-boat and a machine gun. The Vassilakis, or some of them, have been deported. Vassilaki to Imbros and the beautiful sisters to Mudros. . . .It's a blazing, burning day.

Saturday, July 31st, 1915. *Mytilene*. A gaming-house. Moved from my first hotel to a larger and more disreputable one. Lunched with Hadkinson and Compton Mackenzie[73]. At Thasos the Greeks have arrested our agents under the orders of Gunaris. Have worked, and am feeling better.

Later. The three Miss Vassilakis have not gone to Mudros. They turned up this morning, and I was left to deal with them. Not as beautiful, except one, as I had been led to believe. They got Avani out of the room and wept and wept. I told them their brother would be all right. . . . They wanted to know who prevented them from leaving. I said it was the Admiral. That good man is far away.

Sunday, August 1st, 1915. *Mytilene*. Avani went off with the three Miss Vassilakis, in hysterics, last night. They were very angry with us. It seems probable that we shall have a landing on the mainland here to divert attention from the Peninsula. Sir Ian Hamilton is coming down to have a look. A good deal of friction over the

73.   The author, Sir Edward Compton Mackenzie (1883–1972).

blockade. The present system causes much inconvenience to all concerned.

They were enchanting days of golden light or starlit darkness, while one drank health almost in the concrete from the hot pine-scented air and the famous wine of Mytilene. The conditions of others was unfortunately less happy. There were some 80,000 Greek refugees from the mainland, for whom the Greek Government had done practically nothing, while the patriotic Greek communities of England and America had not had the opportunity of relieving their necessities. We all did what we could to help these people.

There was another question allied to this to be considered: whether a Greek Expeditionary Force, largely composed of these refugees, should be sent into Asia Minor. The danger of such a campaign to the native Greeks was obvious; mainly for this reason it was not undertaken. But while no expedition occurred, there was much talk about one. The fact that Sir Ian Hamilton had come was widely known. It was said that great preparations were being made, and these rumours probably troubled the Turks and kept troops of theirs in a non-combatant area.

Diary. Sunday, August 1st, 1915. Mytilene. Lunched with Mavromati Bey. He was very heroic, saying he preferred to die rather than to live under the German yoke, but there were no signs of a funeral at luncheon, which was delicious.

Dined with Hadkinson, and was taken ill, but got all right and went off with him on the motor-boat *Omala* after dinner. H. said that for a long time he had felt that I was coming, and had ordered a lamb for me to be executed the following day; told the cook, too, to get some special herbs.

The object of our journey was to find a wonderful woman, lithe as a leopard and strong as a horse, and put her somewhere near Aivali to gain information.

Monday, August 2nd, 1915. 'Omala.' Off Moskonisi. At dawn this morning we came to Moskonisi, luminous in the sea. A decrepit shepherd led a flock of sheep along the beach. His name is Panayotis and he has a Homeric past; he killed two Turkish guards who courted a beautiful sister-in-law before marriage. Then he killed two others for a pusillanimous brother-in-law after marriage, and he has also sent two other Turks to their rest, though H. does not know the reason for their death.

Hadkinson had collected a large band of Palikaris, but the motor-boat only held a few, the cream of them. He had English names for most of them – Little John, Robin Hood, etc. They were tall men with very quick, clever eyes and lithe movements, picturesquely dressed. One of them had a cross glittering in his kalpak, and A.M. (for Asia Minor) on both sides of the cross. He said to me, pointing to Aivali: 'There is my country; we are an orphan people. For 150 years we have shed our blood and given our best to Greece. Now in her hour of triumph and in our day of wretchedness she denies us help. May she ever be less!' Another Greek had been to Mecca as a soldier and stayed there and in the Yemen for some years. The Captain was a quiet man, but apparently very excitable. They were delighted with their army rifles. The woman, Angeliko Andriotis, did not turn up at Gymno, so we went on to Moskonisi, the men often playing on a plaintive flute, and sometimes singing low together. At breakfast, soon after dawn, we had a sort of orchestra.

We arrived opposite to Aivali. The Turks have sunk three *mauna* . . . Hadkinson saw one of their submarines.

The situation at Aivali is curious. It lies at the head of a bay. Above it there are hills, not high hills, but high enough, the men said who were with us, to prevent its being bombarded by the Turks. They looked at it with longing eyes. Their families were there. They kept on cursing the 'black dogs' and saying they would eat them. There were 35,000 people in Aivali, now only 25,000; 10,000 have left lately. The sword of Damocles hangs over the rest of them, for they might be sent off into the interior at any moment. We went on to the channel between Moskonisi and Pyrgos. There we found the child of the woman, who was sent with a note to her. Men were moving in the olives and the scrub some distance off, whom the Greeks said were their own compatriots.

The boy, who was thirteen, took the letter and put it under his saddle. He went off calmly to get past the Turks, without any air of adventure about him. The others realized the stage on which they were acting, and swaggered finely. I got off on Pyrgos with Hadkinson, and went to a small, rough chapel, where they were bringing the eikons back in triumph.

The beauty of it all was beyond words. I bathed on a silver sand in transparent water between the two islands. Moskonisi, by the way, doesn't mean the Island of Perfume, but takes its name from a great brigand who practically held the island against the Turks about thirty years ago.

After a time the boy returned with a letter from his mother, and a peasant with binoculars. He and the peasant both said that they had seen a great oil-pool in Aivali Bay. We thought that this must be from a submarine, and dashed round there at full speed, but found nothing. Then we decided to come home. We picked up some of the men we had dropped *en route*; and they brought us presents of gran Turco, basilica and sweet-scented pinks. Then they played their flutes as the sun set, and Hadkinson sang Greek, Bulgarian and Turkish songs, singing the 'Imam's Call' beautifully and, to the horror of his Greek followers, reverently.

We might have bagged the twenty-five Turks, or whatever number there were, quite easily, but H. thought this would have produced reprisals. He was probably right.

Tuesday, August 3rd, 1915. Mytilene. We got back last night after dinner and heard that Sir Ian Hamilton, George Lloyd and George Brodrick[74] had been here. One of the poor Whittall boys very badly wounded. They were a fine pair.

August 4th, 1915. Mytilene. Yesterday we heard that the Turks had sent the town-crier to the equivalent of the capital of Moskonisi to say that any Greek going beyond a certain line would be put to death. Miss Vassilaki turned up, and said that she and her sister would come with me to Tenedos. I said they couldn't.

We dined with General Hill and his Staff and slept on the *Canopus*. Mackenzie no better, his neurasthenia was very bad. A good deal of friction in Tenedos. Athanasius Vassilaki has

74.   George Brodrick, 2nd Earl of Middleton (1888–1979).

escaped, and everyone is annoyed. Some men have been arrested for signalling.

Thursday, August 5th, 1915. *Tenedos*. Most of the officers sick. I was asked to stay on at Tenedos, but felt I must get back at once. Christo says that it's dull here, and Kaba Tepé is better than this house. Turkish guns have been firing at our trawlers. A couple of men wounded. Examined a man just escaped from Constantinople. Constantinople is quite cheery: theatres, carriages, boats, etc. The Germans say we can't hold out on the Peninsula when the bad weather comes.

Then I examined a Lebanese French soldier who had arrested a child and an old man for signalling.

Here there are some pages of my diary missing, but the events that occurred are still vividly in my mind.

In company with other officers I went first to Imbros, hearing the thunder of the guns from Helles. In passionate haste we tried every means to get on to the Peninsula for the great battle. I left Christo to follow with my kit, if he could, with the future doubtful before him, and no certainty, except that of being arrested many times.

In the harbour at Imbros on that night there was a heavy sea, and in a small, dancing boat we quested through the darkness for any ship sailing to Anzac. One was found at last that was on the point of sailing, and off we went.

The instructions of my friend Ian Smith were to get to Suvla, and luck favoured him, for at dawn we lay off Suvla, and a trawler took him ashore.

Along the heights and down to the seashore the battle growled and raged, and it was difficult to know what was the mist of the morning or battle smoke. I got off at Anzac, which was calm, realizing that I had missed the first attack.

Diary. Saturday, August 7th, 1915. *Kaba Tepé*. I went out to Headquarters, which are now beyond Colonel Bauchop's old Headquarters. He, poor fellow, had just been hit and was said to be dying. Dix[75] again wounded in the leg and Cator killed when he had just been promoted. I saw the General; on the way out I met

---

75.   Commander Charles Dix CMG DSO. The Naval Beachmaster.

300 Turkish prisoners and was ordered to return and embark them. We came to the pier on the beach, then three shells fell on and beside it; both Sam Butler and I thought we were going to have a very bad time, packed like sardines, with panicky prisoners. Embarking them took time; we were all very snappy, but we got them off. I was glad to find Butler and Woods. All the dugouts here are desolate. I saw General Birdwood, who was very sad about Onslow[76], shot just outside his dugout. He talked of the water difficulties. He was cheerful, as usual, and said he thought we should know which way things were going by 5 o'clock. Sam was less cheerful. I went back to Headquarters, a weary trudge of two hot, steaming miles, past masses of wounded. The saps were constantly blocked. Then back to Anzac for a few hours' sleep, till I can get my kit.

Sunday, August 8th, 1915. Near Anafarta. Slept badly last night at Anzac. The place was very desolate with everyone away. I got up before a clear dawn and went out to the observation post, where I found General Godley and General Shaw. Our assault began. We saw our men in the growing light attack the Turks. It was a cruel and beautiful sight, for it was like a fight in fairyland; they went forward in parties through the beautiful light, with the clouds crimsoning over them. Sometimes a tiny, gallant figure would be in front, then a puff would come and they would be lying still. We got to within about forty yards of the Turks; later we lost ground. Meanwhile, men were streaming up, through awful heat. There were Irish troops cursing the Kaiser. At the observation post we were being badly shelled. The beauty of the place was extraordinary, and made it better than the baldness of Anzac, but we were on an unpropitious hillside, and beyond there were mules and men, clustered thickly.

Then I was sent back to Kaba Tepé, where I found a lot of wounded prisoners, who had not been attended to. I woke a doctor who had not slept for ages. He talked almost deliriously, but came along and worked like a real good man. I saw General

---

76.   Birdwood's ADC, Brian Onslow, a Captain in the 11th Lancers, Indian Army, who had been killed.

Howse, VC, and suggested attaching one doctor to the prisoners, so that we should not get contagious diseases.

Returned to Bauchop's Post and examined a couple of Germans from the *Goeben*. Got a good deal of information. Then I was telephoned for to interrogate a wounded Greek, who had, however, got lost. I went back outside the hospital, where there were many wounded lying. I stumbled upon poor Critchley-Salmonson[77] (a schoolfellow), who had been wounded about 3 am. the day before, and had lain in the sun on the sand all the previous day. He recognized me, and asked me to help him, but was light-headed. There were fifty-six others with him; Macaulay and I counted. It was awful having to pass them. A lot of the men called out: 'We are being murdered.' The smells were fearful and they had not been cleaned. I went down a sap to the north to find the Greek. Fierce shelling began. The sap was knocked down in front and behind.

I came to a field hospital, situated where the troops were going through. There no one knew where Taylor's Hollow, the place where the Greek was supposed to be, was. While I was there shelling was bad. Several of the wounded were hit again. One man was knocked in on the top of me, bleeding all over. I returned to meet Thoms, who said he knew the way. We ran the gauntlet.

I had a curious, beautiful walk, looking for the wounded Greek, going to nineteen hospitals. Many wounded everywhere. First I saw one of our fellows who had met ten Turks and had ten bayonet wounds. He was extremely cheerful. Then a couple of Turks in the shadow of some pines, one dying and groaning, really unconscious. I offered the other water from my bottle, but he refused because of his companion, using Philip Sidney's words[78] in Turkish. Men were being hit everywhere. After going by fields and groves and lanes I came back to where the wounded were lying in

---

77. Captain Arthur Critchley-Salmonson DSO, Royal Munster Fusiliers, attached to the Canterbury Infantry Battalion.
78. 'My mouth doth water, and my breast doth swell, My tongue doth itch, my thoughts in labour be.' From 'Astrophil and Stella', Sir Philip Sidney, circa 1580.

127

hundreds, in the sap going to the sea, near Bauchop's Fountain. There a man called to me in French. He was the Greek I was looking for, badly wounded. He talked a great deal. Said 200,000 reinforcements were expected from Gallipoli. No gas would be used here.

Monday, August 9th, 1915. No. 3 Outpost. Slept uncomfortably on the ground. Went before dawn to observation post; returned to examine prisoners. Had an unsuccessful expedition with Hastings to find some guns which he said had been lost between the lines. Bullets came streaming down our valley, and we put up a small wall of sacks, 3 feet high, behind which we slept. I was sitting at breakfast this morning listening to Colonel Manders[79] talking, when suddenly I saw Charlie Bentinck put his hand to his own head and say: 'By G——, he's killed!' Manders fell back dead, with a bullet through his temple he was a very good fellow.

Sir Ian Hamilton came ashore. I saw him for a moment. Then to Kaba Tepé; going and coming one passes a line of bodies, some dreadful, being carried for burial. Many still lying out. The last wounded have been more pitiful than anything I have seen. Cazalet is badly wounded; I hope he will recover; he is a good boy. Colonel Malone was killed last night and Jacky Hughes wounded. Lots of shelling. Coming back I had to go outside the crowded sap, and got sniped. Thoms and I had a very lively time of it.

Came back for Manders' funeral. I was very fond of him. No chaplain turned up for poor Colonel Manders' funeral, so General Godley read a few sentences with the help of my electric torch, which failed. Four other officers were buried with him. I saw a great shell strike the grave the next day. A cemetery, or rather, many are growing up round us. There are dead men buried or half-buried in all the gullies.

Tuesday, August 10th, 1915. No. 3 Outpost. Christo arrived with my kit and some grapes last night. While we were eating these, two men, one of whom was our cook, were hit, and he being the second cook, it was decided to change our quarters, as a lot of

79.   Colonel Neville Manders, Assistant Director Medical Services (ADMS) New Zealand Division.

bullets streamed down the gully and we had been losing heavily. I was called up in the night to see about some wounded. The General had said they had better go by boat, because of the difficulty of the saps, but there were no boats, and Manders' death had caused confusion at the hospital. The doctor on the beach said he could not keep the wounded there any longer, because of the rifle fire. I woke Charlie and we got 200 men from the Canterbury reinforcements. They had been fighting without sleep since Sunday morning, but evacuated about 300 wounded to below Walker's Ridge. There were no complaints. The Turks still had to be left. They called to me at night and at dawn. I gave them drinks, and later, after sunrise, shifted them into the shade, which made them cheerful. The General had not slept for three nights. The day went badly for us. We lost Chunuk Bair, and without it we cannot win the battle. The Turks have fought very finely, and all praise their courage. It was wonderful to see them charging down the hill, through the storm of shrapnel, under the white ghost wreaths of smoke. Our own men were splendid. The NZ Infantry Brigade must have ceased to exist. Meanwhile, the condition of the wounded is indescribable. They lie in the sand in rows upon rows, their faces caked with sand and blood; one murmur for water; no shelter from the sun; many of them in saps, with men passing all the time scattering more dust on them. There is hardly any possibility of transporting them. The fire zones are desperate, and the saps are blocked with ammunition transport and mules, also whinnying for water, carrying food, etc. Some unwounded men almost mad from thirst, cursing. We all did what we could, but amongst so many it was almost impossible. The wounded Turks still here. I kept them alive with water. More prisoners in, report another 15,000 men at Bulair and a new Division, the 7th, coming against us here. I saw General Cooper[80] wounded, in the afternoon, and got him water. His Staff had all been killed or wounded. In most of my journeys to the beach early in the day I saw some man hit.

80.   Irish Guards. Commanding 29th Irish Brigade.

If the Turks continue to hold Chunuk Bair and get up their big guns there, we are, as a force, far worse off than at Anzac. What has happened is roughly this: we have emerged from a position which was unsatisfactory, but certain, into one that is uncertain but partly satisfactory. If the Turks have the time to dig themselves in, then we are worse off than before, because we shall again be held up, with the winter to face, and time running hard against us, with an extended front. The Turks will still have land communications, while we shall only have sea communications, and though we ourselves shall be possibly better off, because we shall now have a harbour, the Turks some time will almost certainly be able to break through, though possibly not able to keep what they take. But the men at Helles will not be freed as our move proposed to free them.

We have a terrible view here; the lines of wounded are creeping up to the cemetery like a tide, and the cemetery is going to meet the wounded. Between us and the sea is about 150 yards; this space is now empty of men because of the sniping. There are a number of dead mules on it, which smell horrible but cannot be moved. A curious exhibition of sniping took place just below us about 50 yards away. Two men were on the open space when a sniper started to shoot at them. They popped into a dry well that practically hid them, but he got his bullets all round them, in front and behind and on the sides. They weren't hit. The camp watched laughing.

Thursday, August 12th, 1915. No. 3 Outpost. This day a year ago I left England for France. I wish I was doing that again. Last night I had a lot of questioning of prisoners and getting water for the wounded, and shifting the wounded Turks and the English. They caught what they said was a sniper and nearly killed him. I told some Maoris to shift some Turks lying in the sun. They said 'let them die'. Many had fever. I thought one had cholera. One has to give them drinks out of one's own water-bottle. There is no water, not enough for the dying.

At 4.30 in the morning I got up and walked with the General. We went up to Rhododendron Ridge to have a look at the Turks. It is a steep, beautiful walk. He said he was convinced no troops could have done better. Of course if the 9th had been able to advance we should have done the trick, but the Army and Navy appears to have landed them in the wrong place, and Birdwood says the Turks are too good for these mere boys. Fifty broke and ran with two lieutenants in a panic. The Beach Master at Suvla put them under arrest. On the top of the ridge we heard a wounded man calling for water. I asked twice to be allowed to go but the General refused, which as he allowed volunteers to be called for to go out with the Red Cross, he had scarcely the right to do. We are fastening the cliffs up, and camouflaging the trenches.

I took Nikolas the miller round the observation post in the morning. A new Division is supposed to be against us, the 8th. In the afternoon walked into Anzac to get a drink of water as have had fever and a cruel thirst. The dugouts smell, and washing's difficult. Anglesey gave me excellent water.

Friday, August 13th, 1915. *No. 3 Outpost.* Nothing doing. Bullets singing about, but nobody's getting hit. The heat's ferocious, and everybody's feeling ill. Macaulay's wounded. Worked yesterday morning. Also started on new dugout. In the afternoon went with Turkish papers to Anzac. I saw Corbyn. He said that this beach, for cruelty, had beaten the Crimea. Birrell the doctor in charge had come ashore at Anzac and stayed there for about half an hour. They knew the date of the landing, yet they did nothing. The doctors came down here from No. 2 and were then sent back. There were two doctors at Anzac who had joined in order to do their bit; one of these was a very distinguished man and the other all right. What they had to do was to see if the wounded who went off had a blue or a green ticket; a corporal could have done this work; RAMC jealousy put them up to it. Old Birrell has been the man in command. He said a staff officer had come up to him yesterday and said there are sixteen dead men on stretchers there. I don't know if they were dead originally or if they had been forgotten. C. said to him they aren't carrying about dead men these days. One RAMC man refused to have his kitchen moved to make way for the wounded. General Shaw said: 'Damn the wounded, I am not a quarter-master.' Eight bell tents had never been put up

131

that would have protected a lot of men from the sun. The Navy are refusing to evacuate except at night, as they say they have had a petty officer and a coxswain wounded these last days. Savage feeling with the RAMC.

Streams of mules took water out in the evening as the sun set. I met several men with sunstroke coming in. I saw George Hutton, Royal Welsh Fusiliers, who has become a Colonel. He had a hand-to-hand bayonet tussle with a Turk, in the last fight. Another man came up, and killed the Turk with his bayonet. Then, he said, the man, instead of pulling his bayonet out, dashed to another man and asked him for his bayonet, saying: 'I have left mine in the Turk.' The battle-cries, by the way, were for the Turks the sonorous, deep-voiced 'Allah, Allah,' and 'Voor' ('God, God,' 'Strike'); while the New Zealanders used often to shout: 'Eggs is cooked.' This apparently irrelevant, unwarlike slogan had its origin in Egypt. There, on field days in the desert, when the men halted to rest, Egyptians would appear magically with primitive kitchens and the cry of 'Eggs is cooked!'

Diary. Monday, August 16*th*, 1915. *No.* 3 *Outpost.* Christo will spit on my razor strop, otherwise he is very good. Worked yesterday morning and went and bathed with Charlie B. in the afternoon, when Birdwood left. Chaytor is coming back, this means he will take Charlie B's place. I am very sorry as I am very fond of him. I don't think the General can stand the winter here. The big fight ought to come before long, I take it. We shan't get the Balkans in until we get to Constantinople. I don't think we seem to want Roumania in. If she has no ammunition and takes a really bad knock from Germany, it would give Germany a very strong strategic position. It is said that Roumania keeps a percentage of all the ammunition she sends to Turkey. Bulgaria has stated her terms, Monastir and Cavalla. We agree but Serbia don't; can Russia make her? She can't risk the Serbs disobeying her. The Serbs might still do a deal with Austria; anyhow there is bound to be another Balkan war.

The Turks who come in do not really seem very disheartened; they talk in those very quiet soft patient voices, but pat one quite heartily. I am afraid they are beginning to fight without giving quarter. It is very curious the way the men speak of them here. They still can't be made to wear gas helmets because they say the Turks are clean fighters and won't use gas. Last night one man was talking to me in the darkness about his pal who had seen a little trench by Quinn's taken. Then they had to kill the Turks who were in dugouts. 'It had to be,' he said, 'it had to be, and my pal knew that, but he'd had enough fighting after that.' After that he said: 'Let me go back to New Zealand.' Most of these men up here have been sick, dysentery etc.

At about this time the Expeditionary Force entered upon a new phase. The agony of the struggle had passed its crisis. Both sides sat down grimly, to wait for the winter. In many ways our position had distinctly improved. There was more room, and space banished the sense of imprisonment that had afflicted us. The country was not as battle-scarred as Anzac, and walking over the heights at sunset was a feast of loveliness.

We moved our Headquarters again, and I went up to a large dugout in what had been a Turkish fort. The troops quartered in this fort were an Indian Field Battery and sixty-three New Zealanders, all that was left of their battalion. These men had been in the first landing. They had, every one of them, had dysentery or fever, and the great majority were still sick and over-ripe for hospital. As time went on, and illness increased, one often heard men and officers say: 'If we can't hold the trenches with sound men, we have got to hold them with sick men.' When all was quiet, the sick-list grew daily. But when the men knew that there was to be an attack, they fought their sickness, to fight the Turk, and the stream to the hospitals shrank.

I admired nothing in the war more than the spirit of these sixty-three New Zealanders, who were soon to go to their last fight. When the day's work was over, and the sunset swept the sea, we used to lean upon the parapet and look up to where Chunuk Bair flamed, and talk. The great distance from their own country created an atmosphere of loneliness. This loneliness was emphasized by the fact that the New Zealanders rarely received the same recognition as the Australians in the Press, and many of their gallant deeds went unrecorded or were attributed to their greater neighbours. But they had a silent pride that put these things into proper perspective. The spirit of these men was unconquered and unconquerable. At night, when the great moon of the Dardanelles soared and all was quiet except the occasional whine of a bullet overhead, the voices of the tired men continually argued the merits of the Expedition, and there was always one end to these discussions: 'Well, it may all be a—— mistake, but in a war of this size you will have mistakes of this size, and it doesn't matter a—— to us whether we are for it here or in France, for we came out to do one job, and it's nothing to us whether we finish in one place or another.' The Turks were not the only fatalists in those days.

We were now well supplied with water, but food of the right kind was a difficulty. It was very hard to obtain supplies for sick men, and here, as always, we met with the greatest kindness from the Navy. Horlick's Malted Milk and fruit from the Islands did us more good than anything else. Relations of mine in Egypt sent me an enormous quantity of the first, which I was able to distribute to the garrison of the fort. Later, when I was invalided, I bequeathed the massive remnants to a friend who had just landed. Greedily he opened my stores, hoping for the good things of the world – tongues, potted ham and whisky – only to find a wilderness of Horlick's Malted Milk.

Our position had at last been appreciated at home, and we were no longer irritated, as in the early days, by the frivolity and fatuousness of London. Upon one occasion, shortly after the first landing, one of the illustrated papers had a magnificent picture entitled, if I remember right, 'The Charge that Won Constantinople.' The picture was of a cavalry charge, led quite obviously by General Godley – and those were the days when we were living on the edge of a cliff, where only centipedes could, and did, charge, and when we were provided with some mules and my six donkeys for all our transport.

There was a remarkable contrast between our war against the Germans and the Turks. In France the British soldier started fighting good-naturedly, and it took considerable time to work him up to a pitch of hatred; at Anzac the troops from the Dominions began their campaign with feelings of contempt and hatred, which gradually turned to respect for the Moslems. At the beginning the great majority of our men had naturally no knowledge of the enemy they were fighting. Once, looking down from a gun emplacement, I saw a number of Turks walking about, and asked why they had not been shot at. 'Well,' said one man, 'it seems hard on them, poor chaps. They aren't doing any harm.' Then up came another: 'Those Turks,' he said, 'they walk about as if this place belongs to them.' I suggested that it was their native land. 'Well,' he said, 'I never thought of that.'

Diary. Monday, August 16th, 1915. No. 2 Outpost. It's curious the way the men speak of the Turks here. They still can't be made to wear gas helmets, because they say the Turks are clean fighters and won't use gas.

It's good to be high up in this observation post, above the smells, with a magnificent view of hill and valley. We shoot from here pretty often at the Turkish guns. Last night the Dardanelles droned on for hours. This morning the machine guns on both sides were going like dentists' drills. To-day it's absolutely still, with only the whirr of aeroplanes overhead.

Stopford[81] has now gone home. It hasn't taken long to finish him. I am beginning to wonder how long it will take to finish us. Hamilton will continue his policy of pebbles to the end. Well, perhaps it's better from the garrison's point of view to have half a dozen little sieges than one big one. Poor Colonel Bauchop is dead. News came to-night. A gallant man.

On Tuesday I went into GHQ with Levick[82], Guise and another, Bacchante. Levick had got on a wounded boat at Mudros, 800 wounded men, many of them with maggots from neglect; four doctors. Other fleet surgeons were sent but at once recalled, so was he. He refused to obey and stayed four days. When he went back Boyle began cursing him, and he claimed a court martial, heard no more about it. He said he wanted to save the wounded

---

81.   Lieutenant-General the Hon Sir Frederick Stopford KCB KCMG KCVO (1854–1929). Commanded the IXth Corps, formed for the Suvla landings.
82.   George Murray Levick (1877–1956), a Royal Navy surgeon.

in future and punish the responsible people. I said I too was out for vengeance but the only thing to do now was to see if we couldn't save the wounded next time.

When men have gone to the limits of human endurance, when blood has been spilled like water, and the result is still unachieved, bitter and indiscriminate recrimination and criticism inevitably follow. But Anzac had one great advantage. Our leaders were able to see General Birdwood and General Godley every day in the front trenches with themselves, walking about under fire as if they had been on a lawn in England, and the men knew that their own lives were never uselessly sacrificed.

The work of many of the doctors on the Peninsula was beyond all praise, but there was black rage against the chiefs of the RAMC at Imbros and in Egypt. The anger would have been still greater if their attitude of complacent self-sufficiency had been known.

Diary. Thursday, August 19th, 1915. No. 3 Outpost. Returned to the Peninsula with Bettinson and Commander Patch, and Phillips, the navigator. When we had come up to the fort I told them not to show their heads at the observation post, as the fort did not belong to me, and I did not want to become unpopular. I got Perry, Captain of the fort, and he sat them down on the parapet, showing them the lines of our trenches. While we talked, a sniper shot at Patch, just missing him, and hitting the parapet beside him. They were very pleased, though the others said I had paid a man to shoot in order to give them fun. Perry said in a friendly way: 'That's a good sniper; he's thirteen hundred yards off, so it was a pretty decent shot.' Then he talked to them, and they felt what anyone must feel talking to these men. They gave us a lot of things, and are sending all sorts of things to-morrow for the men here.

Before lunch I went to a New Zealand dentist, MacKenzie. He began by telling me two stories about myself, both of them caricatures. I interrupted in the second and told him who I was. He then pierced the wrong gum and I moaned like a dove. The RAMC Colonel there had insulted him by saying they could not have him as an honorary member of their Mess; he knew no one and nightly went up on a hill looking across at the New

Zealanders and moaning his complaint. Roger Keyes he said was a white man; he had shown him the letter of the RAMC Colonel and Keyes had been very abusive. I also was very abusive. I thought he would be less likely to hurt me. I am never going in uniform again. It prevents one making a fuss before one is hurt.

Friday, August 20th, 1915. *No. 2 Outpost*. Last night was the first cold night. This morning I went out with the General, who was like a bulldog and a cyclone. We met Birdwood, who was there to see the last Australians arrive, 17th and 18th Brigades, in Reserve Gully. They looked a splendid lot, and it did one's heart good to see them. Some more officers from the *Bacchante* turned up with stores, and special cocoa for me. I was just going off to find Perry when I met him. He is off out; there is a fight to-morrow. I gave him the cocoa. He was glad to have it. . . .The men are all tired out with heat and dysentery, and digging, and fighting. The General and I went up to Sazli Beit Deri. I didn't think it oversafe for him.

Saturday, August 21st, 1915. *No. 2 Outpost*. Work in the morning. Was to have gone with the General in the afternoon, but prisoners came in to be examined. They said: 'Curse the Germans! We can't go on. There are no more men left.' One of them was killed by their own fire after I left. At lunch George came. Charlie Bentinck, he and I started off together. I felt rather sick. It was very hot. We went at a great pace over two or three ridges, our own guns thundering about us; I finally felt so sick I let them go on and lay down for a bit. Meanwhile the battle developed and the shooting became fierce and general. While I hunted for General Monash's HQ I met Colonel Artillery Johnson. He seemed rather grumpy and very worried. We walked along side by side, and a bullet came between us. He told me afterwards that Colonel Parker had said he would not carry out his instructions and that General Cunliffe Owen had come and upset his whole scheme of artillery bombardment this morning. He was going to Cixs. I said I was going to Monash but lay down behind some rushes. Several bullets buzzed through, and I got up to go back feeling too sick to carry on. I wandered along through deafening noise but quite alone. Then I heard a thud and saw a cloud of dust and knew that shrapnel had hit the ground about ten yards off. Judging the shrapnel had come from the left, as I reached it another burst came hitting the tree on both outer sides and scratching my hand. I felt, however, fairly comfortable until vicious bullets began pecking round me. There was a sniper who was taking an interest in me. I had to move round until I was unprotected from the shrapnel. A lot of stuff sighed and groaned over; it sounded like two currents of air meeting, our shells and the Turks crossing. The sniper wasn't very regular, but I felt uncomfortable and got up and ran, with not much happening, to a very shallow nullah. I walked down this and came to a regular gully and so home. I thought the Turks must be in force from the fierceness of their rifle fire. I lay down, had soup and felt recovered.

Diary. August 21st, 1915. Charlie B. and George came back all right. The Turks had come over in three waves down Chunuk Bair. The first two were destroyed by naval fire; the third got home into our trenches. Charlie B. was full of admiration for one old fellow whom he had seen holding up his finger and lecturing to the men when they hung back. Hutton is wounded again.

That day I saw an unforgettable sight. The dismounted Yeomanry attacked the Turks across the salt lakes of Suvla. Shrapnel burst over them continuously; above their heads there was a sea of smoke. Away to the north by Chocolate Hill fires broke out on the plain. The Yeomanry never faltered. On they came through the haze of smoke in two formations, columns and extended. Sometimes they broke into a run, but they always came on. It is difficult to describe the feelings of pride and sorrow with which we watched this advance, in which so many of our friends and relations were playing their part.

Sunday, August 22nd, 1915. *No. 2 Outpost.* Last night, or this morning at 1 o'clock, I was called up. They said there were 150 Turks in one place and others elsewhere, anxious to surrender. I took the miller, Zachariades and Kyriakidis out to Headquarters. Sent back Kyriakidis and the miller, as there was nothing doing and I wanted to keep Kyriakidis. Went on with Zachariades and guides sent by Poles to Colonel Agnew to his HQ. There we lay on the ground, very cold. They said the Turks had wished to surrender, but there had been no interpreter, and they had been fired on. The Turks were then attacking heavily. Eastwood telephoned that they had fourteen prisoners. I went back to see if they could give any news about our immediate front.

Everyone worried. The 18th Battalion of Australians had gone wrong. Nobody knew where they were. I sent my escort to try and find them. The Hampshires, who ought to have arrived, had not come. They came along gradually. We attacked at about four in the morning. The Turkish fire tarried a little, then got furious. We went towards Monash, and met the Hampshires, very tired and wayworn. Bullets sang very viciously, and burst into flame on the rocks. There was a thunder of rifle fire and echoes in the gullies, men dropping now and then. Lower down the gully I found the Hampshires running like mad upwards to the firing line; beyond this a mixed crowd of men without an officer. . . .My guide, wild as a hawk, took us up a ridge. I fell over a dead man in the darkness and hurt my ankle. We had to wait. There seemed a sort of froth of dust on the other side of the ridge, from the rifle fire, and I told the escort to take us down and round the ridge across the valley. He admitted afterwards we had no chance of crossing the other way. In the valley the bullets sang. We came to the half-nullah where I had taken such unsatisfactory cover in the previous afternoon. There we waited a bit, and then ran across the hundred yards to the next gully. Zachariades and the escort grazed. Found the prisoners; the other Zachariades examined them. Spent bullets falling about, but the Greeks never winked. A surrendered Armenian could only tell us that the Turks were very weak before us. The rifle fire died away in the end, and we walked back at dawn, getting here by sunrise. Examined more prisoners till about 11, and slept till 1. The position is still indefinite. It's on the same old lines, on the hills we are the eyebrows and the Turks are the forehead.

Monday, August 23rd, 1915. No. 2 Outpost. Perry is wounded, but not badly I hope, in the arm. There is hardly anyone in the fort. The interpreter question becoming very difficult. They are all going sick. Had a quiet evening last night, and read on the parapet. It will be very difficult to keep these old troops here during the winter. The Australians and New Zealanders who have been here a long time are weak, and will all get pneumonia. There was a great wind blowing and the sound of heavy firing. I went to Anzac to-day, and found men bombing fish. They got about twenty from one bomb, beautiful fish, half-pounders.

Tuesday, August 24th, 1915. *No. 2 Outpost.* General Shaw has gone sick to England; General Maude has taken his place. He commands the 13th. He and Harter dined here last night. Longford[83] was killed, Milbanke[84] said to be killed or wounded, and the Hertfordshires have suffered.

This morning we talked about the winter seriously and of preparations to be made. I am for a hillside. The plain is a marsh and the valley a watercourse. We ought to have fuel, caves for drying clothes, cooking, etc., and mostly this hill is made of dust and sand. A great mail came in last night, but the machine guns got on to the men as they passed by the beach in the moonlight, killed some and wounded five men. So there are the mails lying now, with the machine guns playing round them. I advised Lawless yesterday at Anzac to move out from the beach, lest the sea should rise and take him like a winkle from his shell.

Saw Doddington to-day. He has a curious story to tell of the other night, when I was telephoned for. He said I was called three hours too late. A lot of Turks had come out of their trenches, some unarmed and some armed, and some with bombs. He had gone out and pointed his revolver at one of them, who shouldered arms and stood to attention. Some of the Turks came right up, and the New Zealanders said: 'Come in here, Turkey,' and began pulling them into the front trench. Doddington had feared that the Turks, who were about 200, might rush the trench, and had waved them back and finally fired his revolver and ordered our fellows to fire. It was a pity there was no one there who could talk. Later I saw Temperley, who said when we took Rhododendron Ridge there were 250 Turks on the top.

83.   Brigadier Thomas Pakenham, 5th Earl of Longford KP MVO (1864–1915). Commanding the 2nd (South Midland) Brigade. Lord Longford was killed leading an attack on 21st August. His last words were reputed to be 'Don't bother ducking, the men don't like it and it doesn't do any good....'
84.   Lieutenant-Colonel Sir John Milbanke VC (1872–1915). Commanding the Nottinghamshire Yeomanry (Sherwood Rangers).

They piled their arms, cheered us and clapped their hands.

To-night I went to Chaylak Dere with the General and saw General Maude[85], and his Staff, who looked pretty ill, also Claude Willoughby, who was anxious to take the Knoll by the Apex. There was a tremendous wind, and dust-storms everywhere. In the gullies men were burying the dead, not covering them sufficiently. My eyes are still full of the dust and the glow of the camp-fires on the hill-side, and the moonlight. It is an extraordinary country to look across – range after range of high hills, precipice and gully, the despair of Generals, the grave and oblivion of soldiers.

On Wednesday the 28th I saw Rochdale[86] early. He said he had been home when summoned to the House of Lords; that he had seen A.J.B, Asquith[87], Bonar Law[88] etc. A.J.B. and B.L. said he had told them nothing new, but the Dardanelles Committee seem to have no suggestion to make in view of a possible disaster. Asquith was very angry with him, and told him he was an officer, had no right to criticize the campaign, and asked him what his solution was. He said that he had never been shown any intelligence papers and therefore wouldn't say what he thought, but he said it would be a good thing to clear Asia of guns. It would indeed. He said we were bound to get a disease in the autumn, both from lack of room for sanitation and the men buried in the gullies; that the distance we had achieved had brought us no nearer to our object and had cost us ten men a yard. He told me that twenty-four hours after landing he had been ordered to take some trenches that the Brigadier of the KOSBs had refused to take. That he had done so at great loss. Later when he was given

---

85.   Lieutenant-General Sir Frederick Maude KCB CMG DSO (1864–1917). Commanding the 134th Division at Suvla.85. George Kemp, 1st Baron Rochdale CB (1866–1945). Lieutenant-Colonel in command the 1st/6th Battalions of the Lancashire Fusiliers and temporarily commanded the 126th and 127th Brigades of the 42nd (East Lancashire) Division.
86.   Arthur Balfour, 1st Earl of Balfour KG OM PC (1848–1930). At that time, First Lord of the Admiralty.
87.   Herbert Asquith, 1st Earl of Oxford and Asquith, KG PC KC (1852–1928). At the time, Prime Minister.
88.   Andrew Bonar Law (1858–1923). At the time, Chancellor of the Exchequer.

a similar order he expostulated to Hunter Weston[89] and said: 'Do you want to wipe out the 42nd?' Hunter Weston said: 'Why not? I have wiped out the 29th, why not the 42nd.' That was the way he always talked. Rochdale said that Hunter Weston never went near the trenches, but I had not heard that before. He thought evacuation was the only possible thing. If we do, we must make some great advertising coup.

Here the diary stops abruptly, and begins again on Saturday, September 23rd.

No. 2 Outpost. After writing the above I had a bad go of fever, and was put on to hospital ship. Went aboard with General Birdwood, General Godley, and Tahu Rhodes. The Generals had come to inspect the New Zealand hospital ship, which was excellent. That night there was a very heavy fire. I felt some friend of mine would be hit on shore, and the next morning I found Charlie Bentinck on board, not badly wounded, hit in the side. My friend Charlie Bentinck had a temper, and was often angry when others were calm, but in moments of excitement he was calm to the point of phlegm. When we were off Mudros there was a great crash, and a jarring of the ship from end to end. I went into Charlie Bentinck's cabin and said: 'Come along. They say we're torpedoed. I'll help you.' 'Where are my slippers?' he asked. I said: 'Curse your slippers.' 'I will not be hurried by these Germans,' answered Charlie, and he had the right of it, for we had only had a minor collision with another boat. At Mudros the majority of the sick and wounded on our hospital ship were sent to England, but my friend and I were luckily carried on to Egypt.

Diary. September 23rd. There was a remarkable man on board the *Manitou*, Major Kelly[90] of the Norfolks was there. He had led 240 men under orders into a Turkish trench; three got back unwounded, but he carried most of his wounded back with eighteen men. The Adjutant was killed on his back. He had already

89.   Lieutenant-General Sir Aylmer Hunter-Weston KCB DSO GStJ (1864–1940). Initially commanded the British 29th Division, during the landing at Cape Helles he had been promoted on 24 May 1915 to Lieutenant-General and given command of the British VIII Corps.
90.   Lieutenant-Colonel John Sherwood-Kelly VC CMG DSO (1880–1931).

been wounded twice. Finally, he left the trench alone, and turned round and faced the Turks at 200 yards. They never fired at him, because, he said, 'they admired me'. I never met a more gallant man, or one so proud of his courage. This officer found a DSO waiting for him in Egypt and has since earned the VC in France, for which he had been previously recommended in South Africa. He and I returned to the Dardanelles together while he still had a long, unhealed bayonet wound in his leg.

At Alexandria, fortunately for myself, I had relations who were working there. I went to the hospital of a friend. It was a great marble palace, surrounded by lawns and fountains, and made, at any rate, gorgeous within by the loves of the Gods, painted in the colours of the Egyptian sunset on the ceilings. The Englishwomen in Alexandria were working like slaves for the wounded and the sick. They did all that was humanly possible to make up for the improvidence and the callousness of the home medical authorities. Thanks to their untiring and unceasing work, day and night, these ladies saved great numbers of British lives.

One day the Sultan[91] came to inspect the hospital where I was a patient. For reasons of toilette, I should have preferred not to have been seen on that occasion by His Highness, but the royal eye fixed itself upon my kimono and he pulled me into a corner and said he was very grieved for the Conservatives in England, because of the Coalition I suppose, and he was also grieved about Gallipoli. There I cordially agreed. He said there were peace negotiations in the air, Franco, Turko, Anglo, Russo peace. He said that France and Syria would be the difficulty. He sent many messages to Birdwood, of whom he is very fond.

I went up to Cairo for a few days, and found the city and life there very changed. Shepheard's was filled with the ghosts of those who had left on and since April 12th.

In Egypt the danger of the Canal had passed, but anxiety had not gone with it. There was much doubt as to what the Senoussi would be likely to do and what consequences their action would

91.   Sultan Husayn Kamil (1853–1917), Sultan of Egypt and Sudan from December 1914–October 1917.

have. They had little to gain by attacking, but all knew that this would not necessarily deter them. I was in Cairo when Fathy Pasha was stabbed, and those in authority feared for the life of the Sultan.

My friend Charlie B. and Major Kelly and I left Alexandria in brilliant moonlight. Our boat could do a bare twelve knots an hour. On the journey rockets went up at night, SOS signals were sent us, all in vain: we were not to be seduced from our steady spinster's course to Mudros. When we again reached that place we found our sister ship, the *Ramadan*, had been torpedoed.

Diary. (Written September 23rd.) General Godley was on the *Lord Nelson*. He had been sick for some time, and had been taking three days off. Roger Keyes desperately anxious to go up the Dardanelles, come what may. He is the proper man to do it, but I think it's only singeing the King of Spain's beard.

At Imbros the General, Charlie B. and I had a stormy row ashore and a long walk to GHQ, where I found Willy Percy, who had been badly wounded, now recovering. I saw Tyrrell, George Lloyd and Deedes. The news had just come through of Bulgaria's mobilization, but they did not know against whom. I wonder if the Bulgars will attack both the Serbs and the Turks. That would be a topsy-turvy, Balkan thing to do, and might suit their book. We ought to have had them in on our side six months ago. From GHQ we came back to Anzac. The General has had my dugout kept for me in the fort, where Christo and I now live in solitude, for all the rest are gone. I found a lot of new uniforms and a magnificent (Foot) Guard's cap full of gold braid waiting. I put this on but Christo cried violently: 'NO, NO, NO, not until we ride into Constantinople as conquerors.'

HQ are on the other side of the Turkish fort, in a tiny valley across which you can throw a stone. They have all the appearance of a more comfortable Pompeii, and are scarcely more alive; it is the quietest town I have ever seen; there lies in front a ridge of valley, a dip of blue sea, and a good deal of the Anafarta plain. The first night on arriving the cold was bitter, also next morning. Pleurisy has already started. This morning the General went up to the Apex and behind it. He was not at all pleased with the fire trenches. He nearly drove Doddington, the officer at that moment instructing the Australians, mad first by criticising everything – I thought pretty justly – and then by standing about in view of the Turks and not worrying about shells or bombs. I did my best to get him in. The Australians were all laughing at Doddington for his caution and fussiness. Incidentally, one of the big mortar-bombs fell in the trench as we arrived. Hastings is Intelligence officer. It's luck to have got him.

Sunday, September 24th, 1915. *No. 2 Outpost.* A lovely morning. There was a bracing chill of autumn and yet warm air and a smiling, southern look across Anafarta Plain, with great hills on the other side, stately and formidable. Swallows everywhere. Up till now it's been very silent. I thought that the noise of war was past, but bullets and shells have been whining and moaning over us. At Anzac yesterday morning they had about twenty men hit by one shell, and I saw a lot of mules being dragged down to the sea as I went in. We walked through the 'Camel's Hump' with Colonel Chauvel and Glasgow, on to No. 1 Outpost, now deserted, with the beautiful trench made by the six millionaires. Poor chaps, I wonder how many of them are alive. Cazalet, of whom I had grown very fond, is dead, Hornby's missing. I was very sad to hear that Reynell was killed on the night of the 27th, when we left. A fine man in every way. His men worshipped him. Poor Reynell was killed charging. He ought not to have been there; he was an extra-ordinarily gallant fellow. A lot of French transports were leaving Egypt as we left, maybe for Asia. We shall do nothing more here unless we have an overwhelming force. We have never done anything except with a rush. Directly we have touched a spade we have ceased to advance, and have gone on adding bricks to the wall which we first built and then beat our heads against.

This morning we had a service in the valley, which is extra-ordinarily beautiful. The flies are awful, horrible, lethargic; they stick to one like gum. The men in the trenches are wearing the head-dresses that Egypt has sent. I went with the General in the afternoon to Anzac. We walked back as shelling began. We had one whizz round us, and a man fell beside me on the beach. I heard a tremendous smack, and thought he was dead, and began to drag him in to cover, but he was all right, though a bullet had thumped him. The flies and their habits deserve to live in a diary of their own. They were horrible in themselves, and made more horrible by our circumstances and their habits. They lived upon the dead, between the trenches, and came bloated from their meal to fasten on the living. One day I killed a fly on my leg that made a splash of blood that half a crown would not have covered.

Diary. Monday, September 27th, 1915. No. 2 Outpost. Last night Ferguson dined. He said the Indians could all get home from Mudros if they gave the hospital orderly ten rupees. The hospital orderly would then certify them as having dysentery. Some did not at all want to go, others did. One old fellow with a great reputation for gallantry left with a self-inflicted wound. When they were reluctant about fighting, he thought it was due to the fact that it was Moslems they were against.

This morning the General and I went round Colonel Anthill's trenches. Billy Hughes was there, as independent and casual as ever. He came out here as a sergeant and is now Acting Brigade Major. I am giving him a shirt. Many of the men are very done. I do not think that they will try to combine to insist on a rest, but I don't know before the winter is out.

Billy Hughes was not the only member of his family who was independent. His father, a well-known Australian doctor, on one occasion gave one of the chiefs of the British RAMC his sincere opinion about the treatment of the sick and wounded. After a while the chief of the RAMC said: 'You don't seem to understand that it is I who am responsible for these things.' 'Oh yes, I do,' said the Australian doctor, 'but it's not you I'm getting at; it's the fool who put you there.'

Diary. Thursday, September 28th, 1915. No. 2 Outpost. Last night I dined with Sam Butler and Harold Woods. Walked back through a still, moonlit night, with the sea and the air just breathing. Very bright stars. We sent up flares. The General was ill this morning, so did not go out. The Greek interpreters have been called up for mobilization. This Greek mobilization ought to do some good about the German submarines. Last night at Anzac they had iron needles dropped from aeroplanes. I always objected to this. This morning over our heads there was a Taube firing hard at something with a machine gun. It produces an unpleasant impression, I suppose because it is unfamiliar, to hear the noise straight above one. Two bombs were dropped – at least, I suppose they were. They fell with a progressive whistle, but not close to us; another big one, however, an 8-inch one, I believe, from the Dardanelles, fell with a tired and sensuous thud just over the ridge.

Wednesday, September 29th, 1915. *No. 2 Outpost.* The General went out at nine this morning, Pinwell and I with him. He went to the Apex and round. In the evening Kettle and I talked in the fort.

Friday, October 1st, 1915. *No. 2 Outpost.* Yesterday morning General Godley, General Birdwood, de Crespigny[92] and I went round the trenches, Apex, Anthill's, etc., from 9.30 until 3. A very hot day; I wish that Generals were a hungrier, thirstier race. We had some light shelling, into which the Generals walked without winking or reason, though they made us take intervals.

George Lloyd has gone home. Ashmead Bartlett wrote a letter to Father Asquith criticising the campaign and saying that Hamilton ought to be recalled. The War Office have now recalled him and he goes back cheerfully. Ross turned up last night; glad to see him again. He said that a statement was to be made almost at once, and that we weren't going to be here for the winter. He had a notion that the Italians were going to take our place. This morning there was a very heavy mist; the hills and the sea were curtained in it. My clothes were wringing wet. The Greek interpreters have been called up by the Greek mobilization and have gone to Imbros, some of them to try to avoid going. They have, says Christo, 'kria kardia' (cold feet). Xenophon, in a moment of enthusiasm, changed Turkish for Greek nationality. He now speaks of the days of his Ottoman nationality with a solemn and mournful affection, as of a golden age. He envies his cousin, Pericles, who was not so carried away. Kyriakidis is too old to go, thank goodness.

Going into Anzac with the General, and glad to be quit of the

---

92.   Lieutenant-Colonel Sir Trent de Crespigny FRCP (1882–1952). At that time Commanding officer of the 3rd Australian General Hospital.

trenches. It's a weary business walking through these narrow mountain trenches, hearing the perpetual iteration of the same commands. The trenches are curiously personal. Some are so tidy as to be almost red-tape – the names of the streets, notices, etc., everywhere – and others, slums. (*Later.*) I went into Anzac with the General to see General Birdwood, but he had gone out to see the bombardment from the sea. The General went off to the New Zealand hospital ship, *Mahino*. I went to get Pinwell off, who was ill. The General and I had a very philosophical talk coming back; I said to the General that it would be difficult to write an article on this campaign. Half the splendour of war was the comradeship, the joy of giving and eagerness for sacrifice; GHQ had destroyed that. No one wanted to get killed to prove that Hamilton was more wrong than everyone had evidence of. He said GHQ had taken birdwood's plans cold, Helles and Suvla. Birdwood would probably have modified his Helles plan in view of the notice the Turks had been given; Birdwood had never had any recognition. It was mainly Braithwaite[93]. Helles was all right in principle, but when they didn't drive the Turk back by pounding him, the obvious plan would have been to have attacked higher up.

There was a radiance over Anzac; the sunken timbership shone against the sunset, with the crew half of them naked. Shells screamed over us, and in the Headquarters hollow parts of them came whimpering down.

Saturday, October 2nd, 1915. No. 2 Outpost. I hurt my eye last night and cannot see occasionally. Had a bad dream about Beb the night before last. Hope he is all right. This morning General Godley, Colonel Artillery Johnson and I went round to see the guns, all across the Anafarta plain. Yesterday they had been shelling a good deal and had killed some Gurkhas. The rest broke and ran for the big sap. We trudged about in the open, the Turkish hills in a semi-circle round us; we kept about 50 yards apart. We

---

93.   Lieutenant-General Sir Walter Braithwaite GCB (1865–1945). Chief of Staff for the Mediterranean Expeditionary Force. Braithwaite left much of the detailed planning to Colonel Skeen who took over from him as Chief of Staff.

found one dead mule that had been sniped. I thought it very risky for the General. However, nothing happened. For almost the first time I heard orders given. Have been meeting various school acquaintances these days. Tomorrow I have to change my dugout and go down to HQ. It's a nuisance. I have now had (1) an original one on the cliff (2) one with Tahu and Jacky Hughes at HQ New Zealand Gully (3) my Louis Quinze dugout looking over the sea (4) the death hole here (5) the Turkish fort, the best of all.

Sunday, October 3rd, 1915. The General and Charlie went to Suvla. I lunched at Anzac with Butler and Woods. Woods had been told he might be asked to take charge of the Turks in Maadi near Cairo. We played chess. There was a good deal of shelling. I saw several poor fellows hit. They had a man killed the other day just below the dugout. Hamilton, in his answering telegram to the King's compliments, has said that the spirit of the troops was fine but their health bad. It's a curious admission to have made unless there was a reason, as it must cheer the enemy up.

Monday, October 4th, 1915. I changed my dugout this morning with an infinity of trouble and dozens of trips. I didn't like the men doing it much as it involved standing on the roof, and if one of them had been shot I should have felt responsible and unduly luxurious. However, we did it all right, and now I am in a half-covered place, all right as long as it doesn't rain. This morning the Turks had a very fierce demonstration. The bullets kicked up the dust at the mouth of the gully in every direction. Colonel Johnson was nearly hit; some came up the gully and only hit one man. They shelled us with big stuff that came over crawling tired and groaning, bursting with a horrid noise and torrents of black smoke. I picked up one bit of high explosive just outside.

General Carruthers[94] lunched. He said people sent curiously inappropriate stores sometimes. In the middle of the summer they had sent us here mufflers, cardigan jackets, and two thousand swagger canes. These were now at Mudros. The General has sent for two Ford cars. I don't know how he will use them. Chauvel

---

94.   Brigadier General R.A. Carruthers, Deputy Assistant Quartermaster General, Anzac Corps.

has taken over command while the General is sick. He borrowed all my novels.

Tuesday, October 5th, 1915. General Cunliffe Owen turned up. He said we are going to attack through Macedonia. Heaven help us! Bulgaria has been given twenty-four hours' ultimatum by Russia. Went into Anzac, to go by boat to Suvla. Met Chamberlain, who was at Arnold's (my private school). He said there was no boat. I went on and played chess, coming back through one of the most beautiful evenings we have had, the sea a lake of gold and the sky a lake of fire; but Chamberlain and I agreed we would not go back to Anzac or to Arnold's if we could help it.

Wednesday, October 6th, 1915. I was going into Suvla with Hastings, but in the morning a Turkish deserter, Ahmed Ali, came in. He promised to show us two machine guns, which he did (one German, immovable, and the other Turkish, movable), and seven guns which he had collected; this he failed to do, and also to produce three more comrades by firing a Turkish rifle as a signal. In the afternoon I had a signal from Sam Butler to say he was leaving, sick, for Egypt. I walked in to see, and found he had gastritis.

Thursday, October 7th, 1915. *NZ and A Div. HQ*. This morning we went up with Ahmed Ali, and lay waiting for the Turkish deserters until after six. One Turkish rifle shot, a thicker sound than ours, was fired at Kidd's Post, but no Turks came. Ahmed Ali was distressed. The dawn was fine; clouds of fire all over the sky. The Turkish deserters and prisoners were put through a number of inquisitions. There was first of all the local officer, who had captured the Turk and was creditably anxious to anticipate the discoveries of the Intelligence. Then there was GHQ, intensely jealous of its privileges, and then Divisional HQ, waiting rather sourly for the final examination of the exhausted Turks. The Turkish private soldiers, being Moslems, were inspired rather with the theocratic ideals of comradeship than by the *esprit de corps* of nationality, and spoke freely. They were always well treated, and this probably loosened their tongues, but Ahmed Ali was more voluble than the majority of his comrades, and I append information which he supplied as an illustration of our examinations and

150

their results. The two sides of Turkish character were very difficult to reconcile. On the one hand, we were faced in the trenches by the stubborn and courageous Anatolian peasant, who fought to the last gasp; on the other hand, in our dugouts we had a friendly prisoner, who would overwhelm us with information. 'The fact is you are just a bit above our trenches. If only you can get your fire rather lower, you will be right into them, and here exactly is the dugout of our captain, Riza Kiazim Bey, a poor, good man. You miss him all the time. If you will take the line of that pine tree, you will get him.'

Diary. Saturday, October 9th, 1915. *NZ and A Div. HQ.* Ahmed Ali proposed coming to England with me when I went there. Last night we had bad weather. I was feeling ill and walked out when a sort of whirlwind came down. It whizzed away part of the iron sheeting over my dugout and poured in a cascade of water, soaking everything. It was not possible to light candles and I thought the rest of the sheeting would come down like razors. Christo never turned up. I resigned myself, but finally Ryrie came and lent me a torch, and I slept, wet but comfortable, under my cloak.

This morning the doctor, Colonel Sutherland, told me to go off to a hospital ship, but I said no, I would stay on here or go to Imbros. I told the General so. He said: 'Better to go, but if you think you can stick it, wait a day and I might take you with me to Alexandria.'

Sutherland came back and said I must go. I thought of Imbros and trying to ride up to Skinoudi, but felt too weak. Finally I settled to go. I told the General I should be offered other work but should not accept it without his consent, and that it had been a great pleasure serving him for the last five months, which is very true. He said that there was no work to do here now, and if there were a push I might come back again. I said: 'Yes, unless I get caught up in Asia Minor work.' I felt awfully reluctant to go but Sutherland said I should be no use for work for a month. Charlie came in after dinner very unhappy, but admitted he didn't think he could stay very long. He is a very good man. A bullet came in. While the General and I talked, it was reported that the Turks had

151

up a gas cylinder opposite to the Gurkhas, but we both thought it pretty unlikely. The rest of the time was one long farewell-taking. I wrote a thing trying to get all the interpreters mentioned, and pointing out they had never wanted Anzac as a permanent job. Zachariades made me flowery speeches, and dear old Kyriakidis.

Diary. Monday, October 11th, 1915. NZ and A Div. HQ. Saturday night was one of the quietest I ever heard; the spirit of peace without sleep breathed. The night before, after the storm, when Turks and English had got alarmed it had been a tempestuous night, and an angry dawn, very windy with the stars paling in the skies, and musketry in a bad mood crackling all round at intervals.

On Sunday morning I saw Chaytor and everyone but Pinwell, and gave away my stores. I said goodbye to the General who was quite delightful, tipped the men, and tottered off with Colonel Sutherland and Charlie; finally having a garland of Colonels to say goodbye[95].

At this point the diary ends, for the writer was evacuated on the hospital ship, and did not return to Active Service for several months. Of all those who had sailed from Egypt with General Godley on April 12th, the General himself remained the only man who saw the campaign through from the first to the last day, with the rare exception of a few days of sickness.

---

95.   In private letters, at the beginning of the Gallipoli campaign, Herbert had complained of being '*locked on the wrong side of a backdoor of a side show*'. On his departure he wrote '*I never want to see again a mule, a monk, or a backdoor, or a sideshow, or Winston or flies or bully beef*'.

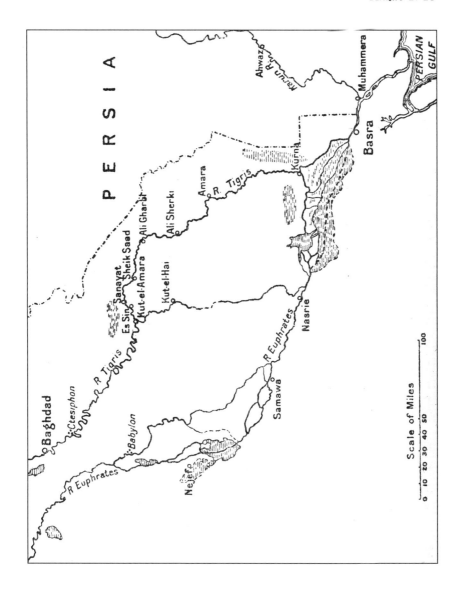

153

Chapter Three

Kut
1916

After some months of convalescence, I was passed fit for Active Service. Admiral Wemyss[97], Commander-in-Chief of the East Indian Fleet, had done me the honour to ask me to serve under him, when I was well again, as his liaison and Intelligence officer. I accepted very gladly, for I knew how devoted to him were all those who served Admiral Wemyss. The unappreciative War Office showed no reluctance in dispensing with my services, but my orders got lost, and it was only late in February when I left. When my weak qualifications in the way of languages[98] were put before the Department concerned, the brief comment was: 'This must be an immoral man to know so many languages.'

About this time the question was perpetually debated as to whether war should be made mainly on the one great front or *en petits paquets*; that is, practically all over the globe. 'Hit your enemy where he is weakest,' said some, while others were violently in favour of striking where he was strongest.

When I left England, she was in a curious state of official indecision. It would then have been, obviously, greatly to our advantage had we been able to get the Turks out of the war, for the collapse of Bulgaria would almost certainly have followed. On the other hand, Russia had been promised Constantinople and the Church of Santa Sophia, and while these promises held it was

97. Admiral of the Fleet Rosslyn Erskine Wemyss, 1st Baron Wester Wemyss GCB CMG MVO (1864–1933).
98. French, German, Italian, Turkish, Arabic, Greek and Albanian.

154

idle to think that the Grand Turk would compromise or resign his position as head of Islam. So the dread in the minds of Englishmen of friction with Russia was unconsciously adding square leagues to the British Empire, by forcing us reluctantly to attack an unwilling foe. In the end, we chose both Scylla and Charybdis, for the Turks remained in the war, Russia went out. Yet we survived, victoriously. Allah is greatest.

The story of this campaign is the most difficult to tell. The writer was in a humble position, but in a position of trust, and can only record what he saw and the things with which all men's ears were too familiar in Mesopotamia.

Diary. Monday, February 28th, 1916. *SS Mooltan. Off Marseilles.* The Germans are by way of not torpedoing our boats until Wednesday, but to-day is St. Leander's Day, a day of ill omen. They have torpedoed four boats these last days near Marseilles. We are off the coast of Corsica, dull and unattractive. Johnny Baird[99] is here. The officers on board have had no orders of any kind. There are very few civilians. If I was OC I should make all officers who have it, wear mufti, and order those who have no mufti, not to appear on deck if a submarine comes along until further orders. Johnny and I have put on life waistcoats like most others. The only thing one notices is that everyone shows a preference for the open air. I wish myself that our cabin was not upon the lowest deck.

Wednesday, March 1st, 1916. *SS Mooltan.* Yesterday Johnny Baird, Captain Cummings[100], and I went ashore at Malta. We heard of the torpedoing of the *Maloja*[101] off Dover. I saw Admiral

99. John Baird, 1st Viscount Stonehaven Bt GCMG DSO PC JP DL (1874 –1941). A Conservative MP, subsequently the eighth Governor-General of Australia.
100. Captain Sir George Mansfield Smith-Cummings KCMG CB (1859 –1923). Cummings was the first director of what would eventually become the Secret Intelligence Service (SIS).
101. A 12,431-ton P&O liner en route to Bombay. Forty people lost their lives, the majority being women or children. A further 147 people were killed when one of the ships coming to their aid, the tanker *Fort William*, also hit a mine.

Limpus[102], an old friend who greeted me with cries of delight, then dined with Admiral de Robeck[103]. I quarrelled rather with Roger Keyes. He still wants to go up the Dardanelles. I told him it was simply Drake wanting to singe the beard of the King of Spain; this seems to me to be a war of ants and attrition, and no one ought to think of the glory of the Army or the Navy before winning the war. I do not think he cares if he is at the bottom of the sea, as long as the country and the Navy is covered with imperishable splendour. He talked about the blizzard as if it had been a zephyr. You can't beat that sort. A lot of old Admirals rolled up. They had rejoined long past the age as Commanders of sweepers, or in any and every kind of capacity. The spirit of their Elizabethan ancestors was not more tough or fine than theirs. They asked me to stay on for the Intelligence Conference, but I said my orders were to report myself to the Commander-in-Chief so must go on. Johnny and Jack Marriott stayed.

Monday, March 6th, 1916. Ismailia. We landed without incident from the *Mooltan.* The last day, at luncheon, there were two tremendously loud bangs, the lids of hatches falling; they sounded exactly like cannon shot. Nobody moved at lunch, which I thought was good. Am staying with O'Sullivan, a nice, kind, earnest, furious, working man, but eighteen years in the tropics have made him very nervous. To-night I went to the Club and found Kettle, alive, whom I thought dead – very glad to find it wasn't true – and crowds and crowds of Anzacs. Then went for a walk with the Admiral; I understand why men like serving him. Afterwards tea with General Birdwood and a yarn about the Peninsula. He, like all of them really, talked of Anzac with a sort of reverence. He said that they had got a grudge against him at the War Office as an Indian soldier. The truth I think was that he wanted to command an Australian Army, and that that would have

102.   Admiral Sir Arthur Limpus KCMG CB (1863–1931). Senior British Naval Officer, Malta, Mediterranean 1915–1916.
103.   Admiral of the Fleet Sir John de Robeck GCB GCMG GCVO, 1st Baronet de Robeck of Naas, County Kildare (1862–1928). At the time of writing he was Acting Vice-Admiral in Command of the Eastern Mediterranean Squadron.

been run on political lines. I dined with General Godley, who was sad about himself. He said that he was going to be left here; that Birdie had proposed leaving the New Zealanders behind until he could command a Division but that he had refused this. I have been doing work between the Navy and the Army; found them very stiff. Yesterday they said: 'What can you want to know?' Also, in my humble opinion, what they are doing is wrong.

Friday, March 10*th*, 1916. *Cairo.* Back again at Zamalek. They have sown a proper, green, English lawn instead of the clover which we put in for economy. Saw Clayton[104] in the evening. Agreed that for the time being our Arab policy was finished. If the Russians go ahead and threaten Constantinople, the French agreement may stand. If, on the other hand, they cannot get beyond Trebizond, then Arabia will probably be a Confederation, perhaps nominally under the Turks. The Powers would probably look favourably at this, as it would be a return to the bad old principle. It would constitute one more extension of the life of the Turk, outside Turkey, made miserable to him and his subjects, during which all his legatees would intrigue to improve their own position. They would go on fermenting discontent amongst the subjects of the Turk, and when it did not exist they would create it. It is the old cynicism that this war has done nothing to get rid of. On the other hand, if annexation follows there will be two results: Firstly, the population in the annexed French and Russian spheres will be rigorously conscripted. I think we ought to do our best to prevent the Arabs being the subjects and victims of High Explosive Powers. They themselves don't realize what it means, and simply look forward to the boredom of having to beat their swords into ploughshares and take up the dullness of civilization. The second result is that we shall have vast, conterminous frontiers with France and Russia, and that we shall be compelled to become a huge military power and adopt the Prussianism that we are fighting. There

---

104.   Brigadier Sir G.F. Clayton KBE CB CMG. Sudan Agent, Head of Military Intelligence and Head of Political Intelligence Egypt and founder of the 'Arab Bureau'.

ought to be a self-denying ordinance about annexation. We should none of us annex.

Wednesday, March 8th, 1916. *Cairo.* I arranged for Storrs[105] to come down the Red Sea with the Commander-in-Chief. In the evening I saw the Sultan at the Palace. He prophesied that the Russians would be in Trebizond in eight days, and that we should be in Solloum in the same time; he put our arrival at Bagdad at the end of May. The snows were melting, he said, and the waters of the Tigris and Euphrates rising; the Turks might be cut off and might have to surrender. He said we did not understand the Moslems or what was their fraternity. In his hall he had two signs, 'God and His Prophet,' and the other, 'I live by God's will.' Any Moslem who entered saw these, and knew him for his brother. He would rather have been a farmer, dressed as a farmer, and, he added, rather quaintly, sitting in his automobile, amongst his fields, than in his Palace with interviews before him all day long. He had accepted the Throne when Cheatham offered it to him after consideration, because the good of Egypt was bound up in our success, and as Sultan he could help us. He regretted he had not been allowed to help more. He was loyal, but neither we, nor any man, could buy his honour. We could throw him over at any moment. So be it; he knew what his honour and individual dignity demanded. He said, Maxwell was the only man who understood the Moslems. Even the Duke of Connaught could hardly have done better in Egypt. He said 'Lady Maxwell, that is a very different question'. It was a great mistake that Maxwell was not trusted and that he himself was not consulted on Moslem questions. He, the Sultan, had deplored Gallipoli, both before and after. We English were *bons enfants*, but did not understand the East. He gave many messages to his friends, especially General Birdwood. He wanted to be remembered to George Lloyd and Sir Mark Sykes.

He is a grand Seigneur and a very attractive one.

Went to the Zoo in the afternoon; extraordinarily beautiful. I

105.   Sir Ronald Storrs (1881–1955), Oriental Secretary of the British Agency in Cairo between 1907 and 1917.

love Cairo. I saw the High Commissioner[106], talked of George Lloyd to him and suggested he should be sent down the Persian Gulf, folly to use a man who knew it like he did for inspecting horses' fetlocks.

Thursday, March 9th, 1916. *Cairo*. Saw Jaafar Pasha[107], a prisoner. He was wounded by a sword-thrust in the arm. They had had a good old-fashioned mêlée. He was just off shopping, taking his captivity with great philosophy. It was beautiful weather. The Bougainvillea was purple and scarlet all over the house. It looked as fairylike as a Japanese dwelling.

Friday, March 10th, 1916. *Cairo*. I lunched with General Maxwell. He is sad. It is a pity that they are taking him away. Two men are wanted for Egypt: (1) like Maxwell, with a name that makes things gracious and (2) a fighter. Now, at the moment when it is apparent that there is not going to be any serious fighting, we are taking away the man with the name. He wanted to know who was responsible for the contradictory orders in Egypt and the chaos at home. He and the High Commissioner are very sick with each other. McMahon has not had the initiative to take any responsibility and yet resents Maxwell's having taken it. Everyone is very sad about Desmond FitzGerald's death. There were very few like him, no one quite like him. He was extraordinarily fine, too fine to be a type, though he was a type too, though not a modern one. I shall never forget him during the retreat; always calm and always cheerful.

The Admiral came up on Thursday night. Bron[108] came. He said his leg troubled him flying, but he loved it. I saw his Colonel, who

106.   Lieutenant-Colonel Sir Arthur McMahon GCMG GCVO KCIE CSI (1862–1949). High Commissioner in Egypt 1915 to 1917, succeeding Sir Milne Cheetham.
107.   Jaafar Pasha was a Turkish Army officer who commanded the Senussi troops during the Senussi Uprising in Egypt. Captured at the Battle of Aqqaqia in February 1916 (which ended the uprising), he was held captive in Cairo until the outbreak of the Arab Revolt. Jafaar Pasha then volunteered to join the forces under Faisal, became commander of the Arab regulars during the revolt and then served as Minister of War and Prime Minister of Iraq under the then King Faisal.
108.   Auberon Herbert, 9th Baron Lucas and 5th Lord Dingwall PC (1876–1916), Aubrey Herbert's cousin. Lord Lucas was a Captain in the Royal Flying Corps and went missing, presumed killed, on the Western Front over German lines.

told me that he was worried, as if he fell in the desert he was done, as he could not walk great distances like the others, with his wooden leg.

I have got a 'Who's Who,' for Arabia, but I want a 'Where's Where.'

Saturday, March 11*th,* 1916. *Ismailia.* The Australians have been at their old games in Cairo, stealing motor cars, looting shops, holding up Despatch Riders with revolvers, and firing the revolver off wounding people. Maxwell ought to have shot them. They will have to do that in France. We have to pay for their extraordinarily fine fighting qualities, but it's a pity that they can't be more quiet. They admire General Birdwood, who's got a difficult job; instead of punishing he calls them 'boys' etc., but I don't think he could have done differently in Anzac. We owed a lot to their initiative when all their officers were killed and it wasn't worth bothering about salutes. In peace they resent General Godley's discipline, and that's natural, but it's inevitable, and they know it, when it comes to fighting. They say his idea is to make them Guardsmen in a given time. Charlie Bentinck came down with us, going home; I hope he gets there all right.

Tuesday, March 14*th,* 1916. *Ismailia.* Maxwell is now definitely recalled. I suppose it will simplify a complicated situation, but it's a pity to take the man away who is everything in Egypt, at the moment when it is apparent that we shall not need to defend Egypt. On Saturday I dined with the Admiral and Captain Potts, late of the Khedive's[109] yacht. Like Jimmy Watson, he loved his Chief. Sunday I lunched with the Admiral and General Murray[110] whom I thought a weak, stiff man. He apparently means to stay at Ismailia which sounds impossible. Saw my old friend Tyrrell. Yesterday the Admiral left with Philip Neville, his Flag-Lieutenant, for Solloum. I should have liked to have been in that show.

We are by way of leaving after the Viceroy comes, that is on the 25th of this month. India will have nothing to do with any aerial

109.   The 'Khedive' was the title used by the rulers of Egypt and the Sudan until 1914 when Husayn Kamil took the title of Sultan.
110.   General Sir Archibald Murray GCB GCMG CVO DSO (1860–1945). Murray commanded the Egyptian Expeditionary Force from 1916 to 1917.

attack on the Turks outside Aden. India is eaten up with jealousy.

Wednesday, March 15th, 1916. *Cairo*. This morning went to the citadel to see Jaafar Pasha for a minute. He is becoming less and less a prisoner. Was off to shop, and said that he heard that Cairo was a nice town. He was unmoved by the war. I said to Mary[111] that the war ought to prevent one's pulses ever fluttering again. Mary said to me: 'Yes, unless it makes them flutter forever.'

Saw Clayton. He was against a Naval Base at Sefaja. Said Alexandria was the place. If we fortified Jaffa or Haifa it was obviously against our neighbours of the future. Alexandria could be improved into a Gibraltar. Sefaja wasn't any use commercially and Port Sudan only a few hours distant would answer both purposes. He thought Jacob of Aden[112] a good man, who would be quite ready to have Aden taken away from India and given to London. Percy Cox[113] of the Gulf, an unrivalled knowledge desired to be the great Pro-Consul of that part of the world, 'and the man who wants that,' said Clayton, 'would like to see it cut adrift from India'. He deplored Maxwell's going.

Wednesday, March 22nd, 1916. *Ismailia*. I have neglected my diary. Yesterday I went and said goodbye to General Birdwood and walked with him to the station talking of Mesopotamia. He said he couldn't believe it was a question of Townshend[114] surrendering. He could leave his wounded and fight his way through to Aylmer. General Godley, he and everybody went to see Maxwell off. It was a very remarkable demonstration; all were there – red hats and tarbouches, blue gowns and the khaki of the private soldier.

---

111.   The Hon Mary Herbert (1889–1970). Aubrey Herbert's wife, she had travelled out to Cairo with him prior to the Gallipoli Campaign.

112.   Lt.-Col H. F. Jacob CSI (1886–1936). 1st Assistant Resident at Aden (1910–1917) and Chief Political Officer, Aden Field Force.

113.   Major-General Sir Percy Cox GCMG GCIE KCSI (1864–1937). Cox was the Acting Political Resident in the Persian Gulf and Consul-General for the Persian provinces of Fars, Lurestan and Khuzestan and the district of Lingah. Years later he was confirmed as the Resident at Bushire, a post which he occupied highly successfully until 1914, when he was appointed Secretary to the Government of India.

114.   Major-General Sir Charles Townshend KCB DSO (1861–1924). Commanded the 6th Indian Division at Kut.

Murray's staff triumphant. Everyone else downhearted because of the old boy's departure.

To-day I rode with Temperley through the groves of Ismailia, out by the lagoon. The desert was in splendid form. The Australians were bathing everywhere and French sailors were paddling. I lunched with General Russell[115] who is a broad-minded fellow. I dined with General Godley. All the talk was of Mesopotamia. He took the opposite view to Birdie about Mesopotamia, and said that no beleaguered force had ever cut its way out. I could only think of Xenophon, whom General Gwynne[116] said wasn't beleaguered, and Plevna, that didn't get out.

Sunday, March 26th, 1916. *Cairo*. This morning we leave for Mesopotamia, by the Viceroy's train. He arrived yesterday, having been shot at by a torpedo on the way. The soldiers are becoming discontented. Their pay is four months due, and when they get it they are paid in threepenny bits for which they only receive twopence in exchange. Hence their irritation. Tommy Howard's brigade has nearly all got commissions. There are now forty-seven officers and only enough soldiers left for their servants. Saw Uncle Bob G., who reminded me of Sayid Talib, the Lion of Mesopotamia and the terror of the Turks, with whom on one occasion I travelled from Constantinople. Sayid Talib once wanted to get rid of a very good Vali of . He went round to all the keepers of hashish dens and infamous houses and got them to draw up a petition: 'We, the undersigned, hear with anguish that our beloved Vali is to be removed by the Merciful Government. He is a good man, has been just to all, and most just to us, who now implore the mercy of the Sublime Porte.' Constantinople was in a virtuous mood. The experts of were summoned. They expressed their horror at the

115.   Major-General Sir Andrew Russell KCB KCMG DSO (1868–1960). Russell has commanded the Australian and New Zealand Army Corps during the evacuation of Gallipoli and went on to command the New Zealand Division on the Western Front.
116.   Major-General Llewellyn Gwynne CBG CBE (1863–1957) was the first Bishop of Egypt and Sudan. Gwynne joined the Army as a chaplain and eventually became Chaplain General to the British Expeditionary Force.

support which the Vali was receiving from all the worst elements in the town. The Vali was removed. Sayid Talib scored. He was on our side, and remained in , but we made him a prisoner and sent him to India, I believe.

Monday, March 27th, 1916. *HMS Euryalus. Gulf of Suez.* Yesterday, Sunday, the Prince of Wales, the Viceroy, General Birdwood and the High Commissioner travelled down to Ismailia. Storrs and I were also of the company. General Godley was at the station to meet the Prince, and a lot of others. Storrs began intriguing with the Viceroy in the train, then with the Prince of Wales on the boat, and now with the Admiral. The Prince of Wales was more imaginative than I expected. He said that he hated being at home, it worried him thinking of the others in the trenches.

Tuesday, March 28th, 1916. *HMS Euryalus.* I wonder what situation we shall find in Mesopotamia. Willcocks[117] in Cairo said that the Arabs were feeding Townshend's people. 'In the old days,' he said, 'Elijah was fed by the ravens – that is, "orab," which means Arabs as well as ravens. Those were the days of faith, to-day we take the second meaning.' That was how he explained that miracle. I still wonder if the Turks won't keep the flag over Mesopotamia.

It is getting hotter and hotter and changed three times yesterday. I am working at Hindustani. The Staff here are all first class. It's luck to find Colonel de Saumarez[118], who was on the *Bacchante*, now promoted.

Thursday, March 30th, 1916. *HMS Euryalus.* Took a bad fall down the ladder and am lame. Storrs sleeps in a casemate. The only ventilation is through a gun whose breech has now been closed. Have been writing précis and political notes. We are bound to make mistakes in dealing with the Arabs, but they need not matter if they are passive mistakes; they can be corrected. If they are active, they are much harder to remedy. Our people divide the world into two categories. The Ulstermen, the Serbs and the Portuguese are good,

---

117.   Sir William Willcocks KCMG (1852–1932). Willcocks had been the head of irrigation for the Ottoman Turkish government, for what was then the greater area of Turkish Arabia and had drawn up the first accurate maps of the region and was thus in a position to advise the British force.
118.   Sir James Saumarez, 5th Baron de Saumarez (1889–1969).

loyal people, because they are supposed to put our interests first, whereas the Bulgars, the Arabs, etc, are beastly traitors, because sometimes a thought of self-interest crosses their minds.

It's raining hard this morning and it's cooler. Hope to get into the trenches at Aden, but doubt there being time. Am learning Hindustani. A number of the same words mean different things. *Kal* means yesterday or to-morrow, i.e. one day distant; but on the other hand *parson* means the day after to-morrow or the day before yesterday. This must occasionally make muddles about appointments.

Friday, March 31st, 1916. Aden. Got up early this morning and went over to the Northbrook. The Turks at Lahej are being bombarded. The Admiral's going part of the way to see it. Six aeroplanes, or rather sea planes, have gone. A heavy, hot, grey day. The Turks are fighting well. There is no ill-will here. They say the Turk is a member of the club, but has not been in it lately. We are feeding the Turks and they feed us. Caravans come and go as usual. There are great difficulties in the way of blockade. We can't hit our enemies without also hitting our friends, and yet if we do nothing our prestige suffers.

A conference this morning. Fifty years ago Colonel Pelly[119] said that the Turks were like the Thirty-nine Articles; everyone accepts them, but nobody remembers them or what they are. India seems extremely apathetic about Aden. We left early this morning. Last night I saw Colonel Jacob, who has been twelve years at Aden and in the hinterland. The Arab here doesn't seem to realize there is a war any more than many in Egypt. An old gentleman went for a walk the other day to see his son in Damascus. He was eighty, nearly blind and blundered across the canal and only got held up at our extreme outposts. He had been in the habit of taking this walk once in two years and knew of no reason why he should not do so now. Wood[120] realizes the difficulty of explaining things to the ordinary soldier. He says you have to treat every case with knowledge and on its merits. On the whole he is sympathetic to

119.   Colonel Sir Lewis Pelly, KCSI (1825–1892).
120.   Maj. W. M. P. Wood, the First Assistant Resident in Aden.

the Arabs, but he and Jacob agree in their dislike of India, and in their liking of the Arabs. Jacob seemed to me a pretty good sort of a man, long service. I should think he was fairly obstinate. The real thing about Aden is that if the India Office disapprove of the suggestions made, they ought to send a man to consider the circumstances, as the Egyptian Government does in the Sudan. The bombardment this morning is supposed to have been effective.

In the evening I went to the Turkish prisoners with Brigadier Walton[121], an awfully stupid man. They weren't at all well kept, but he promised improvements and was not bad. I gave them money for cigarettes. They said they had surrendered because life was impossible in the Yemen. They had been six to seven years without pay, had had bad food, and perpetual fighting. They had then been put on a ship to go back to their families and then taken off and sent to fight us. Human nature couldn't stand it, they said. They could never go back. They liked their Commander, Said Pasha, who was good to the soldiers, but they complained of their non-commissioned officers.

Saw Bradford, the General's ADC, a good man who saw how stupid his chief was. He said that his chief was the fifth in Aden in a short time. None of these men came with a knowledge of the place. Aden is under Bombay, this is small and tiresome, and cannot realize that events outside Aden have much more than a local importance. There was only one officer, Jacob, who talked Arabic, and not a soul that talked Turkish. Wrote to Clayton asking for an interpreter for them.

Sunday, April 2nd, 1916. HMS *Euryalus*. We are steaming through a grey-black gloom, like an English autumn afternoon, only the thermometer is 92 and there are no rooks cawing. There are lowering skies everywhere.

Have been re-reading Whigan's *Persia* and other Gulf books. Wish that I had George Lloyd's memoranda. The present position is unsatisfactory. We have policed and lighted and pacified this

---

121.   Brigadier William Walton CB CMG commanding the Aden Brigade. Walton was Acting Resident in Aden between February–July 1916.

Gulf for a hundred years, and we are entitled to a more definite status. We ought to have Bunder Abbas. Otherwise, if the Russians come down the Gulf to Bunder Abbas, they hold the neck of the bottle of the Persian Gulf and we shall be corked in our own bottle; they would be on the flank of India; they would be fed by a railway, while our large naval station would be cooking away in Elphinstone's Inlet (which is only another name for a slow process of frying), where we should have battle casualties in peace-time from the heat. Elphinstone's Inlet to Bushire is a poor Wei-hai-wei [122] to a first-rate Port Arthur. Then, if the Russians come down, any defensive measures which we may be forced into taking will appear aggressive when the Russians are on the spot. They would not appear aggressive now. We have a prescriptive right to Bunder Abbas, which we ought to strengthen. It doesn't involve territorial annexations.

Monday, April 3rd, 1916. HMS Euryalus. Last night I had a long and rather acrimonious argument with Miller and Burmester [123] on the question of Arab policy. They said: 'You must punish the Arabs if they don't come in on our side.' I said: 'You have no means of punishing them. All you can do is to antagonize them.' They said our men were fools and I told them they could not judge after a month here. They also discussed the most secret things at the top of their voices in the ward room.

There is news of a Zeppelin raid on London. Everybody is anxious.

Tuesday, April 4th, 1916. HMS Euryalus, Muskat. Last night I had my fourth Hindustani lesson, a very easy one. Jack Marriott is extraordinarily quick at languages. My teacher said that his affianced wife is fourteen and that he kept her in a cage at Bushire. Talked over making Bushire a big naval base of the Persian Gulf with the Admiral and Burmester.

---

122.   Known as Port Edward, Weihaiwei sits between the Bohai and Yellow Seas. After Russia had leased Port Arthur from China (on the opposite coast) in 1898, the British obtained a lease on Port Edward which was to run for as long as the Russians stayed in Port Arthur.

123.   Commanding HMS *Euryalus*. Later Admiral Sir Rudolf Burmester KBE CB CMG (1875–1956).

To-day is a wild day, Arabia crouching, yellow like a lion, in a sand-storm, and spray and sand flying in layers on the ship. All the land is lurid and the sea foaming and the sky black. If only there had been some sharks at sea and lions on shore, it would have been a perfect picture. This afternoon it cleared and became beautiful. We passed a desolate coast with no sign of life, where it looked as if a man would fry in half an hour in summer. A few dhows on the sea were all we saw. My last journey here came back vividly and the time at Bahrain after we were wrecked in the *Africa*[124].

Wireless came into to say the spring offensive was beginning. At Muskat the Resident, whose name we haven't made out, called on the Admiral. A tired man. If Curzon had to get his information from such as him, he must have been driven half mad. He knew nothing, and didn't seem to carry anything. It may be only nervousness and he hasn't been here long; anyway he depressed the Admiral more than anything I have seen. Later, when he had left he cheered up and told us how he had been only once to Dublin to propose, and had been refused, which he didn't think he ought to have been. There has been a row at Chahbar, and the *Philomel*, which we expected to find here, has left, telegraphed for this morning. The news here is that the tribes intend to attack Muskat, but it's not believed. We went ashore this evening, and a Beluchi boy took the Admiral and all of us round. The people who had not been to the East before were enchanted by the quiet, the scent of musk, and the evening behind the Sultan's Palace. Last time I was here was on Christmas Day, with Leland Buxton[125]. I was very sick, carrying a huge bag of Maria Teresa dollars. It hasn't gained in attraction. The Portuguese forts and the names of the ships that come here, painted in huge white letters on the cliffs, are the remarkable things about the place. There is a sort of a silent roll-call of the ships. The men like writing their names up in white letters. Matrah is round the corner, and looks bigger than

---

124.   On 31ˢᵗ December 1905 when travelling from Karachi to Bahrain. The *Africa* ran aground on a sandbank six miles off the coast.
125.   Leland Buxton (1884–1967).

Muskat. You have got to get to it by boat. Muskat itself is completely cut off. I saw a straight-looking Arab from Asir who had been with the Turks and had information, and asked the Agent to send him on to Aden.

Wednesday, April 5th, 1916. Muskat. Came ashore early this morning. Then came the Admiral and his Staff, and we went to the Sultan's house. He had about thrity followers. We drank sherbet like scented lip-salve, to the confusion of most of the sailors. The Admiral and the Sultan talked. Later the Sultan came here with seven ADCs and a nephew who talked very good English, which he had learned at Harrow. The Sultan has got a lot of rather nice-looking little horses and a monstrous goat with ears that are about 3 feet long. The Sultan gets 5 per cent of the customs of this place. Jack Marriott went to see a prisoner in the Portuguese fort. He was Sheikh of a village in which a murder had been committed. They had failed to catch the murderer, and so the Sheikh had to suffer imprisonment himself. Not a bad plan, really. It's the old Anglo-Saxon idea. That sort of thing discourages men from pushing for power and makes them very energetic, for their own sakes, when they have power. Everything seems quiet in the hinterland. These people here are Bunhas, who cheat the Sultan, some aristocratic Arabs, and gorilla-like negroes. They are mostly armed to the teeth. Sheets of rain fell this afternoon.

Thursday, April 6th, 1916. Persian Gulf. We left early this morning. Some very fine king-fish were brought aboard, about 4 feet long. Great heat. We had an excellent telegram about Gorringe's[126] offensive in Mesopotamia; the Turks driven back. The Admiral in great spirits. I am tremendously glad, because I have always felt that we were coming to a tragedy. I remember the telegram read out to us at Anzac and the cheers – 'The Turks are beaten! The way lies open to Bagdad!' – and our enthusiasm and the disappointment after it, and I did not think this would succeed. Hanna, on the left bank of the Tigris, is reported taken. That ought

---

126.   Lieutenant-General Sir George Gorringe KCB KCMG DSO
(1868–1945), Commander 3rd Indian Army Corps during operations in
Mesopotamia, March to July 1916.

to open Sinn on the right bank.

Friday, April 7th, 1916. *Persian Gulf.* Yesterday Ghullam Ali came and said that it had caused comment in Muskat that when the Sultan had called on the Admiral at the Residency the Admiral had not accompanied him down stairs to the door. Ghullam Ali had answered that the house was the Resident's, not the Admiral's, but he did not appear satisfied with his own answer. To-day we were told by wireless telegram that we had a slave of the Sultan's on board. Quite true; so we have. He said he had been with the Sultan eight years and that if he were sent back he feared for his throat. He drew his finger across it very tenderly, and everybody roared with laughter. I do not see that the Sultan has a leg to stand on. If the man went to him eight years ago, he went either of his own free will, in which case he can leave, or he was sold, and we do not recognize anything except bondage, no traffic in slavery.

The *Philomel*'s prisoners have been transferred to us. One of them looks like an old nobleman. His name is Shah Dulla. He held up Chahbar for 4,000 rupees, like other old noblemen, and was captured with seven bearded patriarchs by the *Philomel* four days ago. They are dignified people.

Saturday, April 8th, 1916. *HMS Euryalus. Bushire.* A very cold morning with a clear sky. It's a nuisance having lost all my coats. Here I leave Edward[127]. I hope he will be all right. He is to follow by the first opportunity with the other servants and my kit. McKay, who is a jolly fellow, will look after him. The news this morning is that we have again improved our position and have taken the second Turkish line. The Russians are advancing. There was a fight here a couple of nights ago. Our Agent, his brother and four sepoys were killed last night at Lingah.

Sunday, April 9th, 1916. *HMS Imogene. Shat-el-Arab.* Yesterday Commodore Wake came aboard, an aggressive type of sea bulldog, very repellent. He said that an officer had put land-mines down, and that some time after this officer had been

127.   Edward Murphy, AH's servant, an Irishman from Abbeyleix, his wife Mary Herbert's family home.

recalled. People in Bushire naturally wanted him either to remove or mark his land-mines, but he said that they were all right, as they were only exploded by electricity. The following night, however, there were loud explosions when dogs gambolled over these mines, so people still walk like Agag, and walking is not a popular form of exercise round Bushire. To-day we are in a brown waste of waters that I remember well, a dismal hinterland to a future Egypt. We passed a hospital ship early this morning, in these yellow shallow waters. It made one think of Anzac, but there it was better for the sea, sky and land were beautiful and the climate on board very good. Aylmer[128] has apparently been sent home. One can't help being sorry for these processions of disgraced.

The report which we heard yesterday from General Douglas was that when Townshend had to retreat he came across a lot of barley in an Arab village. This he commandeered. He telegraphed some time ago to say that he could only hold out until the 1st April; but if he killed his horses he could hold out longer, as his barley store would not be encroached upon to the same extent. The answer was that he was not to kill his animals as he would be relieved before then. Here we are at the 9th.

Monday, April 10th, 1916. HMS Imogene. Kurna. Yesterday we arrived at . General Cowper[129] and Colonel Winter came aboard. They said we had taken two out of the three lines of trenches, that we had to take in the first attack. Then we had been checked. We were now to take the third line last night. The Sinn position remained to be taken. Both positions were scheduled to be taken by the 12th. My feeling is that if we were successful last night, and we ought to have heard by this morning, we have a chance of relieving Townshend. If not there is little chance, for as far as I have seen, where we do not succeed in the first few days we do not succeed at all. Winter said that the Royal Indian Marine were totally unacquainted with conditions here and only less

128.   Lieutenant-General Sir Fenton Aylmer Bt VC KCB (1862–1935). Commanded the Tigris Corps during the first, failed, attempt to break the siege of Kut.
129.   Major-General Maitland Cowper CB CIE (1860–1932). Quarter Master General of the Indian Expeditionary Force D.

unbusinesslike than the doctors. He said they asked for iron barges from India and were given wooden barges which the banks and the current broke every time. At home we were sending out river craft. They asked here for one type but were told they must have another. They asked them to consult Lynch's[130] people at home and were answered that they were acting on Lynch's advice. Lynch telegraphed from here and found that Lynch in London had never been asked. The troops have only two days' supplies. The soldiers in Basrah were cheerful. They said too that for the first time the wounded were cheerful because they thought it had been worthwhile getting wounded and that we were going to succeed. The Turks fled from the first trench but fought well at the second. There is now a storm getting up. The river is a great rolling flood of yellow water, palm trees beyond, and again beyond them, marshes and glimpses of a skeleton land. Marsh Arabs always in the background like ghouls, swarming on every battlefield and killing the wounded of both sides. The Turks are said to say: 'Let us have a truce and mop up the Arabs and then turn to and fight.' Nureddin, the Turkish Commander-in-Chief, is supposed to have been at Harrow with Townshend. I should think that it was really a *pension* at Lausanne. I saw Cox yesterday and liked him again (he and Lady Cox were very good to me years ago in the Gulf) and thought him pro-consular, but he has evidently made many mistakes that probably were inevitable since he knew nothing of Turkish politics, or the larger Arab question. It seems likely that if we relieve Townshend we could then press on to Bagdad, and it would be desirable to do so because otherwise the Russians will be there ahead of us, though the Russians have not yet met any considerable Turkish force down here. If on the other hand we don't relieve Townshend and have to fall back, we shall be attacked by all the Arabs who are well armed. Gorringe they say is a good man, with rough arrogant manners. Lake[131] stellenbosched Aylmer after his last failure. They say a Royal Commission is

---

130. Lynch Bros, Merchants and Ships' agents of London.
131. General Sir Percy Lake, KCB KCMG (1855–1940), succeeded Nixon as Commander-in-Chief, Mesopotamia.

being sent to India because at home they anticipate a failure here and wish to have a scapegoat, which they have already provided in Nixon[132].

I dined with Gertrude Bell[133], Millborrow, whom I had last seen at Bahrain, and Wilson, whom I had known before in Bushire. We transfer here at Kurna from the *Imogene* on to a tiny Admiralty gunboat, leaving as usual all our kit. It is lucky for us the river bends so continually and runs fast as the Turks cannot drift down mines, for they would explode on every corner. I hope we don't have an expedition to China after this with landing parties, and old steamboats like old-fashioned tricycles and mules etc. I think the Germans must be as bored as we are, too few mules, too many APMs[134], etc. This is the most exciting and most tragic war threshold that I have seen. It's a curious fate which sends us a second time, unprepared, to one of the richest countries in the world, combined fertility and desert, with a stream controlling its future.

Tuesday, April 11th, 1916. HMS Snakefly. On Monday night we got off the *Imogene* on to the *Snakefly*, one of twelve gunboats built for this expedition and sent out here in pieces. One has been captured by the Turks. The *Snakefly* draws 2 feet 9. Webster her Captain, Laws second-in-command. We slept all right. We saw practically no traffic at first on the river and could not understand that we did not pass boats coming back empty for supplies. We passed many Indian troops mainly on the left of the river and isolated stations with telegraph masters in chief. These men go out a couple or four miles into the desert with only a couple of rifles. These small posts contain the maximum of boredom and anxiety, because there is nothing to do, and if any force of Arabs came along they would be cut up. We were fired at once in the

132.   Lieutenant-General Sir John Nixon (1857–1921), Commander-in-Chief in Mesopotamia (April 1915–January 1916), Nixon's overconfidence and subsequent overstretch of his force led to the siege of Townshend's Division at Kut.
133.   Gertrude Bell CBE (1868–1926), the writer, traveller, political analyst and administrator in Arabia. An old acquaintance of AH from his pre-war travels in the region, she was also an eminent archaeologist.
134.   Army Provost Marshals.

night, they thought by an Indian sentry. We passed the dour Arabs in villages and groups on the banks with flocks, herds, buffaloes, goats and dogs, more savage than the Philistines but armed with rifles. We saw a long apparently endless column of our cavalry winding its way through marsh and desert, and the green grass; occasionally fires where meals were cooked. A sight more curious than the Australians at the Pyramids. At 6 p.m. we came to Ali Gharbi. I saw a captain of the 67th Punjabis. He said they were all glad that Aylmer had gone; that Aylmer had looked at an empty position for hours; that the Political Officer had actually been in it and got a bullet through his cap by one of our own men. Aylmer waited to attack until the Turks had come, then on the 8th March we were repulsed. Gorringe was supposed to be a good organizer but they didn't know about him as a fighting man. Lake, too, was new. Townshend was the man they swore by. 4th Devons with John Kennaway[135], he believes, are at the Front. I hope to God he is all right. The day had been fine, but flies that bit like bulldogs everywhere. Every night we have had lightning over towards Kut like a sort of malignant and fantastic star of Bethlehem to take us on.

Wednesday, April 12th, 1916. *HMS Snakefly.* Last night the weather broke. We had a terrific downpour that wetted everything through and through. The Admiral's got a cabin about 6 feet long by 2 1/2 across. He put his head out of the window and said: 'Would any of you fellows like to come in?' My clothes are the lightest on board and I thought my khaki trousers would tear like a veil. There seemed to be people's faces everywhere on deck, though there was a lot of water. I kept my dictionary dry. There was no shelter; but it is now fine and bright and anyway one was 40 per cent better off than the men in the trenches. At 7.00 this morning when I had just turned into a dry bunk, the boy scout, 18, who is one of the crew, went overboard. He was rescued and swam lightly and gallantly. Very lucky with the whirlpools and the sharks. Today is the 12th. On the 12th I went to Mons, on the 12th I sailed for Gallipoli. I wonder what this 12th is going to bring.

135.   Sir John Kennaway Bt (1879–1956).

No kit worse luck. I have one extra shirt and an Acqua Scutum, which I bought for a penny from J. Marriott, one blanket and a Turkish dictionary for a pillow. That is all.

Everything seems greater and greater chaos. Seventeen months of war here and everything as bad as possible. They started with two brigades of Indians who were not good fighters anyhow and never ought if possible to be used on sacred ground. We started with the wrong type of boat, and also Indian Generals who looked on the expedition as a frontier campaign. If we fail to relieve Townshend, I suppose the best thing to do would be to cut our losses and retire to Kurna and hold that line, but if we do that the Turks can fortify the river and make it impregnable. The political situation with the Russians coming on must be risked.

We ran on to the bank last night, and stayed there. We spent an uncomfortable wet night, but got off all right this morning. There was an encampment close by. We couldn't make out if they were friends or enemies; the Admiral didn't bother. We all want a clean pair of socks and fewer mosquitoes.

Thursday, April 13th, 1916. Near Sanayat. It was at noon yesterday that we arrived at Ali Gharbi. The Admiral saw General Lake. We are cruelly handicapped by lacking transport and not being able to get it. In the afternoon I crossed the river and saw General Gillman[136] at Felahiya. I was very glad to see him again. He had been on our left with the 13th Division at Anafarta. One of the best men I have met. We had a long talk. He spoke critically of everything more or less, and that is his job. He blamed Townshend for saying that he could only hold out until the end of January. That was first of all. We then rushed up troops and attacked, without any preparation for wounded, ambulances, etc., and failed. It's easy to be wise after the event. If we had had proper notice this need not have happened. Then Townshend had got five thousand Arabs with him, the *bouches inutiles* told enormously, but Townshend had apparently promised these people his protec-

---

136.   General Sir Webb Gillman KCB KCMG (1870–1933). At that time, a Brigadier and Liaison Officer between the War Office and the Mesopotamia Force.

tion and nothing would make him send them away. A *geste de seigneur*. Many of those with him, especially the older men, were down with nerves. The strain had been too great. He did not think that he had a dog's chance of breaking his way out. Aylmer had sat and looked while the Turks brought up their reserve, then the 13th had been cut up. Robertson removed Aylmer who was spent and broken. The 13th Division were very young. They had had a bad knock at Anafarta. Still in the beginning of this show they were very keen and their officers could not keep them back *on the 8th March*. On the 9th April they could not get them forward, they were very cold and tired. A hot cup of coffee might have made the difference. We should have to face Arab trouble he thought, and to look to the defences of Nasryah which would soon be cut off by marshes from and could easily be turned into another Kut by the Turks. He thought the line that we ought to defend was Nasryah–Amara –Ahwaz. I suggested his going with the Admiral. He agreed. He said strongly that India had starved and ruined the show. That Beecham Duff had wanted him to go and see him, but that he could not on his way out, but that he had heard the apologia pro vita sua, which was that a man called Meyer, the Treasury Member for the Council of India, had absolutely refused to give help. Here in this flat land they needed observation balloons. None forthcoming. They asked for transport from May to Christmas, and then got one launch. He said there had of course been local faults too. Townshend had at first protested against going on. Nixon had told him to, because those were his orders from India, but when a new Turkish Division had come up to Bagdad, Townshend had never been told.

I saw the Admiral in the evening. He had seen Gorringe and was cheered. Gorringe said he had found out the Turks' weak place and was containing their strong force and attacking their weak spot. We walked by the river. We met some of the Black Watch – clean, smart men. There was a great bridge of boats, without rails, swaying and tossing in the hurricane and covered with driven foam from the raging yellow water. Across this there lurched Madrassis, Sudanese, terrified cavalry horses, mules that seemed to think that there was only water on one side, and that they would be on dry land if they jumped off on the other. We are out of range, but shelling is going on and one can fix points in the landscape by bursts. The eternal flatness is depressing.

This morning I saw Leachman,[137] the political officer. He remembered incidents of my stay at Bagdad. He had had a lot of adventures in Arabia – a very good fellow, whom everybody likes, which is rare. He was against our going farther back than Sheikh Saad, both from the point of view of strategy and also because it would be playing a low game on our own friendlies. The Arabs on the bank between Sheikh Saad and Ali Gharbi are, apparently, past praying for.

This afternoon I went out with the Admiral. He said Townshend had telegraphed to India to ask if he might tell his troops that when they were relieved they would all be given leave. The answer was in the negative. Today he telegraphs that the Indians are dying of starvation. The troops here have been on half rations for some time. The boats are many but insufficient. They are everything from Irrawaddy steamers to Gordon relief expedition steamers and LCC boats. We met some of the 6th Devons and I asked them if the road the Admiral was going on was safe. They said: 'We be strangers here zur', as if they were talking of Exeter. The Admiral has been asked if he will allow a boat with provisions to run the gauntlet. He is prepared to if it is guaranteed to him that by so doing there will be a chance not of prolonging the agony but of saving Townshend. He does not think that the boat has much hope of getting through. I asked him to let me go. He said on no account; it was folly. I agreed. The rain is still making the relief almost impossible. There was heavy firing last night and we advanced 2,000 yards, but the main positions are untaken. Tonight I met Percy Herbert. He said he would get me a horse to ride up to the trenches but at the present moment my only trousers have again come to pieces.

137.   Lieutenant-Colonel Gerard Leachman CIE DSO (1880–1920). Leachman served as an Intelligence Officer and Political Officer in Iraq and Arabia. In December 1915, Townshend ordered Leachman to save the British cavalry by breaking out of Kut and riding south. This he did and the cavalry were the only unit to escape before the city fell. After the war, Leachman was the first military governor of Kurdistan.

The Admiral had a message to-night from Townshend by wireless. He welcomed him and said that life at Kut was the limit. I wrote to Colonel Beach[138] after a talk with Gillman, saying if I could be of any use to Townshend I would go and be with him when and if he had to surrender. I told the Admiral first.

Stonefly. *13ᵗʰ April 1916*

> *Dear Colonel Beach,*
> *I saw General Gillman yesterday, who advised me to write to you. Before the war I knew many of the leading Turks very well. Several of them, Talaat, Rahmi etc. were personal friends of mine. The war has of course made a difference in relations of that kind, and the fact of German control will have made an even greater difference. But if things do not go well at Kut and you think that I can be of any use to General Townshend I shall be glad if you will dispose of me as you think fit. Any order sent to the* Mantis *will reach me.*

Friday, April 14th, 1916. HMS *Stonefly.* In the morning I talked to Gillman. He said he wasn't getting on with his work too quickly. Gorringe was uncommunicative, and while this attack was going on and in preparation he couldn't go round and worry the Divisional Commanders. The complaint is the same everywhere: that lack of transport is starving this campaign of supplies and necessaries. Lake is the only man who doesn't complain, and that is because he comes from India and is, I suppose, partly responsible.

A furious wind got up and drove mountains of yellow water before it, against the stream. The skies were black. Captain Nunn, the Senior Naval Officer, wanted to go to Sheikh Saad. I wanted to go to HQ to see Colonel Beach, Chief of the Intelligence, who has written to me to come. We got off with difficulty into the stream. It was like a monstrous snake, heaving and coiling. We

---

138.   Colonel W.H. Beach CB CMG DSO, Head of Military Intelligence in Mesopotamia.

only drew 3 feet and we were very top-heavy with iron, and I thought we were bound to turn over. I said so to Singleton, the captain, who said: 'I quite agree. It serves them d——d well right if we do, for sending us out in this weather.' This thought pleased him, though it did not satisfy me. Nunn said it was the worst weather he had seen in the year. I got off at Wadi thankfully, and went to see Beach, but it was not all over yet. He wanted to go and see how the bridge of boats was standing the strain. The end of the bridge of boats had been removed to let the steamers through, though there were none passing. It was twisting like an eel trying to get free, and going up and down like a moving staircase in agony. There was foam and gloom and strain and fury and the screaming of the timber, but the bridge held. The engineers were calmly smoking their pipes at the end, wondering in a detached way if it would hold. I infinitely prefer fighting to this sort of thing.

I went walking with Beach. He asked me to hold myself in readiness in case Townshend wanted me. I dined with General Lake, General Money[139], Williams, and Dent; capital fellows. Had an interesting time after dinner. The future is doubtful. If we have to retire, we shall have a double loss of prestige, Kut gone and our own retreat. When we want to advance later, we shall find all our present positions fortified against us. A retreat will also involve the abandonment of our friendlies. This campaign has taught me why we have been called *perfide Albion*. It's very simple. We embark upon a campaign without any forethought at all. Then, naturally we get into extreme difficulties. After that, we talk to the natives, telling them quite truthfully that we have got magnificent principles of truth, justice, tolerance, etc., that where the British Raj is all creeds are free. They like these principles so much that they forget to ask if we have guns and throw in their lot with us. Then, principles or no principles, we have got to retreat before a vastly superior force, and the people who have come in with us get strafed. Then they all say *'perfide Albion,'* though it's really nobody's fault – sometimes not even the fault of the Government.

139.   Major-General Sir Arthur Money (1866–1951).

I slept on the *Malamir*, on deck. It was very wet in the night, but I kept fairly dry.

Saturday, April 15th, 1916. Malamir. I went and saw the Turkish prisoners in one of the most desolate camps on earth; some Albanians amongst them. They said there were munitions factories in Bagdad, and that 4,000 Turks had gone to Persia – they did not know if it was to the oil-field at or against the Russians. It's and the oil-field that are important to us.

Lunched aboard the *Malamir* with General Lake who was very kind. I went off on an Irawaddy steamer, a 'P' boat (steamer P6). The captain said that after Ctesiphon they had 900 wounded on board and one doctor. It took them seventeen days to Amara. They had to turn back three times at Wadi and return to Kut, because they were heavily attacked by Kurds. Nixon cursed them the first time for cowardice until he too had to return. The transports were so overcrowded going up the river that the men pushed each other overboard. He said one transport lost five men. On board I met an ex-Bombay Political Officer, now in 82 Punjabis, P.G. Murphy. He said that India had purposely got up trouble on the frontier in order to prevent troops being sent away. That he had been on a couple of these expeditions, one in the Swat Valley. The enemy was not an enemy, had simply come in to get their share of the subsidies which we gave to another tribe. That they or rather the deputation had been captured by this other tribe and that we had said they had been routed etc., and then had stopped all their trade coming across a bridge that was their only road. He had a curious story of how at Abazai he had seen a Pathan wrestling. Before he wrestled he held up his hands and cried: 'Dynamis' (Power). He thought it must have come from the days of Alexander. He knew Greek and quoted the odd verse I remember: '*Partone kori mou, echi kai liras, den ton ethelo echi kai psiras.*' He had been in the Dujaila fight on March 8th. He said they had to advance to attack a shrine, while on their right the Devons had to advance to take a fort which covered the position. They advanced but without the Devons, and were attacked in the flank by the fort, losing 60 per cent. The Sepoys thought that Aylmer was trying to retrieve his reputation, a gambler's last throw. He said that the corruption at was terrific; they were all in the hands of their Babus.

On board our ship there were piles of bread without any covering, but a swarming deposit of flies; good for everybody's stomach.

Sunday, April 16th, 1916. Half a day's food is being dropped daily by aeroplane in Kut. The Admiral has again been asked to send up a ship with supplies. He thinks it is a forlorn hope. There is a strong current, many bends, mines, and guns dug in on the banks at the turnings. He explained all this but it made no difference and everyone volunteered. He refused me with some heat and now appears very angry about the Townshend business. He apparently hadn't realized what I proposed. I hope this ship will not be another *River Clyde* on a small scale. She is to go on the 19th. There is a bright moon. He has stipulated that he would not send the ship merely to prolong the agony. He asked for an assurance that in the improbable event of her getting through, her supplies would make the difference necessary to save Townshend. If what one hears is true, namely that they burnt the whole of the home mail of the Sheikh Saad affair (Jan. 21) to hush it up, it's easily understood why nothing is known at home.

In the morning I went to examine a Turkish prisoner, and talked to Costello[140], a VC, a very jolly Catholic Irishman. He said that when the war broke out he, and many like himself, saw the Mohammedan difficulty. They had themselves been ready to refuse to fight against Ulster; why should Indians fight the Turks? We were fighting for our own lives, but the quarrel did not really concern Indians. They might have been expected to be spectators. Then the orders came for them to go to France. They called up the Indian officers and said to them: 'Germany has declared war, and on second thoughts, a Jehad. She quarrelled with England first and then pretended she was fighting for Islam.' The Indian officers agreed, and came along readily. They were then ordered to Mesopotamia. They again called upon the Indian officers, who said: 'We would sooner go anywhere else in

140.   Brigadier Edmund Costello VC CMG CVO DSO (1873–1949).

180

the world, but we will go, and we will not let the regiment down.' They were told to go to Bagdad, and were willing to go, though their frame of mind was the same. Curious position, he said, for: 'I have often seen men fighting on the frontier, who would as soon shoot the Sepoy beside them as the enemy in front.' He, too, was hopeful.

Then I went off to interrogate prisoners. It was tremendously hot. The prisoners were under a guard of Indians, and I found it hard to make the Indians understand my few words of Hindustani. The morale of the prisoners (wonderful men) seemed good. They said they weren't tired of the war and that they didn't think of disobeying orders, for that would be awful and would mean chaos. They thought what pleased God was going to happen, and they were inclined to think that that was victory for the Turks. They said twenty-seven guns had come up in the last eight days, 17cm. and 20cm. If that is the case they can shell us out of here.

I told the Admiral, and in the evening we walked. We met General Gorringe who said that he could make sure of relieving Townshend if we had ten days more. I am tremendously sorry for these men here. Last year the God of battles was on our side. We ought not to have won, by any law of odds or strategy, at Shaiba, at Ctesiphon, or Nasryah, but we did. They won against everything, and now the luck has turned. They have brought Indian troops to fight on holy soil for things that mean nothing to them. They have been hopelessly outnumbered by the Turks. They have been starved of everything, from food to letters, not to speak of high explosives. They have been through the most ghastly heat and the most cruel cold, and they are still cheerful. I have never seen a more friendly lot than these men here. They have always got something cheerful to say when you meet them. The weather has changed and it's very fine, with a beautiful wind and clear skies, but there are no scents, like in Gallipoli of thyme and myrtle. It's a limitless bare plain, green and sometimes brown mud, covered by an amazing mixture of men and creatures: horses and mules and buffaloes, Highlanders, Soudanese and Devons, Arabs and Babus. Camp fires spring up, somehow, at night by magic. We generally have a bombardment most days, but no shells round us.

Monday, April 17th, 1916. HMS Waterfly. Harris is Captain. While we were having breakfast this morning a German aeroplane flew over and bombed us ineffectually. Bombs fell a couple of hundred yards away in camp, not doing any damage, but they'll get us sometime, as we are a fine target, three boats together.

Tuesday, April 18th, 1916. HMS Waterfly. Last night the Admiral went to Amara. He left Jack Marriott, Philip Neville, Dick Bevan and me here. There was no work down there and a lot here. Last night we did well, took about 250 prisoners and the Bunds that are essential to us. If the Turks have these and want to, they can flood the country to the extent of making manoeuvring impossible. There was peace yesterday at the crimson sunset. Then after that came the tremendous fight. Guns and flares blazed all along the line. Now comes the news that we have lost the Bunds and the eight guns we had taken. The position is not clear. We are said to have retaken most of the positions this morning.

The prisoners'; morale here is much better than in Gallipoli. I asked an Arab if he was glad to be a prisoner. He said that he was sorry, because his own people might think that he hadn't fought well, but that he was glad not to have to go on fighting for the Germans. Jack Marriott wrote for me while I translated. The prisoners could not or would not tell us anything much about the condition of the river. This morning I had an experience. I walked out through tremendous heat to where the last batch of officer prisoners were guarded in a tent. As I came up, I heard loud wranglin, and saw the prisoners being harangued by a fierce black-bearded officer. I said: 'Who here talks Turkish?' and a grizzled old Kurd said: 'Some of us talk Kurdish and some Arabic, but we all talk Turkish.' I picked out Black-beard and took him apart from the others, whom I saw he had been bullying. He was a schoolmaster and a machine-gunner, and fierce beyond words. He began by saying sarcastically that he would give me all the information I wanted. 'You have failed at Gallipoli,' he said. 'We hold you up at Salonica, and you are only visitors at . I do not mind how much I tell you, because I know we are going to win.'

I answered rather tartly that it was our national habit to be defeated at the beginning of every war and to win in the end, and that we should go on, if it took us ten years. 'Ah, then,' he said, 'you will be fighting Russia.' I did not like the way this conversation was going, and said to him: 'Do you know the thing that your friends the Germans have done? They have offered Persia to Russia. How do you like that?' 'The question is,' he said, 'how do you like it?' He then said that he was sick of the word 'German,' that Turkey was not fighting for the Germans, but to get rid of the capitulations. He said they had four Austrian motor-guns of 24cm. coming in a few days. I congratulated him. In the end he became more friendly, but I got nothing out of him. One prisoner had a series of fits: I think it was fright. He got all right when he was given water and food. The river has given another great sigh and risen a foot and a half. We have crossed over from the right to the left bank. It's a black, thundery day. Much depends on to-day and to-night.

Good Friday, April 21st, 1916. HMS Waterfly. I have had no time to write these last days. This morning is a beautiful morning, with a fresh north wind. When we first came here Townshend was supposed to be able to hold out until the 12th. Now the 27th April is the last date. All the reports that we have been getting from the Turks are bad. Masses more men and guns coming up, heavy calibre guns. Still, Townshend is getting some food and money. The *Julnar* is to go up in a few days, when the moon is waning. It looks perfectly hopeless. I tried to find out whether there was a barrier across the river but Costello objected to this as he thought the prisoners might be able to send word to the Turks. I realized the danger, but it is essential to get all possible information. General Browne, generally an ass, agreed on this. Leachman is trying to get it from the Arabs which is really more dangerous. Costello is chief of the Intelligence here, a capital fellow.

The Royal Indian Marine, freed from the obstruction of India, seem to have done pretty well. A lot of the boats and barges sent here have been sunk on the way. The Admiralty goes on building these river Fly boats like anything. The *Mantis*, with Bernard

Buxton[141] captain, draws 5 feet and was intended for the Danube in the days when we were going to have taken Constantinople. On Wednesday, the 18th, we fired a good deal from the *Waterfly*. We are not well situated for firing as we have to fire across hospitals, and if they are shelled we have only ourselves to blame.

The Dorsets and Norfolks, the Oxfords and the Devons, have done the most splendid fighting. Twenty-two Dorsets saved the whole situation at Ahwaz. Harris, the captain of this boat, who is only twenty-five, has been through all this. He was the first up here, with Leachman. It's awfully bad luck on Townshend, being shut up again, the second time counting Chitral. He consults a Napoleonic dictionary at all crises. Since the siege of Chitral he has always worked eight hours a day at his profession. Harris is a good fellow but rather spoilt by everyone saying that he is a great character. Batson the second-in-command was a stockbroker, a quiet fellow, very bored with the war and the Tigris.

On Wednesday there was a tremendous fire. It sounded like a nearer Helles. The Turks are three miles from us. They lollop down mines that go on the bank, but this morning one was found close by the ship. I examined a Turk this morning, who said that three Army Corps were coming up under Mehemed Ali Pasha. I asked him if they could outflank us on the Hai, to try and turn this place into a second Kut. 'That,' he said, 'has always been my opinion.'

Yesterday, the 20th, I went to HQ in the morning, then talked to Dick and got maps revised and borrowed a horse for the afternoon from Percy Herbert, and got another from Costello for Bevan. (Here I should explain that I had promised my friend Bevan, the sailor, to take him up into the front-line trenches. He had never been in a front trench before, and was determined to see what it was like.)

Diary. General Gillman gave Bevan and me luncheon. Then Bevan and I rode out to the camp of the 18th Division, where I found Brownrigg[142], now become a Colonel, with malaria.

141. Commander Bernard Buxton DSO RN (1882–1923).
142. Lieutenant-General Sir Douglas Brownrigg KCB CB DSO (1886–1946).

I congratulated and condoled. I asked if we could get into the front trench, and Colonel Hillard said it was unhealthy. Bevan said that didn't matter, and I asked exactly how unhealthy. Hillard said that there were no communication trenches and we should have machine-gun fire at 80 yards. No rations being sent up till nightfall. We walked first down a communication trench which we had to leave and then across the open to Crofton's Tower which was an observation post in the flat land, of mud walls and a few sandbags; they had dug down about six feet into the ground. The Turks were about 800 to 900 yards away. It is incredible that they leave this place standing or that they allow people to walk about in the way in which they do. It couldn't have been done in Gallipoli. There are other observation posts behind; simply a ladder rising from the flat land and men on it. Going out we passed quail and partridge, and wild flowers, also we came on the smells of the battlefield. When we were at Crofton's Post a furious bombardment by us began. I cursed myself for not having asked what the plans of the afternoon were going to be. Bevan was delighted. Shells rushed overhead from all sides. I heard the scream of two premature bursts and saw the raised filthy great columns of heaving smoke. It was a wonderful picture; the brilliant light of the afternoon, the desert cut by the river, and the gleam of the gun flashes with the smouldering smoke columns. They said that two nights ago the Gurkhas had not broken. They had used all their ammunition, and as many Turkish rifles as they could get, and had then fought with their kukris. At one place an unfortunate mistake had happened. We mistook some Indians for Turks and we bombarded each other. We went back almost deafened by our own guns. I expected a heavy Turkish return every minute, which without a scrap of cover would have been unpleasant; but beyond the ticking of a machine gun nothing happened. Maude said his men had been tired and tired to death, but he thought they were more rested now. His casualties had been heavy with nineteen officers killed and wounded in the last two days, simply trench work, no attack. He said you can't go on doing that with the new Army. It strains regulars if they lose their officers like that, the new Army can't stand it.

The more one sees of this foul country, the more convinced does one become that we are a seafaring people who have been lured to disaster by this river. These lines are quite untenable without two railways, one across to Nasriyah and one up the river to Bagdad. At the present moment, we can be cut off if they can put in guns anywhere down the river and sink a couple of our boats, or one in the narrows, the channel is then blocked. To prevent this we ought to have a patrol up and down the river. All this depends on having a policy and we have none. Lawrence[143] arrived at Wadi on Wednesday. He said Cox had no policy and did not mean to have a policy. I heard from John Kennaway yesterday at Sheikh Saad, asking me to go there. No news obtainable about poor Bobby Palmer[144]. There is not much doubt he must have been killed. I am very sad for his people.

Easter Sunday, April 23rd, 1916. HMS Greenfly. A curious morning, with the whole of Pushti Kuh standing blue and clear. The last two foreigners who visited that place were given the choice of embracing Islam or of being pushed over the precipice. They chose the precipice.

Yesterday morning we attacked. The 19th Brigade, the Black Watch, the 20th and the 28th. We took two trenches, but were driven back to our own. I was sent post-haste to HQ for news. There was a great sand-storm and men and artillery going through it like phantoms. Overhead it was lurid. One could hardly breathe for the sand. High columns of it rushed across the desert. The repulse looks as if the end's very close. I came back to the Admiral and was sent back again. This time they said there was a truce, and if the Admiral would give permission, I was to go to the front at once. I came back and found the Admiral and went on shore. I got a horse and rode up to the front as fast as I could, passing a good many dead and wounded. I went to General Young-husband[145] and asked if I could be of any use to him. He said the truce was ending. The Turks had pushed out white flags, which he

143.   Lieutenant-Colonel T. E. Lawrence CB DSO (1888–1935).
144.   Maj the Hon Robert Palmer (1889–1916). Son of the Earl of Selborne and a cousin of AH by marriage. Killed at the Battle of Um El Hannah on 21st June.
145.   Major-General Sir George Younghusband (1859–1944).

said was very decent of them. We had done the same. They were now taking our kit, and his staff were keen to shoot at them. I asked him to give them notice, which he did. He talked about possible terms for Townshend and whether the Turks would let him and his men go out with the honours of war and be on parole until peace. I said I could see no *quid pro quo*, and even if one existed we couldn't use it because of our ignorance of the Russian situation. He said he had meant to attack across 600 yards but the water had narrowed our front to 300. The Turkish trenches were half full of water, and many of our men fell and got their rifles filled with mud. The Turks attacked again at once. He said there weren't many troops who would do that when a brigade like the 19th had been through them. Not much left of the 19th. Beautiful men, they were. I talked to a lot of them these last days. He said as far as he was concerned there was no Arab question. He gave orders to shoot every Arab on sight, so we weren't bothered with them.

I rode back on a horse that was always falling down. In the evening I crossed the river with the Admiral and rode up to the front with Beach. There was shelling going on, but nothing came near. The river was gorgeous in the sunset. Overhead the sand-grouse flew. We talked about the future. It seems to me that if we have got to retreat 130 miles it's less bad for prestige to do it in one go. The Politicals' point of view is that you should not retreat at all, but that, of course, has got to depend on military consider-ations. The Soldiers' point of view is that you should not do your retreat in one go, because you do not kill so many of the enemy as if you fall back from one position to another; but then, I suppose, that cuts both ways. None of these soldiers have had any decor-ations since the beginning of the war. One of them said to me it made them unhappy, because they felt that they hadn't done their duty. It's an infernal shame. He was wounded and I asked him if he had gone on leave. He said: 'Not much! I should have lost my job'; which would have been a pleasure to a good many men. Lawrence is here, down with fever. Nunn also has had fever these last days. The atmosphere makes shooting difficult. Yesterday the Turks shot quite a lot at a mirage, splashing their bullets in the marsh. We often do the same. Curiously enough, I believe that we won the battle of Shaiba by virtue of a mirage. We saw a lot of Turks marching up against our position, and fired at them; these Turks were phantoms of men miles away; but it happened to be the only road by which they could bring up ammunition, and our firing prevented that. To-night the *Julnar* goes up the river on her journey. She has less speed than they thought.

For various reasons I have barely mentioned the *Julnar* until now, though she had been very much in our thoughts. The *Julnar* was a river boat, and for some days past she had been preparing to set out upon her splendid, tragic mission. In her lay the last hope of General Townshend and his gallant force. Her freight was food, intended to prolong the resistance of the garrison until the relieving force was sufficiently strong to drive back the Turks and enter Kut. The writer of this diary has many heroic pictures in his mind, but no more heroic picture and no more glowing memory than the little *Julnar* steaming slowly up the flaming Tigris to meet the Turkish Army and her fate. Her Captains were Lieutenant Firman[146] RN, and Lieutenant Commander Cowley[147] RNVR, of Lynch's Company, who had spent a long life navigating the River Tigris. When Admiral Wemyss called for volunteers, every man volunteered, for what was practically certain death. I asked again but was refused. Lieutenant Firman and Lieutenant Commander Cowley were both killed and both received posthumous VCs.

Diary. April 23rd. HMS Greenfly. We are alongside the Mantis. I am sleeping in Firman's cabin. He is down-stream, but he comes up to-night. Many men badly wounded yesterday, but all as cheerful as could be; one man with three bullets in his stomach, full of talk and oaths. Fifteen of the Dorsets have died in the nearest hospital and have been buried close by.

This afternoon an Easter Service was held on board. The Padre made a good sermon three minutes long. It was a wonderful sight – the desert covered with our graves, mirages in the distance and the river glowing in the sun. At the end of the service the *Julnar*

---

146.   Lieutenant Humphrey Firman VC RN (1886–1916).
147.   Lieutenant Commander Charles Cowley VC RNVR (1872–1916).

arrived. Firman is an attractive good-looking fellow. King, whom I met last year in Alexandretta, whither he had marched from Bagdad, is also here. When Buxton told the men of the hundred to one chance of the *Julnar*'s getting through, they volunteered to a man. Gieve waistcoats are being served out; the cannon's sounding while they are loading the *Julnar* and the Black Watch are playing on the bagpipes close by. Overhead go the sand-grouse, calling and the river and the desert wind are sighing. It's all like a dream. Even if she does get through, I don't believe we can relieve Kut. The Turks will have time to consolidate their position and we shan't be sent enough men from home to take them. If this attempt fails, I suppose we shall fall back to Sheikh Saad. I see three points: (1) Political. Don't retreat. (2) Military. You've got to retreat, occupying as many positions as possible, in order to attrition the enemy. (3) If you do this last, you give the Turks the chance of saying they have beaten you in a number of battles. Probably retreat as little as possible is the best. A retreat may be more disastrous to us than the loss of Kut. While we hold Sheikh Saad, it's difficult for them to outflank us on the right bank, and while we have the Vali of Pushti Kuh with us, they ought not to be able to get to Ahwaz. One wonders if they realize the supreme importance of at home and that if we no longer hold it we do not hold the Indian Ocean.

Monday, April 24th, 1916. HMS Dragonfly. Firman came last night, and I sat next to him at dinner. A nice fellow but nervous and excitable. The *Julnar* could not start; she starts to-night. She had been held up by the bridge of boats at Sheikh Saad. The Commandant had refused to break it and the *Julnar* arrived here too late. I felt this might be my fault for not having seen to this in liaison work, but it is very difficult: if one worries people about that sort of obvious detail which is their job they are furious, if you don't, this is the sort of thing that happens. To have made a success of this the Admiral ought to have turned it over to the Flag Captain to discuss with the military. Have partially but unostentatiously prepared the boat at Amara, sent her up here to be finally fortified in a night, then drawn a circle round this place to prevent spies carrying information and let her go. She starts to-night. I don't think much chance of getting through, but with luck the men ought to be saved. I said to the Admiral in no case could Kut be saved even if she got through, because we shouldn't be given the men to take the new position the Turks would make in the next three weeks. I also think that the fall of Kut may bring the Government down at home.

I went ashore this morning and saw Leachman, then Colonel Beach. The flies are awful; one black web of them this morning; in one's hair and eyes and mouth, in one's bath and shaving-water, in one's tea and in one's towel. It's a great nuisance being without Edward and having to do everything oneself, besides one's work. It destroys all joy in war.

Tuesday, April 25th, 1916. *HMS Greenfly.* A year ago to-day we landed at Anzac. To-day is the day of the fall of Kut, though the surrender may not be made for some time. Last night the *Julnar* left. I saw old Cowley, an old friend. He is to pilot her. He has been thirty-three years on this river. He is a proper Englishman. He laughed and chaffed with Philip Neville and me on the *Julnar* before starting. Firman was very glad to have got the job, and felt the responsibility. Everybody wanted to go. The sailors were moved. No cheers were allowed. They pushed off, almost stationary, into the river, that was a glory of light with the graceful mehailahs in an avenue on both sides of it, with masts and rigging a filigree against the gorgeous sunset. The faint bagpipes and the desert wind were the only music at their going. The Admiral told me to be ready to go out at any moment.

This morning Colonel Beach came aboard and told me to hold myself in readiness. He proposed going out to see the Turks with Lawrence and myself. He talked about terms. It's a very difficult thing to get terms when one side holds all the cards. If I was a Turk I should ask for unconditional surrender, treating Townshend very well as a gallant and honourable gentleman, but warning him that the future treatment of him and his men would depend on whether he destroyed his guns, etc. Beach said we had to telegraph home, and talked of money possibilities. I didn't think that possible. I think we ought to try to prevent the Arabs being hung by the Turks, but my opinion is that Townshend would make much better terms for himself than we will get for him here.

The *Julnar* has grounded above the Sinn position. Nothing is known of what happened to the crew.

Wilfred Peek[148] turned up here this afternoon, looking prosperous, and having seen John Kennaway down the stream. We have no terms to offer the Turks except money, general or local peace, or the evacuation of territory. I do not think the first is any good. We cannot offer the second because of ourselves and of Russia. The third might be all right, if it was not beyond Amarah. I hope in these negotiations we do not meet a Prussian Turk in Khalil.

After lunch I met Captain Potter of the 6th Jats. In the last attack this had happened: A corporal had gone mad, and after rolling in filth, had come down the trench with a bomb in each hand, screaming that he was after Arabs. The parapet was low and there was much shrapnel and bullets. He threw the bombs into the middle of them, killing one and wounding the Colonel; Potter and the others were knocked out. They collared him, who had got a mammoth strength. Then the attack followed. Potter went as soon as he recovered. They had 600 yards to go under machine-gun fire, up to their knees in mud. The Turks were in the third trench; the first and second were filled with mud. Then the Turks put out a white flag, which suited us very well, as it allowed our men in the Turkish trenches to get away, which otherwise they could not have done. He thought that the Turks did it because they wanted to bring up reinforcements. He now commands a battalion of 84, all that are left of 650 men. He had been in practically every fight. He said they had reached the limits of human endurance. He had three officers, including himself, left. The Black Watch had been wiped out twice, and other regiments simply annihilated. I told him that I thought there would be no more attacks. He said a Turkish prisoner, a friend of his, had said to him: 'Let's have a truce and both kill the Arabs.' Beach says there is no question of

148.   Sir Wilfred Peek, a friend of AH's from Devon and General Townshend's ADC.

191

going out to-day. I see no possibility of terms unless the Turks have got some *arrière-pensèe*. I went our shooting sand-grouse.

Wednesday, April 26th, 1916. HMS Mantis. I am writing in great haste, till the sun goes down, as the mehailahs stream past on a river of fire, in the retreat that is slyly beginning.

The news from home is good and bad. The Admiral read me two Government telegrams re. surrender last night. They are hopelessly optimistic about terms. Gorringe is not to make staying, retreating, etc, part of the conditions. We are to have another 5,000 men but they are to be used defensively. There are other things offered to the Turks. We must, if we can, save the Arabs with Townshend. This morning a telegram was read to me offering my and Lawrence's services to Townshend. He is to carry on his own negotiations, I am to do what I can with the Turks. I read his latest telegrams: pathetic, the rather ostentatious mixture of military erudition mixed up with famine and the stinks of Kut. I hope he hasn't mentioned my name to the Turks. He wired to Peek asking him to give me his valise. I suggested taking Peek as far as we could with provisions to follow if they would give him a safe conduct. I hoped to be able to persuade them to do this. I am nervous about our own safe conduct. If Townshend doesn't make it clear that it's a return ticket, we may be kept. I talked it over with Lake at some length this morning. He thinks that we are safe here or at Sheikh Saad; but of course the Turks may come down, plant a gun anywhere along the river and sink a ship. Burmester, Neville and Miller went off this morning with Dick Bevan. I have to enquire about *Julnar*, exchange of Turkish and English lady prisoners, and twenty-five civil Turkish prisoners. Also about Bobby Palmer.

Friday, April 28th, 1916. HMS Mantis. For the last two days I have been standing by to go to Kut, constantly dressing up for it and then undressing for the heat. A wave of great heat has come and the air is black with flies. Practically no firing, though they tried to shell us yesterday and an aeroplane dropped bombs near here. We have got very little to bargain with, as far as the Turks are concerned, practically only the exchange of prisoners. The operations of this force are not to be reckoned with as a bargaining

192

asset. We are not to retire to save Townshend. Yesterday Townshend saw Khalil at 10 a.m., whom he liked. Khalil said that Townshend would have as great a reception in Turkey as Osman Pasha in Russia, but he demanded unconditional surrender, or that Townshend should march out of Kut. This last is equivalent to an unconditional surrender, and Townshend's men are too weak. We are all sorry for them. Townshend wired privately, but *en clair*, to Wilfrid Peek to tell him to tell his wife that his one desire was to leave the army after the war, that he had been disgracefully treated, and was there by no fault of his own, and that captivity would kill him.

Yesterday morning General Lake sent for me, and talked about the Turks. I said it was quite clear to me that the Turks would procrastinate, if it was only from force of habit, and the end of that must mean unconditional surrender. General Lake was calm. He had been made responsible for things for which other people are answerable. Townshend has telegraphed to say that he has only food for two more days and that Khalil has referred to Enver for better terms. Lake said quite simply that he had expected to be relieved after the last failure and replaced by Birdwood. He said throughout this campaign in India, we had been 60,000 rifles short. Later after lunch a telegram came to Wilfrid from Townshend. In this he told him to tell Repington[149] that it was not his fault that he was there. He said that he was disgusted at the way he was treated and that it was not going to end there. He has had no word of praise through all this time. Eleven honours given for his battles, and forty-six to Gorringe for his 'insignificant' fight at Kurna. He ended, 'show my telegrams to Admiral Wemyss'. I said I had better tell the Admiral alone. This I did. He refused to see the telegrams or Peek. I quite agreed. I told Peek to go to the Army Commander and show him the telegram, and say that the strain had been too much for Townshend and that he, the Army Commander, must send him a telegram to cheer and console him as much as possible. Townshend is very anxious that

149.   Colonel Charles Repington (1858–1925). Military Correspondent for *The Times*.

we should negotiate from his side. I think it ought to come from him. I still think Townshend would get better terms for himself than we shall get for him. He has made a desperately gallant fight of it, and his position has not been taken. Lack of food makes him surrender, not force of arms. We, the relieving force, have been checked by the Turks, but I suppose all these men, Lake, Townshend and Nixon, will be made scapegoats. I have just been over this morning and seen his last telegram. In this he warns us to be prepared in case the Turks attack. He says he cannot move out and that if he did get his weak men to move the Turks would not have enough tents for him there, or transport to Bagdad, and that there will be a terrible drama and that 25 per cent of the sick and wounded will die. He says we must insist on the force being paroled and going to India; but we are not in the position to insist on anything at all. I am very sorry about his telegrams to Peek. The Turkish wireless may very well have caught them up, and the splendour of his defence be covered with shoddy jealousy if the telegram is published in Berlin. But there can be no doubt his mind is touched. One has seen enough men and soldiers go off their heads or be affected by shock.

Sunday, April 30th, 1916. HMS Mantis. The Events of Saturday: Yesterday morning Colonel Beach came to the *Mantis* at seven and took me off. We rode across the bridge to General Younghusband's HQ. Nothing that I have ever seen or dreamed of came up to the flies. They hatched out until they were almost the air. They were in myriads. The horses were half mad. The flies were mostly tiny. They rolled up in little balls when one passed one's hand across one's sweating face. They were on your eyelids and lashes and in your lips and nostrils. We could not speak for them, and could hardly see.

We went into General Younghusband's tent. The flies, for some reason, stayed outside. He put a loose net across the door of the tent. They were like a visible fever, shimmering in the burning light all round. Inside his tent you did not breathe them; outside you could not help taking them in through the nose and the mouth. We left General Younghusband and went on to the front trenches, where we met Colonel Aylsmee. There Lawrence joined us. We three went out of the trenches with a white flag, and walked a couple of hundred yards or so ahead, where we waited, with all the battlefield smells round us. It was all a plain, with the river to the north and the place crawling with huge black beetles and singing flies, that have been feeding on the dead. After a time a couple of Turks came out. I said: 'We have got a letter to Khalil.' This they wanted to take from us, but we refused to give it up, and they sent an orderly back to ask if we might come in to the Turkish lines. Meanwhile we talked amiably. One of the Turkish officers, a Cretan, had left school five years ago and had been in five wars. He reckoned that he had been in 200 attacks, not counting scraps with brigands and *comitadjis*. The Turks showed us their medals, and we were rather chagrined at not being able to match them, but they and we agreed that we should find the remedy for that in a future opportunity.

Several hours passed. It was very hot. I was hungry, having had no breakfast. Again they asked us to give up our letter. I said that our orders were to deliver it in person and, as soldiers, they knew what orders were, but that Colonel Beach would give the letter up if their CO would guarantee that we should see Khalil Pasha. This took a long time. The Turks sent for a tent. A few rifle shots went off from our lines, but Beach went back and stopped it. The Turks sent for oranges and water, and we ate and drank. We had to refill these bottles from the Tigris, and up and down the banks were a lot of dead bodies from shot-wounds and cholera. After some time they agreed to Beach's proposal. We were blindfolded and we went in a string of hot hands to the trenches of the Turks. When it was plain going the Turks, who talked French, called: 'Franchement, en avant,' and when it was bad going, over trenches, 'Yavash Dikatet.' We marched a long way through these trenches, banging against men and corners, and sweating something cruel. Beyond the trenches we went for half an hour, while my handkerchief became a wet string across my eyes. Then we met Bekir Sami Bey. He was a very fine man and very jolly, something between an athlete and old King Cole. He lavished hospitality upon us, coffee and *yoghurt*, and begged us to say if there was anything more he could get us, while we sat and streamed with perspiration. He told us how he had loved England and still did. He was fierceness and friendship incarnate. He said it was all Grey's fault, and glorified the Crimea. Why couldn't we have stuck to that policy? Then, as we were going off, I said that he would not insist on our eyes being bandaged, showing him my taut, wet rag of a pocket-handkerchief. He shouted with laughter and said: 'No, no; you have chosen soldiering, a very hard profession. You have got to wear that for miles, and you will have to ride across ditches.' Then he shook hands and patted us on the shoulder.

My eyes were bound, and I got on a horse that started bucking because of the torture of the flies. The Turk was angry and amused. I heard him laughing and swearing: 'This is perfectly monstrous. Ha, ha! He'll be off. Ha, ha! This is a reproach to us.' I was then given another horse that was not much of an improvement, and off we three went with a Turkish officer, Ali Shefket, and a guard. Lawrence had hurt his knee and could not ride. He got off and walked, a Turkish officer being left with him. Colonel Beach and I went on. Then our eyes were unbound, though as a matter of fact this was against the orders I had heard given. The Turk Ali Shefket and I talked. He knew no French. He said to me: 'Formerly the Arabs would not take our bank-notes; now they take them. Once upon a time they would not take *medjids;* two days ago they took them. To what do you put that down?' I knew he meant the fall of Kut, but it was not said maliciously. I said that I put it down to the beautiful character of the marsh Arabs, 'yerli bourda beule' ('here the native are thus'). He laughed and agreed. We passed formidable herds of horses and mules, our road a sand-track. The escort rode ahead of us. The heat was very great, but we galloped. The Turks we met thought that we were prisoners. They saluted sometimes at strict attention, sometimes with a grin, and later our Indians were told in return to salute the Turkish officers, who looked at them as black as thunder.

At last we came to Khalil's camp, a single round tent, a few men on motor cycles coming and going, horses here and there and the camp in process of shifting. Later on, Khalil said that the flies bored him and that he meant to camp beside the river. Colonel

Beach asked me to start talking and get on terms. I said to Beach that I thought we had better begin with the unimportant points. I said to Khalil, whose face I remembered: 'Where was it that I met your Excellency last?' And he said: 'At a dance at the British Embassy.' Khalil, throughout the interview, was polite. He was quite a young man for his position, I suppose about thirty-five, and a fine man to look at – lion-taming eyes, a square chin and a mouth like a trap. Kiazim Bey, who was also courteous, but silent, was his CGS. These were the points to be discussed:

> a. *The Exchange of English and Turkish ladies, plus our surrender of twenty-five Turkish civil officials.*
> b. *Our sick and wounded to be brought down from Kut.*
> c. *The exchange of sound prisoners.*
> d. *What happened to the* Julnar?
> e. *Terms: guns, men and money.*
> f. *Permission to send up drugs.*
> g. *An appeal, on various grounds, neither to hang nor to persecute the civil population of Kut.*

The Turks had taken the English ladies in Bagdad. Their husbands were sent across to Alexandretta, where I met them last year; some of them, worse luck, are now prisoners again. We had Turkish ladies at Amara and also twenty-five Turkish civilian officials. This exchange was arranged. They were to meet each other at Beyrout.

I went on to speak of the *Julnar*. He said that there had been two killed on the *Julnar*. He was afraid it was the two Captains. He was sorry. It made Beach and me very sad. Poor, nervous, gallant Firman, he had had forty-eight hours' leave in four years, and fine old Cowley, a splendid fellow. Well, if you are to be killed trying to relieve Townshend it is not a bad end.

After that, I began talking of the treatment of the Arab population in Kut. I asked Khalil to put himself in the position of Townshend. I said that I knew that he could not help feeling for Townshend, whose lifelong study of soldiering was brought to nought through siege and famine, by no fault of his own. I said that the Arabs with Townshend had done what weak people always do: they had trimmed their sails, and because they had feared him, they had given him their service. If they suffered, Townshend would feel that he was responsible. Khalil said: 'There is no need to worry about Townshend. He's all right.' He added that the Arabs are Turkish subjects, not British, and that therefore their fate was irrelevant, but that their fate would depend upon what they did in the future, not upon what they had done in the past. We asked him for some assurance that there would be no hanging or persecution. He would not give this assurance, for the reasons already stated, but said that it was not his intention to do anything to the Arabs. Then Lawrence turned up.

We discussed the question of our sick and wounded. He said that he would send 500 of them down the river, but he required Turkish soldiers in exchange. Beach and I said that he gained by having sound men instead of wounded, to which he agreed. He wanted us to send boats to fetch these men; he said that he was sending them drugs, doctors and food. We shied away from the *Julnar* because we felt he would say that her stores had been burnt or destroyed. We asked him for the exchange of our prisoners in Kut against the Ottomans we had taken. He at first said that he would exchange English against Turk, and Arab against Indian, neither of whom were any use. I said that some Arabs were splendid fellows and very brave. He then pulled out the list of the Turkish prisoners of ours, and went through the Arab regiments, swearing. He said: 'Perhaps one of our men in ten is weak or cowardly, but one in a hundred Arabs is brave. Look! These brutes have surrendered to you because they were a bally lot of cowards. What are you to do with men like that? You can send them back to me if you like, but I have already condemned them to death. I should like to have them to hang.' That ended that. We must see that Arabs are not sent back by mistake.

He then said that he would like us to send ships up to transport Townshend and his men to Bagdad; otherwise they would have to march, which would be hard on them. He promised to let us have these ships back again. Colonel Beach said to me, not for translation, that this was impossible. We have already insufficient transport. He told me to say that he would refer this to General Lake. We then talked about terms and the exchange of the sick and wounded. On this, Khalil said he would refer to Enver or Constantinople as to whether sound men at Kut would be exchanged against the Turkish prisoners in Cairo and India. He did not think it likely. He was going to give us the wounded in any case, at once. He would trust us to give their equivalent.

Guns: Townshend had destroyed the guns. Khalil was angry and showed it. He said he had a great admiration for Townshend, but he was obviously disappointed at not getting the guns, on which he had counted. He said: 'I could have prevented it by bombarding, but I did not want to.' Later, one of his officers said to me: 'The Pasha's a most honourable man; all love him. He was first very pleased and said that Townshend should go free. After that something happened, I don't know what, and now Townshend will be an honoured prisoner at Stamboul.'

I said that the third condition we had offered was financial support for the civilians of Kut. I said we had offered one or two million, purposely adding on one million on my own. This he brushed aside, and again returned to his proposal that we should send up boats to transport Townshend's sick and wounded to Bagdad. Beach said we could not look at it, we simply had not enough ships for ourselves at the moment and no reserve supplies. This, of course, he said to me. I then spoke of the generally difficult situation and asked him if all this was possible without an armistice. He said very strongly indeed that he was entirely against an armistice, and that he wanted his assurance given to General Lake that even if there was a 'general offensive', the ships could still come and go. Beach told me to say that we also had no idea of an armistice. He yawned, I thought more rudely than negligently, and I said the heat made us all sleepy. He apologized and said he had had much work to do. He had seen Townshend that morning. He was all right, but had had slight fever.

Our final understanding with Khalil was that we were to notify him when we were sending up boats, so that he might clear the river. He laughed and said that he had forgotten all about the mines. I laughed and said I had remembered them, but had not liked to speak of them.

We ended with mutual compliments; I told him that we admired his name as a soldier and his chivalry, and that we thought the Turks clean and splendid fighters. He answered with appropriate compliments, and we said good-bye to him and Kiazim Bey. He called me aside and said that he hoped we should be comfortable that night, and that we were to ask for all we wanted. He was glad to continue an acquaintance that had been begun at the Embassy in Constantinople on the occasion of a dance. We rode away; all the Turks saluting. I talked to Ali Jenab Bey who now seemed a fast friend, and said how angry the Germans would be to see us together. Our final understanding with Khalil was that we were to notify him when we were sending up boats so that he might clear the river.

We rode on, and before sunset, came to the Turkish camp. There the three of us sat down and, as far as we could for the flies, wrote reports.

The Turks gave us their tent, though I should have preferred to sleep out. They gave us their beds and an excellent dinner. We all sat and smoked after dinner for a few minutes under the stars, with camp fires burning round us. The Turks and I talked like old friends. Muezzin called from different places and the sound of flutes and singing came through the dusk. Then Colonel Beach decided that I had better stay and go to Kut, where I was to meet him and Lawrence, who would come up with the boats to take our prisoners away. I didn't believe that Khalil would accept this sort of liaison business. Beach wanted to go straight back, but would not let Lawrence or me. We pointed out that, if he got shot in the dark by our people, it would upset everything.

I dictated a French letter to Lawrence, asking for permission for me to stay and go across to Kut. I cannot think how he wrote the letter. The whole place was one smother of small flies, attracted by the candle. They put it out three times. Beach and I kept them off Lawrence while he wrote. We got an answer at about two in the morning. Khalil said that it was not necessary. All this happened on April 29th.

200

To-day. April 30th. We left at 4.30 this morning, and this time rode all the way with unbandaged eyes. We ended up on the river bank amongst dead bodies. We walked across to our front line and Colonel Beach telephoned to HQ. While he was doing this a Turkish white flag went up and we went out again. After several palavers, Ali Shefket came out and said that the river was clear of mines. Beach and Lawrence went back to HQ.

Our boat could go up if it arrived by 2 o'clock in the afternoon. I, with the Cretan, the man of a hundred fights, Ali Shefket and others, went across. A fierce bearded Colonel came out, arrogant and insolent, talking German. He boasted that he knew Greek, but when I talked to him in Greek, he could not answer. He then harangued me in bad German, talking rot. I said, in Turkish: 'Neither you nor I can talk good German, therefore let us talk Turkish.' 'Yes,' said the other Turks; 'it's a much better language.'

The ship tarried. At 5 o'clock in the evening she was in sight, but she could not have arrived for another hour. It was decided that we could do nothing that night and that she would have to be put off until next day. A monstrous beetle, the size of half a crown, crawled up my back. The Turks were as horrified as I.

Monday, May 1st, 1916. HMS Mantis. I came back last night. I saw General Lake this morning to report. I told him I had the strongest instinct that Khalil had got something up his sleeve. I didn't think that it was a knavish trick or that he would use his permission for the evacuation of our wounded to cloak a manoeuvre, but I felt certain he had some near thing in view. A letter came in from Khalil. The ships could go. He wanted boats to send the prisoners to Bagdad, and 20,000 tons of coal as some of his ships had been sunk. General Money first proposed to reply that we needed our ships as we were bringing up reinforcements, which I thought a good answer, but Money finally rejected it, and left it that His Excellency would understand that we ourselves needed all our boats these days. Beach went up this morning with two boats, but they stopped him at No Man's Land.

Tuesday, May 2nd, 1916. HMS Mantis. Last night I went on the P23 bound for Kut with a rather tiresome Padre whom Beach asked e to get through. It rained and blew in the night and was uncomfortable on deck. I got up at 4.00 and we started at 4.30. They opened the bridge of boats for us. A launch followed for me, for I was to get off before entering neutral territory. At the Neutral Zone I found white flags and Major Anderson of the 19th Brigade, who seemed tired and nervous. All the way up there had been a sort of feeling of expectancy and uncanniness, from the Indians shading their eyes from the rising sun, and our own troops staring at us. There was something eerie in the air, and the curious spidery observation posts in that flat land heightened this atmosphere. Anderson said the Turks would allow the boats to go out. I telephoned to Beach who was leaving and he told me to do the best I could; also that he had telephoned about my going to India to see prisoners. I took a white flag and went out into No Man's Land and found the man I had talked to before, the Cretan's brother. I said: 'What does it mean? This is neither peace nor war.' He said it was our fellows shooting on the right bank, and there was quite enough shooting to make one feel uncomfortable. I said that Khalil had given me his word that the boats could go up, even if there was an offensive. This was telephoned to him. Then our men loosed off with a machine gun while I was talking. The Swine and the Cretan then came out to say they had done it, and later the Cretan alone to say that our boats could not go through until the others had returned from Kut. It might not be necessary. I gave him Bobby Palmer's photograph and asked him to read Ali Jenab's writing. He told me that Bobby Palmer was dead, very kindly and sadly. I went back again very tired, and found a number of burying parties which I stopped from going further. There were several bodies on the river bank that looked to me like cholera. There has, by the way, been 150 cases in the last three days. Then I shaved while the Turks looked on in the distance, and telephoned to Beach who was then leaving. He said 'bring the boats back', which I did, all four of them. The only other news is that the Turks have dug in below us at Sheikh Saad, so there is something more ahead. I expected that.

Wednesday, May 3rd, 1916. HMS Mantis. Oh, you foul land of Mesopotamia! This morning poor bodies raced by on the stream, and I have spent most of the day walking amongst the ruin of battle. I was sent a couple of messages and went ashore to see General

Brown and General Gorringe. They said that they wanted to know why our boats hadn't come, that the Turks had been shooting on the right and had sent out 200 men strong white-flag parties to bury the dead. I said I thought that it would be all right about the ships, and if nothing happened I could go and see Khalil himself to-morrow. The fact that they didn't want us to send more proved that they were playing the game, but I also thought that they would like to nag us into doing something indiscreet, and asked Gorringe to give orders that there should be no firing except under instructions while they had our hostages. He sent me off to see the Turks.

I rode fast through suffocating heat, with an Indian orderly. At the bridge I found our two ships, the *Sikhim* and the *Shaba*, which had come through from Kut. They were banking above the bridge, which was being mended. This altered the whole situation, since the General had sent me out to complain that they had not been let through, and I galloped back. After a talk at HQ, it was decided that I was only to thank Khalil.

I jumped the trenches and finally arrived at the main trench, where my horse stared down at a horrified circle, lunching. The circle said that no horses were allowed there and that none had ever been there, and that my horse, or rather Costello's, would be shot immediately by the Turks. So I went to General Peebles, who was lunching farther along in the same trenches, and he had her sent back. I then walked out with a white flag. Anderson wouldn't come; I don't know if was pique or nerves. I saw a couple of Turks. They wanted us to send up two ships to-morrow. I asked them not to send out the bearded Colonel and said I could not stand him, and they agreed. It was blazing hot; a Turkish officer and I sat out between the lines.

There is one incident not recorded in the diary that is, perhaps, worth mentioning, as it had a curious result that will find its place in the sequel to this journal, if it is ever published. On one of the occasions when I was talking to the Turks between the lines, a general fire started from the British and the Turkish trenches. The Turks, for the honour of their country, and I, for the honour of mine, pretended to ignore this fire, and we continued to discuss our business, but in the end the fire refused to be ignored, and, with loud curses, we fell upon the ground and there attempted to continue the discussion. I suggested to the Turks that the whole proceeding was lacking in dignity and that it would be better for each to retire to their own trenches and resume negotiations when circumstances were more favourable.

Next time I returned I was informed that one of the Turks had been hit whilst returning. I naturally said how sorry I was, and that I hoped they would not think it was a case of *mala fides*, as it might have happened to one of us, and wrote a note explaining my regret.

Diary. It was curious and bitter sitting in that peaceful field talking amicably with the Turks between the lines, with maize round us. The river murmured and the larks were singing, while the stiff clay held the knee-deep prints, like plaster of Paris, of the Black Watch and the others, who had charged across that foul field, when it had been a trap and a bog.

Thursday, May 4th, 1916. HMS Mantis. Very tired to-day. I rode back last night from the Turks, very fast. The flies made it impossible to go slow, horses couldn't breathe. At the bridge, I found that the traffic was going the other way and had to hold up an unfortunate brigade to get across, hating to do it.

I met Green Armitage, who had just come from Kut. He had got Townshend's three terriers, who barked like mad. He said that there were three Turkish officers on board the *Sikhim*, who were asking for me. I didn't know what to do, as I wanted to go to HQ, but dashed on board and found they were Ali Shefket and Mehmed Jemal and Salahedin Bey, inspector to the Agricultural Bank of Smyrna. Our people on board wanted me to stay. I told them I would come back. I saw the sick and wounded Indians being carried away, terribly emaciated. I reported at HQ, where, apparently, half a dozen entirely contradictory orders were being prepared for me. I then went back in a launch to the Turks, who were reported to be taking notes of our position from the bridge. On the *Sikhim* I found crowds of our officers with the Turks and a general jollification going on. I did not understand how or why they had been allowed to come down. All the Intelligence came along to see what the Turks could tell them. I was fed-up with the whole business, and disliked the Turks being on deck. I said to them: 'Of course, it's a pleasure to have you here, as guests, but we would much rather give you hospitality in London, for there we can show you everything, and, unfortunately, that's not the case here. So in future, if you please, Turkish officers will not accompany the boats down.' They agreed to that.

The same tiresome Padre, Clerk Gibson, came bumbling up again. I think he wanted to go to Kut for the adventure, and I had no sympathy, as he would have meant another mouth to feed. The Turks made no particular objection to his going, but they said there was already a clergyman there, so I told the Padre he could go if he liked, but that if he went he ought to stay and let the other chaplain come back, as the other had had all the hardships of the siege. He thought I was brutal, but cleared out and gave no more trouble. It seems to me, however, that he runs a fair risk, like the rest of us, of being made a prisoner.

I wish the Admiral was here. The Turks on board said that they had hung seven Arabs. I said that Khalil had said he had no intention of doing so. The Turks answered that these men were not natives but vagabonds. I felt Khalil meant to do it when I talked to him. It makes me angry. We talked of the future. I said it wouldn't be easy for Turkey to disassociate herself from Germany, even if she wanted to. They replied: 'How long did it take the Bulgars and Serbs to quarrel?' They said Khalil had sent special messages to me; and I asked them to return them and arrange that in case of necessity I should be able to get straight through to him. I didn't sleep much. This morning I went up with them to Sanayat, where Husni Bey took their place. Then I came back by launch to the bridge and found a motor, which I took to HQ.

At dinner to-night Reuter's came in, and the doctor, in a perfectly calm voice, read out to us that there now seemed some chance of checking the rebellion in Ireland. Somebody said: 'Don't be a fool. Things are bad enough here. Kut's fallen and we shall probably be prisoners. Don't invent worse things.' The doctor said: 'It's an absolute fact,' and read it out again. Then somebody said: 'Those cursed Irish.' Then an Ulsterman leapt to

205

his feet and said: 'You would insult my country, would you?' Then there was a general row. After that, everything seemed so utterly desperate that there was nothing to be done but to make the best of things, and we had an extremely cheerful dinner. We must have missed a lot of news. Let's hope this Irish business is the bursting of a boil. I am more afraid of the treatment than the disease.

Friday, May 5th, 1916. *HMS Mantis*. Vane Tempest[150] came back from Kut with unpleasant stories. He said that our officers had been looted at the point of the bayonet by the Arabs. He had seen four men hanging and one man hanged. This was a curious incident. This man, as he was going to execution, threw Vane Tempest his *tesbih* (his rosary), the ninety-nine Beautiful Names of God. Vane Tempest had still got it. It means 'I commend my cause to you. Take up my quarrel.' I told Vane Tempest if he was superstitious he ought never to part with it.

Now there is a new position. They can float down all their guns and stores. There is a fight coming, but I wonder where. There are 800 men, Arabs and Turks, below Sheikh Saad with three guns. The country is up behind us. We have only half a day's provisions in reserve. It is going to be very difficult to hold this line. The guns have begun booming apparently behind us. I wish Edward was here, and hope he is all right, with my kit. I want it badly, but I got some stuff from Percy Herbert this morning who, if he can honourably avoid it, does not mean to give enemy shellfire any encouragement. It seems to me we have a most excellent chance of being cut off, and that I personally shall have another Mons, Anzac experience. These men here are starved in every way, ammunition excepted. They are not even given cigarettes and have to pay six times their price to the Arabs. Last night the Arabs were looting all over the place. One man told me this morning a sick officer in the 21st Brigade found five Arabs in his tent and lost everything. Lucky for him he remained alive.

---

150.   Lieutenant Charles Vane-Tempest (1896–1917). Durham Light Infantry and Royal Flying Corps. Died of wounds at Ligny in a German camp, a few hours after being taken prisoner.

Saturday, May 6th, 1916. *HMS Mantis. Sheikh Saad.* Yesterday my typewriter broke. A jolly mechanic more or less repaired it and refused money. 'It's all for one purpose,' he said. HQ suddenly determined to come down to Sheikh Saad in the afternoon. General Gorringe and General Ratcliffe went off, strafing like mad. Then the *Mantis* sailed. I found Edward on board the *Blosse Lynch*, with 200 'sea-gulls,' as he called the sepoys. He was very upset about the Irish news, but glad to have found me.

I walked at night with Bernard Buxton into the Arab village to find HQ. A curious sight: Devons and Somersets, Gurkhas, Arabs and frogs all mixed up together. The Somersets were very glad to meet a friend. This morning, after going through the evidence with the other officers about Bobby Palmer, I sent a telegram to Lord Selborne. They did not doubt the evidence of the Turks that he was killed.

This morning I walked along the banks of the Tigris, while bodies floated down it. After a time I found the 4th Devons and John Kennaway, Acland Troyte[151] and the rest, also half a dozen Dulverton men, Webber amongst them. I promised them cigarettes and that I would send messages home. The newest ones were depressed. They complained of shortage of food. Their camp isn't too bad. Three miles away, one can see Lot's Tomb, with generally, they say, a Turkish patrol on it. Sheikh Saad is supposed, J.K. says, to be Sodom. If you took our troops away, another dose of brimstone would do it and its inhabitants a lot of good.

Then I saw Captain Beck of the Indian Supply and Transport, an ex-Irish Guardsman. He was miserable at the way that his men were treated. He said: (1) The drivers did not receive pay equal to sepoys, nor did they receive allowances, which mountain battery drivers and ammunition column drivers did receive. The work the transport drivers did was equally dangerous and more onerous. (2) There were no spare men. A transport driver went sick and the next man had to look after his animals. (3) They got no fresh clothes. Their clothes were in rags. (4) They had 21-lb. tents for

---

151.   Lt.-Col. Hugh Acland-Troyte (1870–1918). A friend and neighbour of AH from Devon.

four men. In a hot or a cold climate this is unhealthy; very bad here. Also they have only one flap, so later on they'll be bound to get sunstroke. (5) They do not get milk, cigarettes, or tobacco. (6) They get no presents, such as the other Indian regiments have received. (7) The treatment of transport officers is not equal to that of a sepoy officer. *Vide* Subadar Rangbaz Khan, about thirty years' service. Recommended with many others. No notice taken. Only two recommendations given, those for actual valour. This man, if he had been with his relations in the cavalry, would probably have done less good work, but would have been covered with medals.

I walked back through rain, with frogs everywhere, a plague. It's a pity we can't get our men to eat them. One can't even teach the officers to eat them. John said the Arabs sniped them most nights, but they were well and not too uncomfortable. Jack Amory was there, but I didn't see him. He was out shooting sand-grouse.

Sunday, May 7th, 1916. HMS Mantis. Harris came up last night in the *Waterfly*. He said all was quiet down the river. Subhi Bey, with a good many troops, had tried to cut us off at Kumait, but the floods were out. He said that last year Cowley prophesied that when the hot weather came the river would fall and that five-eighths of our transport would be useless. Cowley was generally right. If he was wrong then, he will probably be right now. Harris had been fishing the other day, when two of the Devons suddenly appeared, naked, beside him. They had swum the river, being carried a mile and a half down, and intended to swim it again. It's very dangerous. They are wonderful fellows.

Early this morning a telegram arrived to say the Corps Commander wanted me at once. I spoke from the flying station on the telephone to Cassel. He said: 'We have fired on the Turks and they have collared the *Sikhim*. We want you to get her out.' The whole thing seemed foolish and undignified, but I transferred to the *Waterfly*. Here I saw Costello and said to him that I had told the General that this would happen. He said he agreed with me. Four bullets had been fired by the Turks at the *Sikhim*. The

Turkish officer was very angry with the Turks who had fired this shot, and rigid orders had been issued. After all this we had begun firing. The General apparently wanted it. I saw General Browne who didn't tell quite the same story, but who kept on saying 'we can't have this and we can't have that'. In the end I said: 'It's simply a question of worthwhile. If you think the fact that the Turks are wiring in their positions, which we don't mean to attack, and also that they are sniping us so important that we must fire our guns at them, then do so, but make up your mind to lose the *Sikhim*.' He said: 'Yes, you are right. They have all the cards in their hand. You are our only card.' I said: 'If they see much more of this card, they will soon say "snap".' We are amazing. We get ourselves into this awful mess and then apparently think that it is the Turks' moral duty to get us out, and for some reason the Turk apparently agrees.

I have had several contradictory orders: (1) go to India at once to investigate Turkish prisoners, by order of Army Commander (2) report immediately to the Admiral (3) stay at Felahiah and hold yourself in readiness to go to Khalil.

Tuesday, May 9th, 1916. Felahiah. The last boatload of wounded is coming down and the truce will, I suppose, end. The *Sikhim* has made her last journey. One thing seemed clear: that the Admiral meant me to return at once. He telegraphed that I was to get on board the *Lawrence*, sailing the 12th from and join him at Bushire. I went to Browne who said the General won't let you go. I saw Gorringe after a two-hour wait. He began by telling me to look him in the face, which I did. He said I had been given to him. I said 'no, that couldn't be, the Admiral was my Chief'. He roared like a bull. I gave him clearly to understand that it was a pleasure to serve Lake, but that it was only duty which had made me serve him. I also said I meant to telegraph to the Admiral to explain why I was not carrying out orders. He couldn't prevent that, but said he must see the telegram. I telegraphed: 'Corp Commander says he cannot spare me until all sick have left Kut. Much regret I cannot be with you. Herbert.' That again apparently made him furious. He is one of the worst cads I have ever met in my life, and it has been a real pleasure saying what others were not in the position to say to him[152]. I retired to Powers Mehailah, where I spent a calm and cool day. In the evening I said good-bye to Browne, and told him I didn't ever want to see his chief again as I had been accustomed to deal with gentlemen. Leachman brought Gorringe down in the *Louis Pelly* when he, Gorringe, was wounded. Leachman had to steer for five nights while Gorringe had his cabin. He never said thank you.

There is a lot of cholera. General Rice died last night. There are many bodies floating down the river. It's tremendously hot. I have just seen Williams, the doctor of the *Sikhim*. He says the Turks have been good throughout. The Arabs have looted at the beginning, but this has been put an end to. It's not going well with the Arabs. We must largely depend on them for supplies.

I saw MacPherson in despair about the orders given for destroying Arabs. General Cleary had sent in an order to say that in consequence of thefts, five of the Mehailah men were to be shot. Any five. The thefts are the work of the tribes, not the Mehailah men, and if we shoot the Mehailah men we shall get no more lightermen; also Gorringe has said that aircraft are to drop shrapnel on bodies of Arabs; this will not tend to make the friendlies more friendly, and we can't do without the Arabs. We must largely depend on them for supplies and other things. Gorringe and Tatray have gone off strafing to Sheikh Saad, where I follow them en route for on *S1*.

Wednesday, May 10th, 1916. HMS Mantis. There was a witness of the roaring scene between Gorringe and myself, who reported it, and I found myself the most popular man in camp; implored to stay and insult him once again. Wilson Johnson said 'we can do with the Turks, and the flies and the cholera and the climate, and being forgotten, if only they will send us a sahib as General'. All the same Gorringe, though he is a cad, is also rather a great man. Those who hate him put the Dujeila redoubt and March 8th down to his credit. They say he so tied Kemble up with orders that the

152.   AH wrote to his wife, Mary Herbert, describing this interview: '*I was very glad as I felt I was avenging a whole horde of poor devils that this swine has brow-beaten.*'

latter did not dare move, though he knew the Turkish position was empty, and would soon be full.

I was to have left on *S1*, but when it was apparent that it would not start that night, I went off to the *Mantis*. Buxton telephoned from Sheikh Saad that he would take me to Amara, if I could get there by 4.30 a.m. I came down with Colonel James of the Indian Medical. Many bodies in the river and much cholera at Wadi. Our men lack every mortal thing. I should like to send a telegram like this to Austen Chamberlain[153], but don't expect I should be allowed to:

From my experience of this country, I see that, unless certain action is taken immediately, consequences that are disastrous to the health of the troops must follow. All realize here that the past economy of the Government of India is responsible for our failure (vide Sir William Meyer's Budget speech). Unless this is realized in England and supplies taken out of the hands of the Government of India, altogether, or liberally supplemented from home and Egypt, the troops will suffer even more during this summer than last year. Condensed milk and oatmeal are essential to the troops. India cannot provide these under three months, by which time we shall have sustained great and unnecessary losses. Supplies of potatoes and onions will cease at the end of this month. If cold storage is found to be impossible, a substitute, e.g. dried figs, must be found. India cannot provide these substitutes in time. Sufficient ice-machines and soda-water machines are as essential to prevent heat-stroke in the trenches as to cure heat-stroke in the hospitals. India, unless ordered to commandeer these from clubs, private houses, etc., cannot provide them. Many Indian troops are in 21-lb. tents, single flap, one tent to four men. Numbers of these will

153.   Sir (Joseph) Austen Chamberlain KG (1863–1937), Secretary of State for India 1915-1917. AH knew Chamberlain well, although he thought little of him, writing in a private letter: '*he has his father's eye glass and the next man's mind*'.

*get sunstroke. If you mean to hold this country, you can't do
it on the lines of Sir William Meyer. A railway is essential. A
fall in the river would render half our present transport
useless, above Kurna. Many of the troops here are young and
not strong. If a disaster to their health, which, in its way, is
as grave as the fall of Kut, and due to the same reason, lack
of transport, is to be prevented, supplies must be taken in
hand from England and Egypt.*

Thursday, May 11th, 1916. HMS Mantis. Amara. Yesterday one
of the most beautiful days I have seen in Mesopotamia. We came
very fast down the river, with a delicious wind against us. On both
banks there were great herds of sheep, cattle and nice-looking
horses. Every horse here is blanketed by the Arabs, only our horses
not blanketed. The Arabs vary a lot in looks, one naked man
towing a bellam and looking over his shoulder, was more like a
hyena snarling than anything I have seen many; handsome; mostly
clothed, some naked.

We came to Amara in the evening and found a good deal of
cholera. I went into the bazaar and bought what things I could for
John Kennaway and his mess. Amara looked beautiful in the
evening, fine picturesque Arab buildings, and palm groves and
forests up and down either side of the lighted river. At night we
anchored to a palm and slept well, in spite of occasional great gusts
of wind, which roared through the palms, and bursts of rifle fire
on the bank by us at Arabs, who were stealing or sniping us. Jackals
cried in a chorus on the bank.

To-day the river has been enchanted. Long processions of
mehailahs, perfectly reflected in the water, drifted down, often
commanded by our officers. The river turned into a lake, almost
without a land horizon. We passed the *Marmaris*, which the Turks
fought until she caught fire. Arab villages were half afloat. There
was a look of peace everywhere, and the flood is much too high
for an attack on us.

There was a beautiful, dangerous sunset. The sky was a bank of
clouds that caught fire and glowed east and west over the glowing
water. The palms looked like a forest drawn by magic from the

river. It was like the most magnificent Mecca stone. Pursefield got nervous as the usual lightning began. I think he was afraid of bad luck on his last night in Mesopotamia. He asked me how much I wanted to get on. I said I could not see the people I wanted that night or before 8.00 the next morning so it made no odds to me, and we tied up in mid-stream, which had the advantage that we couldn't be sniped. No flies, thank heavens.

Friday, May 12th, 1916. HMS Lawrence. The Army Commander and General Money were both away, and I only spent twenty minutes at . I saw Bill Beach and Captain Nunn and wrote a line to Gertrude Bell and George Lloyd. I wish I could have seen them both. The *Sikhim* is there, in quarantine, her Red Cross looking like a huge tropical flower. I got on to the *Lawrence*. Cleanliness and comfort and good food. I wish the others could have it too.

Aubrey Herbert maintained his diaries only intermittently on his journey home. The following, undated, extracts, cover the period between his departure from until his arrival, a week later, via Bombay, in Aden.

The Admiral came, and with him a mail, bringing me bad news. I breakfasted with Commodore Wake. The Admiral had had a long letter from Lady Wemyss who is in Switzerland. Rifaat Pasha and many other Turks were staying in the same hotel at Ouchy. Rosetti, the Roumanian, came to her saying that Turkey wanted peace. The Admiral wanted me to go home and see if anything was possible. He said: 'Constantly I have thought that a thing was so obvious that there must be an appointed person to do it, and constantly I have seen what was right and proper neglected. If you can do anything, go home and do it.' He said he would want me again. Meanwhile, I gave him my telegram to Austen Chamberlain. He wanted first to send a similar telegram to Arthur Balfour himself, but I said (1) these were only my opinions, though it is true that they represented the opinions of all the doctors and soldiers with whom I had talked (2) that it had not been my business to make an enquiry of this kind (3) if he also sent a telegram it would

213

almost inevitably create friction with the Army and destroy his power of helping. He then decided to go at once to Simla, and I wrote a report for him to show the Viceroy; a record of my instructions etc., with general observations at the end of it.

General Douglas came on board and talked. Very bitter about India. He said that it had taken them four months' correspondence in Mesopotamia to get the orders for the boats they wanted, i.e. flies, I suppose. He wanted to get forward as far as Shiraz, punish one or two enemy tribes and liberate O'Connor, who is at Ahram, only thirty-five miles away. Poor O'Connor is mad to get out. Douglas has 2,000 more troops coming. Has sent me his plan of campaign.

On Tuesday the 18th I had an answer from Beach to say that my telegram to Austen had been sent to the Chief of Staff, Skeen, for censorship in India[154]. I should have had a pleasant time if I had been staying in India. It was the worst practical joke I have ever had played on me. I wish I had stayed in . Gullam Ali the interpreter tells me that we are unpopular in . In the days of Turkish rule the Arab boats were taxed eight annas a month, to-day we tax them a rupee. There used to be no house tax. We have started a house tax. Booking has collected many taxes at Nasryah. He is the inventor of the mat hut. This would do for higher up the river, but the material must be supplied.

The Admiral had wanted to send a telegram home on the lines of my report. I advised him strongly not, as it would only create friction. Burmester agreed. I trust Burmester.

154.   AH's telegram caused a significant degree of angst among the hierarchy of the Government of India. Admiral Wemyss wrote to AH explaining: '*I found them all in a great state of perturbation about your telegram. I think they had all hoped that you would accompany me as they would have liked to have had your blood, and I think it is as well for you that you went off when you did. The Viceroy told me that your telegram was looked upon as a political attack on the Financial Member of the Council, but I told him that he knew you quite well enough to be able to refute any such idea, and that even supposing you were wrong all through, there was one thing that they could be certain of, and that was the purity of your motives ..*'. The Government of India subsequently tried to have AH court-martialled for breaching military discipline – the War Office refused.

On Monday 22nd May the mail came in with bad news. The Worcester Yeomanry wiped out, the Gloucesters mostly captured; Ego[155] either wounded and a prisoner or killed with his brother-in-law. I am very sorry Micky Hicks Beach[156] was killed, as apparently he knew he was going to be. He was very fond of his wife, who had died a short time before him .

On May 25th the Admiral left for Simla. I implored him not to let promises of future good behaviour on the part of the Government of India cancel the past from his mind. I drove to the Towers of Silence with de Saumarez.

On Tuesday I saw Hopwood and Wason[157] after lunch; and bought masses of food and fishing rods for John Kennaway, then went on board the *Salsette*. There is a telegram to say that we are running into a cyclone which is an awful bore, but no sign of it yet. Also there are two German raiders, one Dutch and one Danish boat, but no sign of them either. A lot of prickly heat. Blackburn[158] on board. He said that Ctesiphon had stocked him with nightmares for his life. There was one ambulance there, the wounded had to come in on springless carts over the rough desert. There were five doctors to 4,000 wounded. Hathaway, the chief doctor, never did anything. I have heard him cursed before. There may be another side, but there ought to be a reckoning for someone.

I had a talk with Blackburn this morning, who said that Nunn had always been against an advance beyond Kurna unless we had more transport; but as a matter of fact the river is constitutionally unsuited to transport. You could put more on it, probably not more than a dozen boats, and the Turks by breaking the bunds might starve us of water altogether in the summer. If the river is to be any use there ought to be a lot more dredging. With proper dredging there should be a thirty foot draft of water at Fao. Sir G. Buchanan, whose business this is or ought to be, is at Simla, said

155.   Hugo Charteris, Lord Elcho (1884–1916).
156.   Michael Hicks-Beach, Viscount Quenington (1877–1916).
157.   Commander C. R. Wason RN, commanding HMS *Odin*.
158.   A RNAS pilot.

Blackburn, drawing a large salary. He said that twenty white men took Amara in June 1915. Eighty men altogether took 3,000 Turks. He complained of shortage of food recently. Twice they had not received anything before 3.00 p.m. because of the lack of transport.

He said that if Townshend had had white Cavalry at Kut he could have captured the Turkish army. He criticized Aylmer's generalship at Sheikh Saad. He attacked on both sides of the river, when he could have got round the Turks on the right bank. Balloons ordered by the Admiral are at last arriving at Sheikh Saad. The fraud and corruption going on in are very great.

Simcox of Bombay tried to see Austen (Chamberlain) and others when he was home, but was not able to do so. He wanted to tell them what was happening. Charmers, whose boat was the *Ariel*, offered a filtering appliance which could produce 30,000 gallons of water a day. His letter was never answered. Blackburn didn't know to whom he made his offer. His boat was the only hospital boat at the front, though there were many down at . He ought to have had the VC many times. He was made to pay for his own rations and never recognized. He paid for everything, besides providing the boat. 50,000 rupees a week were dropped by aeroplane into Kut.

The battle of Shaiba, according to him, was one of the great battles of the world. We should have been utterly done if we had not had luck with us. All the afternoon we fired at a mirage; it happened that this mirage shone upon the only road by which the Turks could bring up their reinforcements.

Yesterday the alarm went and everyone collected rapidly, thinking of the raiders. The captain, however, made a speech saying there would be danger in a week's time, and suggesting that the extra men should look after the superfluous women. Nobody cared about it much.

Yesterday I breakfasted at Aden with General Walton[159], and Colonel Douglas, Chief of the Police of the Andaman Islands. Douglas had been sent the 15th Lancers and was furious about it.

159.   See Footnote 121.

216

He said they were a splendid regiment, one of the only two pure Mahometan regiments of the Punjab, and that they had done very well in France. They said they would not fight in Mesopotamia because it was holy ground. They were now condemned to imprisonment for life[160]. Their native officers had sides against the men. Two British officers were broken men. Walton made him furious. He said they should be ready to attack Mecca if necessary. Jacobs and Walton are evidently at the point of quarrelling.

Feel the journey is ending for the moment[161].

160.   In February 1916, the Pathan Muslim Squadrons of the 15th Bengal Lancers (Cureton's Multanis) refused to march from Basrah to fight the Turks near the holy city of Karbala, requesting instead to be sent anywhere, except there, which they believed would violate their beliefs. Of the 429 soldiers involved, three Non Commissioned Officers (NCOs) were given life sentences, the remaining NCOs fifteen years and the soldiers seven years, to be served in the Andaman Islands. They were released in 1917.

161.   AH reached Cairo on 2nd June and England in early July. Returning to Parliament almost immediately, he took up the cudgel and pressed the Prime Minister to devote time to discussion of the conduct of the campaign in Mesopotamia, speaking a total of five times on the subject. Eventually, with a groundswell of support growing behind Aubrey Herbert, the Prime Minister, Asquith, succumbed and a Royal Commission was appointed to investigate the conduct of the Mesopotamia campaign.